Tick..

Hear that clock ticking? It's the countdown to the AP European History Exam, and it'll be here before you know it. Whether you have one year or one day to go, now's the time to start maximizing your score.

The Test Is Just a Few Months Away!

Don't worry—you're ahead of the game! But you should still begin preparing now. Follow the **Strategies for Long-Term Preparation** (page 161) to make the most of your time so you'll be well prepared for test day.

Actually, I Only Have a Few Weeks!

There's still plenty of time for a full review. Turn to the **Comprehensive Strategies and Review** (page 15), where you'll find a **diagnostic test** to help you identify your areas of weakness, **Multiple-Choice Strategies** (page 95) for advice on how to approach test questions, and in-depth **content review** chapters on each topic covered on the AP European History Exam.

Let's Be Honest. The Test Is Tomorrow and I'm Freaking Out!

No problem. Review the **About the Exam** section (page 5), so you know what to expect when you arrive to take the test. Then take a **practice exam** (pages 173 and 235). Don't worry about the scores— just focus on getting to know the test. Before you go to bed, review the **Multiple-Choice Strategies** (page 95) and **Essay Strategies** (page 97). This information provides a crash course in successful test-taking.

Relax. Make the most of the tools and resources in this review guide, and you'll be ready to earn a top score.

My Max Score

AP EUROPEAN HISTORY

Maximize Your Score in Less Time

Ira Shull and Mark Dziak

Published by Sourcebooks EDU, an imprint of Sourcebooks, Inc.
P.O. Box 4410, Naperville, Illinois 60567-4410
(630) 961-3900
Fax: (630) 961-2168
www.sourcebooks.com

Library of Congress Cataloging-in-Publication Data

Shull, Ira D.
  My max score AP European history : maximize your score in less time / Ira Shull and
Mark Dziak.
      p. cm.
1. Europe—History—Examinations—Study guides. 2. Europe—History—Examinations,
questions, etc. 3. Advanced placement programs (Education)—Examinations—Study
guides. I. Dziak, Mark. II. Title. III. Title: AP European history.
  D16.3.S58 2012
  940.076—dc23

2011048932

Printed and bound in the United States of America.
VP 10 9 8 7 6 5 4 3 2 1

Also Available in the My Max Score Series

AP Exam Study Aids

AP Biology
AP Calculus AB/BC
AP English Language and Composition
AP English Literature and Composition
AP U.S. Government & Politics
AP U.S. History
AP World History

SAT Subject Test Study Aids

SAT Literature Subject Test
SAT Math 1 & 2 Subject Test
SAT U.S. History Subject Test

ASVAB Study Aids

ASVAB: Armed Services Vocational Aptitude Battery

Contents

Introduction

We're not going to lie to you: the AP European History Exam is no walk in the park. It's a tough examination that requires a significant commitment from you. Unlike some of the other examinations you'll take as part of your high school career, you're only going to get one opportunity to ace AP European History. And even if you're quite familiar with other AP examinations, AP European History can feel intimidating because it covers such a huge swath of time and geography. You need to be familiar with pretty much everything that has happened and everyone who has played a significant role in the last six centuries of European history, from about 1450 to about 2001.

Consider for a moment: to do well on this examination, you need to know the timeline of all important events in countries as diverse as Britain, Russia, Germany, and Italy. You must be familiar with historical figures as dissimilar as William Shakespeare, Karl Marx, Michelangelo, Peter the Great, and Lech Walesa. You must be able to discuss the cultural drivers and touch points of eras as diverse as the Renaissance, the Counter-Reformation, and the Scientific Revolution. You must know which countries participated in which conflicts, and you must be able to analyze the causes and resolutions of conflicts as diverse as the Seven

Years' War, the Eighty Years' War, the Napoleonic Wars, and World Wars I and II.

No matter how you look at it, that's a lot of information! However, you should feel confident. With your knowledge of European History and this text, you have all of the tools and strategies you need to be successful.

Visit mymaxscore.com for an additional practice test for the AP European History Exam, as well as practice tests for other AP subjects.

THE ESSENTIALS: A LAST-MINUTE STUDY GUIDE

So, it's a night or two before the exam and you just don't feel ready. Should you panic? No! This is the time to take a deep breath and prepare. If you've been taking an AP European History class, or preparing in other ways throughout the year, you're just about at your goal. All you need to do now is settle your nerves, review a few strategies to refresh your mind, and get your ducks in a row for test day. It's not too late to maximize your score!

First, take your focus off your nerves and put it on the things you can do to get ready. You don't have much time, so you should make the most of the time you do have. Turn off your phone, your computer, and any other electronic gadgetry. Stop texting and stop surfing the Internet. Ask your family not to disturb you unless it's really important. Close your door and get ready.

Review the Test-Taking Tips

You should already be familiar with the test, but if you're feeling in need of a refresher, start by getting to know the test. The speediest way to do this is to review the **Quick Test-Taking Tips** in this section (page 7). If you have more time, get more detail in the **Multiple-Choice** and **Essay Strategies** chapters in the next section (pages 95 and 97).

Review the Big Ideas in European History

If you don't have time for a full review, go over the basics. These are provided for you in the **Big Ideas** chapter that begins on page 11. This section covers the broad themes and key events you're going to encounter in both the multiple-choice and essay sections of the test.

Take a Practice Test

The only way to *really* get to know the test—and to try out your test-taking strategies—is to take a practice test. Time yourself as if the exam was real, moving on to the next section when time runs out. When you finish, go over your answers, looking particularly for areas where you struggled. (Watch for themes or trends.) If you still have time, go over the sections that cover your problem areas. Use the comprehensive review chapters provided in this book.

Gather Your Materials the Night Before

The last thing you want to have to do on the morning of test day is rush around trying to find everything you need. So, make sure you get together everything you need beforehand. Put together a backpack or small bag with the items listed below (and anything else you think you need). Have this bag ready so that you can grab it and go in the morning, knowing you're properly equipped. Listed are some things you might put inside your backpack, as well as other suggestions to help you prepare for test day.

- Place your photo ID in a side pocket or zippered compartment so you can find it easily. You'll be required to show proof of identity.

- Do you know your school code? This is especially important if you're testing in a different school than you attend. Get this information from your school beforehand. Write it on a piece of paper and pack that paper in your bag with your photo ID.

- Pack several pencils, a good eraser (test it first to make sure it erases without marking the paper), and several black or blue pens. Use erasable pens if you want, but make sure they aren't going to smudge. There should be a pencil sharpener available in the testing room, but you might want to pack a portable one just in case.

- Include a small, easy-to-eat snack. Test day is going to be long and you may need nourishment. Go for a snack that's high in protein with a lower carbohydrate count. Avoid messy substances like chocolate, as it could melt and get on your hands and desk. Avoid loose nuts, as they can trigger allergies in other testers. Some good choices might be an energy or protein bar or drink, an easy-to-eat piece of fruit such as a banana, or some crackers.

- Pack a bottle of water. You'll want something to drink at some point and it's best to avoid substances with a lot of sugar or caffeine. You may think they'll give you energy, but they're more likely to make you jittery.

Other Tips

- Don't stay up all night studying. You're as ready as you'll ever be! Instead, get a good night's sleep, so you'll be alert and ready.

- Eat a light but satisfying meal before the test. Protein-rich foods like eggs, nuts, and yogurt are good choices as they'll fill you up but won't leave you crashing from heavy starches or high sugar content. Don't eat too heavily—you don't want to be sleepy or uncomfortably full. If you must have coffee, don't overdo it.

- Dress in comfortable layers. The testing room might be too hot or it might be too cool. You'll want to be able to easily adjust what you're wearing to the temperature. And, make sure your clothes are of the comfortable variety. The last thing you want is to be annoyed by pants that are too tight or irritated by fabrics that look quite nice but feel really itchy.

Checklist for Test Day

- Avoid bringing things you can't have. For example, cell phones, pagers, and other electronic devices are prohibited in the testing room because they could potentially be used to communicate outside the room.
- Bring your photo ID and make sure you know your school code (both are especially important if you're testing in a school you don't attend).
- Wear or bring a watch. If your watch has any alarms, buzzers, or beepers, turn them off.
- Relax! Once you get to the testing room, take a few deep breaths and try to channel some relaxation. Remind yourself that you're well prepared. It's natural to be nervous, but it's better to channel that anxiety into energy for the test ahead.

Once the test begins, set your worries aside and do your best. You've done all you can to prepare. Time to make that preparation pay off!

About the Exam

The AP European History Exam lasts for three hours and five minutes and consists of a multiple-choice section and an essay section. Section I is multiple choice. It includes 80 questions/ incomplete statements, each of which is followed by five suggested answer options. You'll have 55 minutes to complete this section. Because there is no longer a penalty for guessing incorrectly, it's best to answer all questions and avoid leaving any items blank. This section is worth about half your final grade.

Section II is the essay portion of this test. For Section II, you'll write three essays. The first essay is the *document-based question* (DBQ). The DBQ tests your ability to analyze evidence in primary source documents and use that evidence to craft a well-written, cohesive essay. Primary source materials are provided for you and can run the gamut from historical documents, letters, and narratives to political cartoons, photographs, charts, and maps. You're expected to critically analyze all of the primary source material. Your essay should demonstrate your understanding of the materials as well as your ability to logically synthesize it in response to a prompt provided. You'll have 15 minutes to review the source materials before you begin working on your essay. You'll have 45 minutes to write the DBQ.

You'll also write two other essays as part of Section II. These *free-response questions*, or FRQs, test your knowledge of European history and your ability to analyze and synthesize information thoughtfully. This section is broken into Parts B and C; in each part, you'll be given three prompts. You'll select one prompt from each grouping. The prompts are usually designed to span history, concepts, and ideas, so you should select those topic areas with which you feel most comfortable. You'll have 70 minutes to write your FRQs.

That's a total of 130 minutes (2 hours, 10 minutes) to complete the three essays in Section II.

Exam Scoring

Each section is worth about half of your total score. Within Section II, the DBQ is worth about 45 percent of the essay score, and the FRQs together are worth about 55 percent.

Each of your essays will be graded on a scale of 1 to 9, with 9 being exceptional and a 0 or 1 being incoherent, off topic, or otherwise unacceptable. These scores are combined and converted to an AP grade as follows:

5   Extremely well qualified
4   Well qualified
3   Qualified
2   Possibly qualified
1   Not recommended for AP credit

To earn a score of 3, you'll need to answer roughly 60 percent of the multiple-choice questions correctly and score at least a 5 on each of the essays.

Quick Test-Taking Tips

Your score on the AP European History Exam depends a lot on your knowledge of European history. It also depends on your ability to ace this kind of test. Here are a few easy tips to get you started.

When practicing for the test, simulate the testing environment as closely as possible. The smartest way to get comfortable with a particular style of test is to practice taking that test frequently. Each time you test, simulate the testing conditions as closely as possible. For the AP European History Exam, this means testing in a similar environment (a quiet area with no or few distractions), under similar circumstances (closed book exam: just the test and you), and within the allotted time frame (55 minutes for Section I, 130 minutes for Section II). It might seem silly to take multiple "pretend" tests, but don't underestimate the comfort level you'll derive from being familiar with the testing circumstances. More importantly, this type of practice will teach you how to pace yourself appropriately for each part of the test.

Don't be an island; get others involved. Because more than half of your grade will be derived from your essays, which can be quite subjective, it's important that you allow at least one knowledgeable person to review and critique your work. It's convenient if this person is also familiar with European history, but it's critical that this person understand what goes into a well-written essay. You'll also need to be open to the feedback, and work to improve your style over time.

Spread out your studies. Assuming you have some time before your examination and you aren't cramming for a test next week, it's best if you can spread your studies out over a period of time. Build a formal schedule of study for yourself. Mark off two- or three-hour blocks of time and use that time to review content and take practice examinations. An ideal schedule might utilize two three-hour blocks of time twice per week for a number of weeks prior to the examination.

Study different material in different locations. Recent research suggests that you can actually increase your retention of material simply by choosing to study in different locations. This research suggests that the brain's ability to associate topic areas with unique environments can increase retention.

Relax! As testing day approaches, it's normal to feel nervous and anxious. However, it's important to avoid getting overwhelmed or paralyzed by anxiety. It's true that AP European History is an important test; however, it is, after all, just a test. Don't waste energy worrying about it. Instead, use that energy to fuel your studies. Focus on testing to the best of your ability.

On test day, take care of your body. That means get a full night's rest the night before the test and eat something nutritious in the morning. If you're hungry, tired, or if you're fueled on sugar and caffeine, it will be much more difficult for you to concentrate.

Arrive early. If you're testing in an unfamiliar location, make sure you know how to get there *before* the day of the test. Regardless, on the day of the test, get to your school or testing center early. Rushing around will produce adrenaline and fuel anxiety.

Take a deep breath and pace yourself. When the test begins, recognize that this is the moment when all of your studying and practice will pay off. You've worked within the time limits and you know how to best spend that time. Take a deep breath, and do it.

Answer the questions in order. Some test prep materials suggest that you go through a test and answer the questions that seem easy to you. In theory, that might seem like a good idea. However, in practice, this approach is generally a time waster; as you'll have to spend a lot of time later searching for the questions you skipped. Additionally, jumping around on the test increases the possibility that you'll (a) miss questions or (b) fill in the wrong spaces on the answer sheet. (This last option is especially scary and to be avoided at all costs.) Take the questions in order. If you're unsure of an answer, make an educated guess and move on. Flag the question on the test so that you can return to it later if you have time. (For example, you might place a question mark in the margin next to the number of the question.)

Don't be afraid to make an educated guess. Again, try not to leave any questions unanswered. Use elimination strategies when you're unsure.

Don't be afraid to change your answers. Some test preparation material cautions against changing your answer options, as conventional wisdom suggests your first answer option is usually correct. Although this may be true when you're reasonably sure of the answer, it's not necessarily true when you're unsure. If you've flagged an item, don't be afraid to review your answer option and change it later.

Big Ideas in European History

It's important to recognize that although the AP European History Exam covers a wide swath of history, the goal of the examination is not to force you to memorize a bunch of names and dates. Rather, the goal is to develop a global perspective of history and be able to analyze themes and ideas. The AP College Board says,

> In addition to providing a basic narrative of events and movements, the goals of the AP program in European History are to develop (a) an understanding of some of the principal themes in modern European History, (b) an ability to analyze historical evidence and historical interpretation, and (c) an ability to express historical understanding in writing.

Let's break that down a little. In order to be successful on this examination, you need to be able to

- Recognize major themes in the course of history
- Analyze historical evidence in support of those themes
- Express your understanding of those themes in writing

The major themes of history are the big ideas that have changed the world over time.

Intellectual and Cultural History

Broadly speaking, the fields of *intellectual* and *cultural history* involve studying ideas and intellectual patterns over time. They also look at the intellectual, social, and artistic aspects of a culture, people, or nation. Some of the intellectual and cultural history topics you can expect to come across on the AP European History Exam include

- The relationship of intellectual and cultural movements to social values and political events
- Changes in social and cultural attitudes toward religion, the family, and work
- The secularization of society, including education
- Transformations in religious thought, practices, and institutions
- Social, economic, and political ideologies and their impact
- Cultural trends in the arts
- Advances in science and technology and their impact
- Progress in literacy, education, and communications
- Globalization

Political and Diplomatic History

Political and *diplomatic history* are concerned with political ideas, events, leaders, and movements, as well as the relationships between nations. Political and diplomatic history study the public affairs of a country, both within itself and with other nations. Some of the political and diplomatic history topics you can expect to come across on the AP European History Exam include

- Political parties and ideologies
- Relationships among Europe's nations
- Political evolution to the modern state
- Personal, civil, economic, and political rights and liberties
- Political and personal persecution

- Nationalism, imperialism, and colonialism
- Revolution, political protest, and governmental reform
- Domestic and foreign policies and relations
- Peacekeeping efforts: treaties, diplomacy, and international organizations
- War and civil conflict

Social and Economic History

Social and *economic history* involve the study of ordinary people, the economy, and the struggles of day-to-day life. Some of the social and economic history topics you can expect to come across on the AP European History Exam include

- Cultural values and social relationships
- Agricultural production and organization
- Urbanization
- Social structures, from traditional hierarchical models to the modern class system
- Sanitation and health care practices and their impact on society
- Distribution of wealth
- Commercialization, industrialization, mass production, and consumerism
- Social attitudes and norms toward social classes, races, and ethnicities
- Demographic structures and reproductive patterns
- Gender roles, the family, and work
- Global competition and interdependence
- Private and state roles in economics

THE MAIN COURSE: COMPREHENSIVE STRATEGIES AND REVIEW

If you have a few weeks to go before the exam, there's plenty of time to brush up on your skills using the tools in this book.

Note that throughout the book, you will find many italicized words. Italics are used to help identify the key vocabulary terms and concepts you need to know to be successful on the AP European History Exam. Whenever you come across one of these terms, stop and consider: Are you familiar with this term? Can you define it? Do you know what it means and how it applies? Use the italicized listing to build an inventory of vocabulary for additional study.

Here's a plan of things to do to prepare in the weeks ahead.

- Go over the **Multiple-Choice** and **Essay Strategies** chapters (pages 95 and 97) to get familiar with the exam. Really think how you can apply these strategies, as they are known ways to perform the best on this type of test.

- Test out these strategies and assess your knowledge by taking at least one **practice exam** (there are two in this book, plus the diagnostic test). As you go through the answers, note any areas of weakness. Read the answers and their explanations. Watch for trends in your answers. If you missed a question, find out why so you can avoid doing so in the future.

- Read through this **Comprehensive Strategies and Review** section. Pay special attention to any areas of weakness you've identified in your practice tests.

- Take at least one more practice test before test day. You can download one at mymaxscore.com.

- A few nights before the test, go back over the section on **The Essentials** (page 1) for a refresher on test-taking tips and the Big Ideas of AP European History.

- Do everything on the checklist on page 4.

Pack your materials for the next day, get a good night's sleep, and you'll be ready to earn a top score on the exam.

Diagnostic Test

How Ready Are You?

This part of your book includes a full-length diagnostic test. This test has been designed to help you identify and correct potential problems with AP test taking, ultimately helping you to improve your score. After taking the diagnostic test, you might realize you are spending too much time answering multiple-choice questions, or that you are not using document-based materials to their fullest extent in the construction of your essays. Or, you might discover that you consistently struggle with certain types of questions or with questions that address specific centuries, historical figures, or cultural movements. All of these issues are resolvable. However, to identify them, it is essential that you complete the diagnostic test in an environment that closely mimics the actual testing environment.

Therefore, you should follow these guidelines:

- Block out a full three-hour time period to take the diagnostic test. AP examinations are broken into sections, and each section must be completed within a designated amount of time. Make sure you stay within allotted time frames.
- Select an environment that is quiet, with a minimal amount of distraction, such as a quiet room in your home, at your school, or in the local library.

- Turn off your cell phone and your computer. Ask family and friends to avoid disturbing you during the testing period.
- While taking the test, have *only* the examination open.
- Don't cheat! Even though you may be tempted, looking up the answers will only hinder your progress.
- As you take the test, have a highlighter available. Use it to quickly mark any term or concept that seems unfamiliar to you. Later, you will be able to use this information in your studies.
- Finally, each section of the test provides instructions for you to follow. Make sure you follow them.

Once you have completed the examination, assess your score by checking your answers against the key provided at the end of this section. More information about assessing your performance is provided in the chapter that follows.

Good luck!

AP EUROPEAN HISTORY
SECTION I
Time—55 minutes

80 Questions

Directions: Each of the questions or incomplete statements below is followed by five suggested answers or completions. Select the answer that is best in each case. *Take no more than 55 minutes to complete this part of your test.*

1. How did the fall of the Byzantine Empire to the Turks in fifteenth-century Europe contribute to the development of humanism?

    A. It ushered in an age of social pessimism.
    B. It divided Roman Catholicism from Greek Orthodoxy.
    C. It drew attention to the need for authoritarian governments.
    D. It brought social contract theory to the Greco-Roman world.
    E. It provided primary text material previously unknown in the West.

2. In comparison to Portuguese explorers in the Age of Discovery, the most distinctive feature of Spanish conquistadors was their

    A. lack of military skill.
    B. low level of state support.
    C. use of religion as a motivation for conquest.
    D. desire to find a less perilous route around the Cape of Good Hope.
    E. use of scientific discoveries such as the astrolabe and compass.

3. In the Age of Exploration, which of the following best characterizes the spread of goods and ideas under the Columbia Exchange?

   A. Europeans brought diseases to the New World and returned with horses.

   B. Europeans brought tomatoes, maize, and potatoes to the New World and returned with diseases.

   C. Europeans brought corn, peanuts, and potatoes to the New World and returned with diseases.

   D. Europeans brought horses, cattle, and sheep to the New World and returned with corn, potatoes, and tobacco.

   E. Europeans brought tobacco, Christianity, and gold to the New World and returned with horses, cattle, and sheep.

4. The image shown above represents which artistic innovations of the Renaissance?

   A. Grisaille and sfumato

   B. Collage and classicalism

   C. Mannerism and refectory

   D. Proportion and perspective

   E. Chiaroscuro and abstraction

"I think it casts a brilliant light on our estate and it seems to me that the monies were well spent and I am very pleased with this."

5. The quotation above best reflects the Renaissance view of uniting artistic patronage with political power demonstrated by

    A. Machiavelli.
    B. David Hume.
    C. Michelangelo.
    D. Leonardo da Vinci.
    E. Lorenzo de' Medici.

6. As Spanish and Portuguese explorers colonized the New World in the sixteenth century, Native Americans experienced all of the following EXCEPT

    A. loss of language.
    B. epidemics of disease.
    C. religious conversions.
    D. unequal balances of trade.
    E. forced labor conditions.

7. Niccolò Machiavelli (1469–1527) contributed most to the rise of "new monarchs" who centralized political authority and unified their nations by

    A. advocating the Divine Right of Kings.
    B. supporting social Darwinism on a political level.
    C. writing a polemic tract supported by the Church.
    D. suggesting monarchs needed to be shrewd and ruthless.
    E. proposing monarchs serve as the "first citizen" of their people.

8. Which of the following factors led most immediately to the defeat of the Spanish Armada (1588)?

   A. Mutiny
   B. Equipment failure
   C. Poor weather
   D. Lack of fresh water
   E. Invention of the cannon

9. All of the following are associated with the Agricultural Revolution in the sixteenth and seventeenth centuries EXCEPT

   A. the rise of the middle class.
   B. the introduction of soil rotation.
   C. an increase in the standards of living.
   D. the invention of new agricultural machinery.
   E. an increase in the economic power of Venice and Genoa.

"Speak the speech, I pray you, as I pronounced it to you, trippingly on the tongue: but if you mouth it, as many of your players do, I had as lief the town-crier spoke my lines. Nor do not saw the air too much with your hand, thus, but use all gently; for in the very torrent, tempest, and, as I may say, the whirlwind of passion, you must acquire and beget a temperance that may give it smoothness."

10. Which of the following Elizabethan value(s) is represented by the directions above?

    A. Denial of lunacy
    B. Physical endurance
    C. Emotional temperance
    D. Dramaturgy and stagecraft
    E. Pronunciation and speech patterns

11. The Edict of Nantes helped end the French Wars of Religion (1562–1598) by

    A. bestowing substantive rights on Huguenots.
    B. providing French support for the Inquisition.
    C. granting property rights to Catholics.
    D. creating political separation between Church and state.
    E. offering religious tolerance to Jews and Muslims.

12. All of the following were causes of the Dutch Golden Age in the seventeenth century EXCEPT

    A. the creation of a monopoly on Japanese trade.
    B. the widespread availability of cheap energy from windmills.
    C. the support of Prince Henry the Navigator for maritime exploration.
    D. the development of multinational corporations and a stock exchange.
    E. the influx of Protestants from Antwerp under the Peace of Westphalia.

13. Martin Luther's Ninety-Five Theses helped change the social roles of clergy in the sixteenth century by

    A. instituting literacy tests for the clergy.
    B. supporting public confession for clergy.
    C. abolishing the right of clergy to accept taxes and tithes.
    D. suggesting clergy should fall under the rule of the state.
    E. arguing that clergy were not needed for religious experience.

14. Which of the following corresponded with the Acts of Union in 1707 and united the kingdoms of Scotland and England?

    A. The Scottish Enlightenment
    B. The rise of John Knox as a public figure
    C. The creation of an independent Scottish Parliament
    D. The loss of religious freedom in the Scotland
    E. Public protests against the English monarchy

15. The artistic values of which of the following movements are best demonstrated in the image above?

    A. Realism
    B. Baroque
    C. Fauvism
    D. Art Nouveau
    E. Impressionism

16. Huldrych Zwingli and John Calvin chiefly influenced Europe outside of Switzerland by

   A.   launching the Inquisition to identify and punish heretics.
   B.   creating church councils to provide safe havens for the discussion of religious matters.
   C.   challenging the social and political supremacy of the Roman Catholic Church.
   D.   supporting the mass immigration of Swiss Protestants to Roman Catholic areas.
   E.   forming religious armies to enlarge the borders of Protestant Switzerland.

17. What was the main goal of the Peace of Westphalia?

   A.   Ending the military conflict between France and Spain
   B.   Legalizing the use of privateers and letters of marquee
   C.   Establishing the Netherlands as a territory of the Holy Roman Empire
   D.   Confirming the power of the Holy See to rule the Holy Roman Empire
   E.   Reaffirming the right of princes to determine the religion of their own states

18. Historians would most likely cite the marriage of Martin Luther to Katherina von Bora as an example of

   A.   the flexibility of the Roman Catholic clerical hierarchy.
   B.   the egalitarian class structure of the Holy Roman Empire.
   C.   the power of the arranged marriage in the sixteenth century.
   D.   the success of international alliances forged between political families.
   E.   the changing role of women as a result of the Protestant Reformation.

19. Which of the following religious groups was strongly influenced by the writings of William Bradshaw and Cotton Mather?

    A. Puritans
    B. Calvinists
    C. Anabaptists
    D. Presbyterians
    E. Roman Catholics

20. Between 1772 and 1786, Frederick the Great of Prussia demonstrated enlightened absolutism by all of the following EXCEPT

    A. the creation of a constitution.
    B. the formation of a bureaucracy.
    C. the support of religious tolerance.
    D. the abolition of the death penalty.
    E. the humane treatment of prisoners of war.

21. Which of the following corresponded to the end of mercantilism in Europe?

    A. Decline in free trade
    B. Decline in entrepreneurship
    C. Increase in capitalist policies
    D. Increase in the use of hard currency
    E. Increase in state tariffs and export duties

22. Which of the following was the Catholic Church's major objection to heliocentric theory?

    A.   Polytheistic belief systems were reflected in the labeling of Jupiter's moons.

    B.   Planetary rotation contradicted key passages in the Bible.

    C.   Telescopes caused distorted views and could not be relied on for accurate data.

    D.   Observations of the tides were not accurate in the Southern hemisphere.

    E.   Galileo's personal life rendered him ineligible as an authority in Church courts.

23. Which of the following is true regarding the relationship between Ireland and England during the English Civil War (1642–1651)?

    A.   Cromwell found significant support among Irish Royalists.

    B.   Ireland's alliance with Scotland prevented major English sieges and attacks.

    C.   English confiscation of Irish Catholic property caused lasting religious tension.

    D.   Ireland was incorporated as part of the United Kingdom following the war.

    E.   English intervention led to the ultimate political division of Ireland.

24. The Pragmatic Sanction of 1713 allowed for all of the following EXCEPT

    A.   female rulers succeeding to the Austrian throne.

    B.   female succession only when male lines were extinct.

    C.   Hapsburg lands to be administered by unmarried women.

    D.   continued integrity and indivisibility of Hapsburg territories.

    E.   equal training for male and females in line for the throne.

25. Which of the following would most likely have been favored by the empiricist philosophers of the seventeenth and eighteenth centuries?

  A. Abstract art
  B. Rationalism
  C. Emotional argument
  D. Libertine lifestyle
  E. Scientific method

26. Which of the following was an outcome of the Glorious Revolution of 1688?

  A. An Anglo-French political alliance
  B. A parliamentary democracy in England
  C. The execution of King James II by William of Orange
  D. The legal establishment of Catholic monarchial traditions in England
  E. A restoration of power to Catholics previously stripped of lands and titles

27. In the eighteenth century, political debate, social gatherings, egalitarian class structures, and newspapers like *The Spectator* and the *Tatler* were components of

  A. union halls.
  B. parliament.
  C. gaming halls.
  D. coffeehouses.
  E. pleasure gardens.

28. The seventeenth-century picture above illustrates

   A.   Blaise Pascal's calculator.
   B.   Galileo Galilei's telescope.
   C.   Robert Hooke's microscope.
   D.   William Oughtred's slide rule.
   E.   Evangelista Torricelli's barometer.

29. The National Constituent Assembly, formed in the early stages of the French Revolution, was primarily interested in

   A.   declaring a republic.
   B.   overthrowing the king.
   C.   implementing constitutionalism.
   D.   supporting universal male suffrage.
   E.   executing counter-revolutionary individuals.

30. Which of the following groups was instrumental in the early stages of the French Revolution?

    A.　Clergy and women
    B.　Women and rural farmers
    C.　Jacobins and the middle class
    D.　Dragoons and *sans-culottes*
    E.　Monarchists and *sans-culottes*

"Mothers, daughters, sisters [and] representatives of the nation demand to be constituted into a national assembly. Believing that ignorance, omission, or scorn for the rights of woman are the only causes of public misfortunes and of the corruption of governments, [the women] have resolved to set forth a solemn declaration the natural, inalienable, and sacred rights of women in order that this declaration, constantly exposed before all members of the society, will ceaselessly remind them of their rights and duties…"

31. The quotation above is from a work by

    A.　Jane Austen.
    B.　Aphra Behn.
    C.　Olympe de Gouges.
    D.　Madame de La Fayette.
    E.　Mary Wollstonecraft Shelley.

32. Which of the following factors most immediately led to the sale of the Louisiana territories to the government of the United States?

   A. France's inability to apply the Napoleonic Code to Native American inhabitants
   B. Napoleon's need for military funds to support his return from exile
   C. France's need for funds after waging almost continuous warfare
   D. Napoleon's desire to gain American support for the Continental System
   E. The general French policy of limiting geographical expansion

33. The Industrial Revolution altered family structures in urban centers during the eighteenth century by

   A. favoring labor over education for children.
   B. dividing the family based upon marketable skills.
   C. assigning household and childcare duties to men.
   D. requiring women to work to support their families.
   E. providing opportunity for women to become breadwinners.

34. All of the following were aspects of the Luddite anti-industrialization movement EXCEPT

   A. smashing machinery.
   B. elevating handcrafted products.
   C. rejecting the industrialized way of life.
   D. favoring piecemeal over set-price work.
   E. drawing attention to poor working conditions.

35. Peter the Great of Russia founded the city of St. Petersburg for the purposes of

    A. establishing a naval base on the Black Sea.
    B. creating a city that embodied his ideas of Westernization and progress.
    C. providing employment for the landless serf population.
    D. replacing the older, structurally unsound city of Moscow.
    E. offering an urban center to the land-owning elite in the west of Russia.

36. Which of the following philosophers would most likely describe life as "poor, nasty, brutish, and short"?

    A. Voltaire
    B. John Locke
    C. Immanuel Kant
    D. Thomas Hobbes
    E. Jean-Jacques Rousseau

37. The close relationship between the Scientific Revolution and agrarian practices during the eighteenth century is demonstrated by the development of

    A. genetically modified foods.
    B. telescopes and microscopes.
    C. industrial machinery for export production.
    D. selective domestication programs for livestock.
    E. pasteurization procedures for dairy products.

38. Which of the following British figures actively sought to prevent the loss of colonial territories in the eighteenth century?

    A. King George I
    B. King George III
    C. Lord Oliver Cromwell
    D. Diplomat James Porter
    E. Lord Charles Cavendish

39. From 1726–1727, which of the following commodities experienced a dramatic spike in price, driven by inflation and the desire to appear wealthy?

    A. Tulips
    B. Roses
    C. Daisies
    D. Rosemary
    E. Marigolds

"For all good poetry is the spontaneous overflow of powerful feelings…"

40. This quote, from *Prologue to Lyrical Ballads*, is characteristic of the thought and art of

    A. Spiralism.
    B. Beat poetry.
    C. Romanticism.
    D. magical realism.
    E. Gothic literature.

41. After the Napoleonic Wars, Great Britain attempted to protect grain producers in England and Ireland from foreign imports by

    A.   taxing ships and other modes of conveyance.
    B.   regulating agricultural conditions and methods.
    C.   eliminating all trade regulations to foster free trade.
    D.   making it illegal to import cereal grains from abroad.
    E.   raising the minimum wage to increase purchasing power.

42. The terms "less eligibility" and "workhouse test" would most likely be discussed in which of the following studies?

    A.   A monograph on child labor laws
    B.   A work on international economic law
    C.   A treatise on gender equality in the workplace
    D.   A book on capitalism and laissez-faire economics
    E.   A book on the English Poor Laws

43. Which of the following statements is best supported by the novels of Jane Austen?

    A.   Strict social stratification during the Regency era posed problems for young women.
    B.   Novel writing was considered a suitable female employment during the Regency period.
    C.   Women faced social censure by participating in social events outside the home.
    D.   The abolition of property entailment made women less concerned with marriage during the Regency period.
    E.   The decline of love matches among the nobility led to a gradual reemergence of arranged marriage at this time.

44. All of the following occurred after Napoleon's defeat at the Battle of Waterloo EXCEPT

    A.   Napoleon's exile to the island of Elba.
    B.   the restoration of the Bourbons to the French throne.
    C.   France's forced reparations to the European allies.
    D.   the granting of the right to the king to dissolve parliament.
    E.   the return of French geographical borders to 1790 lines.

45. In the nineteenth century, which of the following figures engaged in a successful public campaign to abolish the slave trade in Great Britain?

    A.   Edward Said
    B.   William Wilberforce
    C.   Sir Thomas Bertram
    D.   Admiral Lord Nelson
    E.   Charles Watson-Wentworth

46. In nineteenth-century intellectual circles, liberalism primarily revolved around new concepts of

    A.   rationalism.
    B.   nationalism.
    C.   gender equality.
    D.   individual rights.
    E.   social stratification.

47. Which of the following is a true statement on the political authority of the Holy Roman Empire during the nineteenth century?

    A. The Holy Roman Empire's political authority slowly eroded as it lost territory to France.
    B. The Holy Roman Empire successfully resisted French advances with superior military campaigns.
    C. The Holy Roman Empire maintained a single religious system longer than any other state in Europe.
    D. The Holy Roman Empire drew support from the Prussian Junkers to win the War of Spanish Succession.
    E. The Holy Roman Empire lost its ability to participate in international treaties when the Holy See revoked support for the state.

48. Prior to 1882, women had access to which of the following legal rights?

    A. Right to vote
    B. Right to personal property
    C. Right to a shorter work day
    D. Right to run for political office
    E. Right to equal pay in the workplace

49. The article of feminine clothing seen above, the corset, contributed to the social subordination of women in the nineteenth century by

   A. interfering with a woman's ability to bear children.
   B. physically preventing a woman from exerting herself.
   C. limiting the amount of food a woman could eat.
   D. creating economic dependence on the manufacturing industry.
   E. forcing the purchase of expensive artisan products.

50. A central feature of the Concert of Europe was

   A. the application of nationalism.
   B. the repudiation of conservatism.
   C. a chance to limit the power of the Holy See.
   D. a desire to balance power in Europe.
   E. the possibility of applying the egalitarian principles of the French Revolution.

51. Which of the following corresponded with the origins of the Great Famine in Ireland?

    A.   The repeal of the Corn Laws
    B.   The prevention of crop exportation
    C.   The creation of an Irish parliament
    D.   The widespread cultivation of maize
    E.   The nearly universal potato blight

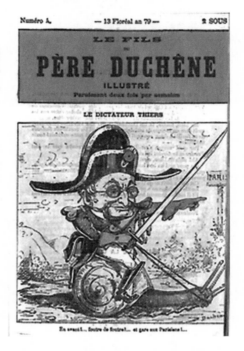

52. The French political cartoon shown above, from the era of the Paris Commune, ridicules the failure of

    A.   the French press to report events accurately.
    B.   the Communals to implement social reforms quickly.
    C.   the Communals to expand their control outside Paris.
    D.   the French government to quickly put down the insurrection.
    E.   the French government to provide modern weaponry and transport.

53. The fundamental concept of the Greek War of Independence was the desire for

   A. socialism.

   B. imperialism.

   C. republicanism.

   D. constitutionalism.

   E. self-determination.

54. The fresco above, *Germania* by Philipp Veit, is characteristic of the thought and art of the Revolutions of 1848 because of its emphasis on

   A. conservatism.

   B. the role of women.

   C. just war theory.

   D. Marxist ideology.

   E. the theme of nationalism.

55. Which of the following corresponded with the rise of Impressionism in Paris?

    A.   The desire to depict the lives of the nobles
    B.   The decline of still life and imagery of nature
    C.   The invention of the camera, with its ability to create life-like images
    D.   The inclusion of female painters in the Académie des Beux-Arts
    E.   The abolition of the Académie des Beux-Arts under Napoleon III

56. All of the following were aspects of the Decembrist Revolution in Russia as it unfolded in 1825 EXCEPT

    A.   the goal of achieving universal suffrage.
    B.   the rejection of court excesses and lifestyle.
    C.   the desire to curtail the power of the monarchy.
    D.   the conscious mimicry of reform movements abroad.
    E.   the wish to free the serfs from lives of hardship and drudgery.

"The Governing Senate…has deemed it necessary to make known…that the landlords' serfs and peasants…owe their landlord proper submission and absolute obedience in all matters, according to the laws that have been enacted from time immemorial…"

57. The quotation above best illustrates the ideology of

    A.   Karl Marx.
    B.   Leo Tolstoy.
    C.   Alexander II.
    D.   Varvara Nelidova.
    E.   Catherine the Great.

58. The writings of Charles Darwin strongly influenced which of the following intellectual movements?

    A. Capitalism

    B. Modernism

    C. Imperialism

    D. Isolationism

    E. Malthusianism

59. The Opium Wars helped establish the role of the British in nineteenth-century China by

    A. creating a mutually beneficial economic coalition and trade system.

    B. establishing an unequal balance of unequal trade with a limited role for the Chinese.

    C. presenting the British as moral governors willing to abolish the opium trade.

    D. importing large amounts of Chinese silver in exchange for European manufactured goods.

    E. demonstrating the British willingness to acculturate themselves for mutual benefit.

60. All of the following resulted from the creation of the Panama Canal
EXCEPT

A. the decline of France's economic control over maritime trade
routes.
B. the creation and widespread implementation of new industrial machines.
C. the establishment of U.S. dominance over South American
foreign affairs.
D. the development of new port cities in Europe catering to
water trade.
E. the dramatic increase in economic goods transported solely
by water.

61. A historian would be most likely to cite the image above as an
example of

A. Impressionism.
B. Cubism.
C. Realism.
D. Dadaism.
E. Art Nouveau.

62. Which of the following factors led most immediately to the military coup that launched the Spanish Civil War?

    A.   The execution of Calvo Sotelo by the Assault Guards

    B.   A decrease in external foreign intervention in Spain's diplomatic affairs

    C.   The failure of the Catholic Church to provide adequate social services

    D.   An increase in agricultural production that led to arguments over export taxes

    E.   The forging of a political alliance between the Catalan Republicans and Germany

"I should feel the air move against me, and feel the things I touch, instead of having only looked at them. I'm sure life is all wrong because it has become much too visual—we can neither hear nor feel nor understand, we can only see. I'm sure that is entirely wrong."

63. The excerpt presented above best reflects the key themes and writing style of the work of

    A.   Ezra Pound.

    B.   Beatrix Potter.

    C.   D. H. Lawrence.

    D.   Charles Dickens.

    E.   Ernest Hemingway.

64. In early twentieth-century Europe, women were less likely to have the right to vote because of the belief that women

    A. were not interested in politics.
    B. would vote for extreme liberal social programs.
    C. should express their political opinions at home.
    D. were not educated enough to make informed decisions.
    E. should not leave their children in order to participate in elections.

65. In comparison to the early modern international system, the most distinctive feature of the early twentieth century was its

    A. use of all-volunteer armies.
    B. fear of the Socialist and Communist threat.
    C. development of militarism as a foreign policy.
    D. use of diplomacy to solve international conflict.
    E. reliance on permanently stationed peacekeeping forces.

66. To which of the following did the failure of the German Schlieffen Plan in World War I primarily contribute?

    A. The rise of Nazism
    B. The arms race
    C. U-boat warfare
    D. Trench warfare
    E. Desertions of the German army

67. As the Lost Generation developed intellectually after World War I, it emphasized all of the following EXCEPT

   A.   social aimlessness.
   B.   themes of self-exile.
   C.   traditional religious thought.
   D.   difficulties with consumerism.
   E.   lack of morality in modern life.

   "War alone brings up to its highest tension all human energy and puts the stamp of nobility upon the people who have the courage to meet it. All other trials are substitutes, which never really put a man in front of himself in the alternative of life and death."

68. Which of the following philosophies is represented in this quotation?

   A.   Deism
   B.   Fascism
   C.   Pacifism
   D.   Anarchism
   E.   Republicanism

69. Which of the following resulted from the rigid adherence to the gold standard during the interwar period?

   A.   The decline of mercantilism
   B.   An increase in the production of fine jewelry
   C.   A worldwide economic depression
   D.   An increase in the value of the U.S. dollar
   E.   A reparation of damages stemming from the silver standard

70. Which of the following accurately describes Germany under the Weimar Republic in the 1920s?

    A.   Many people lived in fear of the Black Shirts.

    B.   Most German citizens lost the right to vote.

    C.   The president was reduced to a political figurehead with little power.

    D.   Censorship of the press limited the information available to the people.

    E.   Hyperinflation made it difficult for citizens to provide for themselves.

71. Which of the following best describes the leadership of Adolf Hitler (1933–1945)?

    A.   Liberal

    B.   Fascist

    C.   Democratic

    D.   Socialist

    E.   Dictatorship

72. A central feature of the Marshall Plan was the

    A.   creation of the League of Nations to prevent future world wars.

    B.   use of antiquated technology to ensure full employment levels.

    C.   implementation of trade barriers to increase national profits through tariffs.

    D.   marshaling of standing armies along the borders of Communist countries.

    E.   desire to reduce the economic devastation in areas liable to Communist takeover.

73. The image above, *The Peacock Skirt,* is characteristic of the thought and art of

  A. Dadaism.
  B. Fauvism.
  C. Minimalism.
  D. Art Nouveau.
  E. expressionism.

74. Which of the following events was instrumental in the division of Berlin in 1949?

  A. An armed rebellion against Soviet rule in Czechoslovakia
  B. A referendum among Berlin's population to separate two sides of the city
  C. A Soviet blockade on access routes and trade
  D. A need to balance Communist and non-Communist forces in the former capital
  E. An agreement to allow Germany to rearm and reclaim the Rhineland

75. In Soviet Russia, motherhood was often glorified through state pro-
    paganda because of the belief that children

    A. provided a useful employment for nonworking wives.
    B. gave psychological insight in the Communist philosophy.
    C. were essential for expanding the Communist power base.
    D. offered an opportunity to showcase gender equality in childcare.
    E. served as a metaphor of the new Soviet state to the rural
        population.

76. Which of the following studies would most likely discuss the con-
    cept of "domino theory"?

    A. Transcripts from the Yalta conference
    B. Press releases from the U.S. White House
    C. A scholarly article on Polish art and culture
    D. A first-person account of life in the Soviet Union
    E. A personal diary from an inhabitant of rural England

77. Why was the North Atlantic Treaty Organization (NATO) formed?

    A. To introduce a common European currency
    B. To reallocate the resources of the Rhineland
    C. To form a free trade alliance in Western Europe
    D. To unify the Soviet states against Western influences
    E. To create a collective defense pact against Communism

78. The close relationship between television and popular opinion during the late twentieth century was demonstrated by the public's reaction to

   A. the fireside chats and speeches of FDR.
   B. the conversion of the Eiffel Tower to a radio receiver.
   C. the vivid televised images of the Vietnam War.
   D. the destruction of German televisions as Western inventions.
   E. the international loss of programming during the 1994 World Series.

79. Which of the following was a chief outcome of the widespread availability of the Internet after the 1990s?

   A. The loss of real social opportunities
   B. The rise of accelerated human interaction
   C. The replacement of physical mail systems
   D. The decline in collaborative projects and decision making
   E. The development of Internet content restrictions in the West

80. Which of the following statements is true regarding the collapse of the Soviet Union in 1991?

   A. Democratization led to the gradual weakening of the central government.
   B. Soviet leadership was overthrown to end the Great Purge of intellectuals and dissidents.
   C. The living conditions in the Soviet Union immediately improved.
   D. A lack of job opportunities led to the destabilization of the workforce.
   E. A lack of funds for international defense led to the fall of the Soviet government.

END TIME: _____

END OF SECTION I
TAKE A FIVE-MINUTE BREAK

EUROPEAN HISTORY
SECTION II
Part A
Planning time—15 minutes

Writing time—45 minutes

Directions: The following question is based on the accompanying Documents 1–7. The documents have been edited for the purpose of this exercise. Write your answer on lined notebook paper. *(During the actual examination, you will be given lined answer sheets for this exercise.)*

Record your Part A start time: _____

This question is designed to test your ability to work with and understand historical documents.

Write an essay that:

- Provides an appropriate, explicitly stated thesis that directly addresses all parts of the question and does NOT simply restate the question.
- Discusses a majority of the documents individually and specifically.
- Demonstrates understanding of the basic meaning of a majority of the documents.
- Analyzes point of view or bias in at least three documents.
- Analyzes the documents by explicitly grouping them in at least three appropriate ways.

You may refer to relevant historical information not mentioned in the documents.

1. Using the documents provided, analyze the image and perceptions of Napoleon Bonaparte from the period 1789 to 1815.

DOCUMENT 1

Source: Napoleon Bonaparte, from a speech to his troops, 1796

Soldiers, you are naked, ill fed! The Government owes you much; it can give you nothing. Your patience, the courage you display in the midst of these rocks, are admirable; but they procure you no glory, no fame is reflected upon you. I seek to lead you into the most fertile plains in the world. Rich provinces, great cities will be in your power. There you will find honor, glory, and riches.

DOCUMENT 2

Source: Napoleon, writing of his coup d'état, 1799

On my return to Paris [from Egypt] I found division among all authorities, and agreement upon only one point, namely, that the Constitution was half destroyed and was unable to save liberty…

They crowded around the president, uttering threats, arms in their hands they commanded him to outlaw me; I was informed of this: I ordered him to be rescued from their fury, and six grenadiers of the Legislative Body secured him. Immediately afterwards some grenadiers of the legislative body charged into the hall and cleared it.

The factions, intimidated, dispersed and fled. The majority, freed from their attacks, returned freely and peaceably into the meeting hall, listened to the proposals on behalf of public safety, deliberated, and prepared the salutary resolution which is to become the new and provisional law of the Republic.

Frenchmen, you will doubtless recognize in this conduct the zeal of a soldier of liberty, a citizen devoted to the Republic. Conservative, tutelary, and liberal ideas have been restored to their rights through the dispersal of the rebels…

DOCUMENT 3

Source: Napoleon Crossing the Alps, *a painting by Jacque-Louis David, 1801*

DOCUMENT 4

Source: From the Napoleonic Codes, a series of civil laws instituted by Napoleon, 1804

Book I: Of Persons

Title I: Of the Enjoyment and Privation of Civil Rights

The exercise of civil rights is independent of the quality of citizen, which is only acquired and preserved conformably to the constitutional law.

Every Frenchman shall enjoy civil rights.

Chapter VI: Of the Respective Rights and Duties of Married Persons

212. The wife is obliged to live with her husband, and to follow him to every place where he may judge it convenient to reside: the husband is obliged to receive her, and to furnish her with every necessity for the wants of life, according to his means and station.

213. The wife cannot plead in her own name, without the authority of her husband, even though she should be a public trader, or noncommunicant, or separate in property.

215. A wife, although noncommunicant or separate in property, cannot give, pledge, or acquire by free or chargeable title, without the concurrence of her husband in the act, or his consent in writing.

DOCUMENT 5

Source: Napoleon, *a painting by Anne-Louis Girodet de Roucy Trioson, 1812*

DOCUMENT 6

Source: Political cartoon, 1814

"Oh, Papa, you've made beautiful soap bubbles!"

DOCUMENT 7

Source: Political Cartoon (Napoleon), 1815

END TIME: _____

END OF SECTION II, PART A
IMMEDIATELY BEGIN NEXT SECTION

EUROPEAN HISTORY
SECTION II
Part B
Time—35 minutes

Directions: You are to answer ONE question from the three questions below. Make your selection carefully, choosing the question that you are best prepared to answer thoroughly in the time permitted. You should spend five minutes organizing or outlining your answer. Write your answer on lined notebook pages. *(During the actual examination, you will be given lined answer sheets for this exercise.)*

Record your Part B start time: _____

Write an essay that:

- Has a relevant thesis.
- Addresses all parts of the question.
- Supports a thesis with specific evidence.
- Is well organized.

2. Analyze TWO of the following economic areas in Europe during the Renaissance:

- Agriculture
- Commerce
- Banking
- Industry

3. Analyze the technological developments that made the Industrial Revolution possible in Europe in the eighteenth and nineteenth centuries.

4.   Analyze economic and social developments in Russia during the reign of Peter the Great.

END TIME: _____

END OF SECTION II, PART B
IMMEDIATELY BEGIN NEXT SECTION

EUROPEAN HISTORY
SECTION II
Part C
Time—35 minutes

Directions: You are to answer ONE question from the three questions below. Make your selection carefully, choosing the question that you are best prepared to answer thoroughly in the time permitted. You should spend five minutes organizing or outlining your answer. Write your answer on lined notebook pages. *(During the actual examination, you will be given lined answer sheets for this exercise.)*

Record your Part C start time: _____

Write an essay that:

- Has a relevant thesis.
- Addresses all parts of the question.
- Supports a thesis with specific evidence.
- Is well organized.

5. Compare and contrast the origins and beliefs of the Anglican and Calvinist branches of Christianity that formed during the Reformation period.

6. Assess the origins, goals, and effects of European imperialism in the sixteenth and seventeenth centuries.

7. Describe and analyze the urbanization of Europe during the eighteenth and nineteenth centuries.

END TIME: _____

END OF EXAM

Diagnostic Test Answers and Explanations

Section I: Multiple-Choice Questions

ANSWER KEY

1.	E	24.	E
2.	C	25.	E
3.	D	26.	B
4.	D	27.	D
5.	E	28.	C
6.	A	29.	C
7.	D	30.	B
8.	C	31.	C
9.	E	32.	C
10.	E	33.	B
11.	A	34.	D
12.	C	35.	B
13.	E	36.	D
14.	A	37.	D
15.	B	38.	B
16.	C	39.	A
17.	E	40.	C
18.	E	41.	D
19.	A	42.	E
20.	A	43.	A
21.	C	44.	D
22.	B	45.	B
23.	C	46.	D

47. A	64. C
48. C	65. C
49. B	66. D
50. D	67. C
51. E	68. B
52. E	69. C
53. E	70. E
54. E	71. E
55. C	72. E
56. A	73. D
57. E	74. D
58. C	75. C
59. B	76. B
60. D	77. E
61. B	78. C
62. A	79. B
63. C	80. A

ANSWER EXPLANATIONS

1. **E.** Early humanism relied on the critical examination of primary texts, such as the Greek and Latin religious texts that had formed the foundations of Christian beliefs. Early humanists such as Erasmus used those texts brought by Byzantine refugees to popularize the ideas of humanism.

Difficulty Level: Hard

2. **C.** During the Age of Discovery, both the Portuguese and the Spanish launched a series of exploratory campaigns that revealed much about the world across the Atlantic. However, the two countries had

very different motivations for these campaigns. The Portuguese were primarily interested in Eastern trade, specifically spices, and used state support and advanced technology to develop trade lines. The Spanish were more interested in a social conquering of the New World. To accomplish this, they merged military skill and religious evangelicalism to support the mass conversion of local populations.

Difficulty Level: Hard

3. **D.** *Columbia Exchange* is a term used to describe the exchange of goods and diseases between Europe and the New World during the Age of Discovery. As part of this exchange, Europeans brought horses, cattle, and sheep to the New World. These animals were domesticated by Native American civilizations and became major components of the American economy. Europeans also brought new germs and viruses to the New World, decimating large populations. On the other side, the Europeans returned to Europe with corn, potatoes, and tobacco. The humble potato would eventually become a staple of the European agricultural system, supporting the populations of entire nations.

Difficulty Level: Hard

4. **D.** *The School of Athens* (by Raphael) is an emblematic example of High Renaissance Italian art. It prominently features both proportion and perspective, new concepts that came into the art world during this historical era. Like other Renaissance artwork, this painting builds on classical themes. However, it does not use found materials (such as in a collage); it does not feature shades of gray; nor does it break figures into abstract shapes.

Difficulty Level: Hard

5. **E.** This quote is drawn from a letter by Lorenzo de' Medici, in which he discusses how artistic patronage (namely his own) enhances both social and political prestige. The Medici family was famous for its vast sponsorship of the arts; some historians argue this support was a direct factor in the origination of the Italian Renaissance. Additionally, the Medicis were responsible for political machinations that resulted in

the election of popes and political leaders on the basis of social clout. Michelangelo and Leonardo da Vinci were artists, not artistic patrons. Machiavelli did not support the arts.

Difficulty Level: Medium

6. **A.** Spanish and Portuguese exploration in the New World had a universally devastating effect on native populations as the explorers sought the three G's (*gold, God, glory*) at any cost. The explorers often instituted forced labor conditions and unequal trade balances to secure for themselves the economic riches of new lands. Their very presence led to repeated epidemics of disease among natives, who had not previously been exposed to many of the germs and viruses they carried. The Spanish and Portuguese were also intent upon converting natives to Roman Catholicism, often by force. This drive, however, led many of the early explorers to learn and use native languages, because it was often easier to convert a native population in their own tongue. Spanish would not become the official language of many colonies until the seventeenth and eighteenth centuries.

Difficulty Level: Medium

7. **D.** Machiavelli's book *The Prince* provided a blueprint for the politically minded "new monarchs" of the sixteenth century who preferred to rule through political prowess rather than divine right. His text was extremely controversial and was condemned by the Church.

Difficulty Level: Hard

8. **C.** The Spanish fleet was decimated in 1588 due to a combination of poor weather and British naval superiority. The Spanish entered the conflict with damaged ships; they did not run out of supplies such as fresh water until forced to retreat.

Difficulty Level: Medium

9. **E.** The Agricultural Revolution in the sixteenth and seventeenth centuries was characterized by higher agricultural output driven by the use of scientific methodologies and new machinery. Cities with large agricultural hinterlands, such as London, Paris, and Amsterdam, rose to

power on the basis on these developments. They were able to eclipse the older economic centers of Venice and Genoa.

Difficulty Level: Medium

10. **E.** These directions, from Shakespeare's *Hamlet*, represent the Elizabethan perspective on the way actors should best employ their craft (i.e., dramaturgy and stagecraft). Elizabeth I supported many acting companies, including Shakespeare's, as part of her cultural revitalization movement. While many of the other themes represented by the answer choices were common topics for Elizabethan works or present in *Hamlet*, this quote pertains directly to the presence, behavior, and comportment of actors on the stage.

Difficulty Level: Hard

11. **A.** The Edict of Nantes ended the French Wars of Religion by granting Huguenots substantive rights, including the right to protection from the Inquisition, the right to places of safety, and freedom from persecution based on religious practices. While the Edict represented a step towards religious tolerance, it did not extend complete freedom of religion, because Jews and Muslims were still persecuted. It also did not create a separation of Church and state, because the government of Paris continued as Catholic.

Difficulty Level: Hard

12. **C.** The Dutch Golden Age in the seventeenth century involved the dramatic flourishing of economy and culture due in part to the large influx of immigrants from territories divided under the Peace of Westphalia. These immigrants brought new ways of thinking to the Netherlands, such as collective economics (corporations), trade monopolies, and energy creation. Prince Henry the Navigator was a fifteenth-century Portuguese prince.

Difficulty Level: Hard

13. **E.** Martin Luther challenged the Catholic Church with his position that the institutional structure of the Church, including the clergy, was unnecessary to individual religious experience. When

Luther made his challenge, he did not have the authority to instate guidelines for the Catholic clergy (being only a monk). He did not address the right of the Catholic Church to accept tithes, focusing instead on the sale of indulgences.

Difficulty Level: Medium

14. **A.** The Acts of Union in 1707 are often credited with ushering in the Scottish Enlightenment, which featured the works of Adam Smith, David Hume, James Hutton, and Sir Walter Scott. Via the Acts, the Scots gained access to the English public school system and economic free trade alliances. This union stipulated that Scotland be allowed to retain its religious preferences, but would answer to England politically.

Difficulty Level: Hard

15. **B.** The elaborate allegorical content of this image, in addition to the presence of contrapposto, marks it as an example of the Baroque movement. Art Nouveau, Impressionism, and Fauvism favored more abstract images, while realism was not characterized by allegorical representations of major themes.

Difficulty Level: Medium

16. **C.** Zwingli and Calvin challenged the supremacy of the Roman Catholic Church on political and religious levels. Their example spread outside of Switzerland to other European countries, such as, England, Scotland, and the German states. Although their followers were occasionally forced to defend themselves, Zwingli and Calvin did not directly advocate the formation of religious armies or mass immigration.

Difficulty Level: Medium

17. **E.** The Peace of Westphalia reaffirmed the earlier Peace of Augsburg (1555), which stated that each prince had the right to determine the dominant religion in his territory. Violations of this rule had led to an increase in conflict between Catholics and Protestants in the Holy Roman Empire (the Thirty Years' War). The Peace of Westphalia reaffirmed the ultimate sovereignty of princes. The Netherlands were formally recognized as independent and the use of privateers was outlawed. Spain

and France continued to wage war for another thirty years after the Peace of Westphalia.

Difficulty Level: Medium

18. **E.** The marriage of Martin Luther to Katherina von Bora would most likely be cited by historians as an example of the changing role of women as a result of the Protestant Reformation. The fact that Martin Luther advocated clerical marriage, as well as the blueprint of spousal assistance demonstrated through his marriage, represented a significant departure from previous belief systems.

Difficulty Level: Easy

19. **A.** William Bradshaw and Cotton Mather were prominent proponents of the Puritan cause and advocated a strict interpretation of religious doctrine, congregationalism, anti-Catholicism, and the zealous pursuit of heresy. Cotton Mather was also deeply involved in the American Salem witch trials, using Puritanical belief systems to issue punishment.

Difficulty Level: Hard

20. **A.** Frederick the Great of Prussia implemented a serious of social and political reforms aimed at creating a freer, more egalitarian, more tolerant Prussian state. However, he stopped short of instituting a constitution, as doing so would have impeded his ability to implement reforms without opposition. His formation of a bureaucracy, support for religious tolerance, abolition of the death penalty, and humane treatment of prisoners of war are often attributed to influence from his friendship with Voltaire.

Difficulty Level: Hard

21. **C.** Mercantilism was an economic system governing international trade in the Age of Exploration/Expansion. It relied on an artificial and unequal balance of trade between well-off countries and their colonies, in which the colonies were required to supply raw materials to the mother country under unfavorable conditions. This system was replaced by capitalism, prominently advocated by Adam Smith, which

argued for laissez-faire economic policies that were mutually beneficial to all trading partners.

Difficulty Level: Hard

22. **B.** Galileo faced opposition from the Roman Catholic Church for his heliocentric theory (derived from the work of Copernicus) on the basis that this theory contradicted key Biblical texts. Galileo was eventually brought up on charges of heresy and sentenced to house arrest because his theory seemed to challenge Church teachings, not because of any perceived factual or scientific errors.

Difficulty Level: Easy

23. **C.** During the English Civil War, religious tensions flared between the predominantly Catholic population of Ireland and the predominantly Protestant English invaders. At the conclusion of the war, all Catholic lands were confiscated and given to Protestant supporters of the English. The sharp division between religious groups, rooted in land, continues to be contentious to this day.

Difficulty Level: Hard

24. **E.** The Pragmatic Sanction of 1713 was issued in order to allow Holy Roman Emperor Charles VI to pass the Austrian throne and undivided lands to his daughter in the event he did not have male heirs. This sanction did not support political training for women, a fact that left Maria Theresa (his daughter) without much of the knowledge she needed to rule effectively.

Difficulty Level: Hard

25. **E.** Empiricism is a belief in the idea that the experiences of the senses reveal truth. This belief is the core ideology behind the scientific method, which was developed and honed during the seventeenth and eighteenth centuries. Empiricism is opposite to rationalism, which argues that sensory evidence can be misleading and only innate leaps of the mind are valid. Empiricist philosophers did not trust emotions and generally opposed lifestyles associated with emotionality.

Difficulty Level: Medium

26. **B.** The Glorious Revolution of 1688 (so termed due to the limited amount of bloodshed) saw William of Orange and his wife Mary come to the throne of England. Their rise to power deposed James II and made Catholicism illegal for any future leader of England. Most importantly, the Glorious Revolution of 1688 instituted a parliamentary democracy in England, through which the power of the king could be checked.

Difficulty Level: Medium

27. **D.** The eighteenth-century coffeehouse was defined by its open nature, as anyone with a penny could purchase a drink. These institutions were important sites of social and political debate where people could gather to discuss the latest news. Unlike gaming halls, pleasure gardens, and union halls, coffeehouses accepted individuals from *all* classes of society. The debates held in these locations were often spontaneous, lively, and informed by the popular press, making them markedly different from the formal debates of parliament.

Difficulty Level: Medium

28. **C.** The image shows a microscope, which can be identified by its optical viewer pointing toward a small slide. This general setup is still used for modern day microscopes. This particular microscope belonged to Robert Hooke, who published a book with early illustrations of small items viewed through it.

Difficulty Level: Easy

29. **C.** The National Constituent Assembly, or National Assembly, was primarily interested in implementing a constitutional monarchy in France to prevent a return to the excesses of divine rule. This moderate attempt at reform was eventually overrun by more radical movements, including those that eventually overthrew and executed the king, implemented universal male suffrage, and led a wave of mass executions.

Difficulty Level: Hard

30. **B.** The early French Revolution is remarkable for the participation of women and the rural poor. In fact, a march on Versailles led by a group of women is often considered the starting point of the French

Revolution. The rural poor were also heavily involved in early protests, and early discontent revolved around the price of foodstuffs. The *sans-culottes* and the Jacobins would become a major political force later in the Revolution, once the movement gained traction and radicalized.

Difficulty Level: Medium

31. **C.** The quotation is drawn from the famous work of Olympe de Gouges, *Declaration of the Rights of Women* (1791). This work was a response to the failure of the French Revolution to grant substantive rights to women. Olympe de Gouges's work emphasized Enlightenment ideas of individual rights and stressed that women should also be recognized as individuals.

Difficulty Level: Medium

32. **C.** The almost continuous warfare waged by Napoleon, in continental Europe and Haiti, forced him to sell the Louisiana Territory to the United States. He needed the funds in order to continue running the French empire. Napoleon sold the Louisiana territory prior to his exile; he did not attempt to apply the French social systems to the territory.

Difficulty Level: Medium

33. **B.** During the Industrial Revolution, whole families needed to work in order to provide for the basic necessities of life. Unlike traditional labor in a rural setting, in which all members worked to support the family, survival in an industrialized urban center meant dividing the family so that each family member could seek the most profitable employment. Family members did not generally work together. In terms of gender roles, the Industrial Revolution tended to perpetuate dominant male ideologies: women made less money than men, were expected to take care of all household duties, and were not given the opportunity to become breadwinners.

Difficulty Level: Easy

34. **D.** The Luddites were anti-industrialists who argued that mechanized production, based on piecework, destroyed their livelihood, way of life, and working conditions. They led many armed uprisings in major factory

towns. During these uprisings, the Luddites would smash the machinery that found so threatening to their artisan production methods.

Difficulty Level: Hard

35. **B**. Peter the Great was interested in recreating Russia in the image of Enlightenment Europe. One of the main expressions of this policy was the founding of St. Petersburg, a new capital along Russia's Western border. St. Petersburg served as Peter's "window to the West." During the construction of the city, Peter was criticized for relocating the capital even though Moscow was still a thriving urban center, for requiring the elite to move, and for forcing serfs to work under hazardous conditions.

Difficulty Level: Medium

36. **D**. The description of life as "poor, nasty, brutish, and short" fits with the philosophical outlook of Thomas Hobbes. In his most famous work, *The Leviathan*, Hobbes argued that human societies need strong governments to reign in the disreputable tendencies of humankind.

Difficulty Level: Medium

37. **D**. The relationship between the Scientific Revolution and agrarian practices can be best viewed through the development of domestication programs for livestock. These programs involved applying scientific knowledge to farming practices in order to increase yield and output. Domestication and selective breeding programs were the only agrarian practices given as answer choices to be instituted in the eighteenth century. Pasteurization and genetic food modification occurred much later in time.

Difficulty Level: Hard

38. **B**. King George III is remembered by history for his active resistance of colonial bids for independence, most notably in the context of the American Revolution.

Difficulty Level: Easy

39. **A**. From 1726–1727, Europe and the Ottoman Empire experienced what has been called the "tulip craze." Tulips became the symbol of

upper class status and wealth. Price inflation continued until it became necessary for governments to establish price controls.

Difficulty Level: Medium

40. **C.** The quote demonstrates the emphasis on emotions that came to define the Romantic movement. Overall, Romantics were interested in the indefinable aspects of human existence, such as high emotion, and spent their lives actively seeking to experience life to the fullest. A cultural example of the Romantic lifestyle is found in Lord Byron, who was a flamboyant and wild adherent to hedonistic Romanticism.

Difficulty Level: Medium

41. **D.** The Corn Laws (1815–1846) were meant to support local industry by limiting the availability of grain from abroad. These laws applied to all cereal grains. The Corn Laws were met with opposition, however, because imported grain was often much cheaper than the homegrown variety. The ban on cereal imports was eventually repealed after the Great Famine in Ireland demonstrated that less expensive grain products were needed to support the population.

Difficulty Level: Medium

42. **E.** The terms "less eligibility" and "workhouse test" would most likely be used in a book on the English Poor Laws; these terms were used to determine how the law itself was applied.

Difficulty Level: Hard

43. **A.** Jane Austen's novels stressed the difficulties encountered by young women in a socially stratified society. Austen critiqued the customs and social issues of her day, ultimately drawing the reader's attention to the need for reform. Her novels were published anonymously, as novel writing was not considered a suitable employment for a lady.

Difficulty Level: Medium

44. **D.** Napoleon's defeat at the Battle of Waterloo allowed the European allies to implement a serious of changes they believed would limit the power of France and prevent the rise of Napoleon-like figures in the future. The allies reduced French borders to their 1790 levels; they restored

the Bourbons to the throne; and they exiled Napoleon Bonaparte to the island of Elba. The Allies also ensured that the new Bourbon king was responsible to a parliament for all decisions.

Difficulty Level: Medium

45. **B.** William Wilberforce led a heroic twenty-year campaign to abolish the English slave trade against vocal opponents such as Charles Watson-Wentworth. As a result of these efforts, slaves could no longer be imported or exported out of England or transported on English ships. Complete emancipation was to come in the following years.

Difficulty Level: Medium

46. **D.** As an intellectual movement, classical liberalism was primarily concerned with the rights of individuals and the relationship between individuals and the state. While thinkers were concerned with individuals, they did not often address issues of gender or social status. Rationalism is not a nineteenth-century intellectual movement.

Difficulty Level: Hard

47. **A.** The Holy Roman Empire began a rapid decline in the nineteenth century after its political base was eroded through a series of French land grabs. Without the territory to back up his claim to authority, Emperor Francis II abdicated the throne and dissolved the Empire. Napoleon reorganized existing territory into the Confederation of the Rhine.

Difficulty Level: Hard

48. **C.** In the nineteenth century, women were considered legally subordinate to their husbands. Under this system, women did not have the legal right to personal property, because everything they owned technically belonged to the spouse. Women did not have a political voice and could not vote or run for office. Women were also paid approximately half as much as men when they worked outside the home. The only legal right possessed by women during this time was the right to a ten-hour workday, a reform granted to women and children via the Ten Hour Act of 1847.

Difficulty Level: Medium

49. **B.** Corsets severely restricted the abdomen in order to shape the female body into the fashionable "hourglass" figure. As a social tool, corsets represented the subordinate position of women by physically restricting movement and making women more dependent on others for daily functions. The tightly laced version (shown) had the most severe effects on the body. The extreme silhouette created by these garments was considered the mark of an upper class women participating in the "cult of domesticity," with servants to complete manual household labor. She could focus on appearing attractive for her husband.

Difficulty Level: Hard

50. **D.** The Concert of Europe was a European coalition led by Metternich. It focused on creating a political balance of power in Europe in order to head off widespread revolution and political expansion. Members of the coalition stood against the new values of nationalism and egalitarianism and favored conservatism at all levels. The Concert of Europe also had a religious component, as many of its members wished to maintain Christian social value systems in the empire.

Difficulty Level: Medium

51. **E.** One of the major events that corresponded with the beginning of the Great Famine in Ireland was the almost universal spread of a potato blight. During the nineteenth century, potatoes were the main crop of the Irish population as other crop growth was tightly regulated by the English government under the Corn Laws.

Difficulty Level: Easy

52. **E.** The image shown ridicules the French government for its slow reaction in the face of the Paris Commune. As shown through the formal clothing of the rider and the presence of a snail, the image projects the idea that formal upper class systems (the opposite of the Communals) were incapable of moving quickly.

Difficulty Level: Hard

53. **E.** The Greek War of Independence was fought primarily because of the Greek desire for self-determinism. This political principle states that

native populations have the right to determine their own governance. In order to achieve self-determination, the Greeks needed to gain their independence from the Turks.

Difficulty Level: Hard

54. **E.** The fresco represents nationalism through its use of symbols, such as the German flag, the two-headed eagle, the crown of oak leaves, and the sword. This particular image was displayed in the Frankfurt Parliament of 1848. It is representative of the spirit of nationalism that characterized the revolutions of 1848. During this time period, many nations chose to symbolically represent their nation allegorically in the form of a woman (such as Lady Liberty in America, Germania in Germany, and Marianne in France). The use of the female was strictly allegorical, however, and did not represent the desire to grant rights or authority to women.

Difficulty Level: Medium

55. **C.** Impressionism was an art movement that grew from the invention of an accurate camera. Because a camera could depict life images with a degree of detail unreachable to ordinary artists, those artists chose to emphasize emotions in their work. Artists such as Monet, Manet, and Degas painted their "impressions" of nature and ordinary life scenes.

Difficulty Level: Easy

56. **A.** The Decembrist Revolution in Russia, partially inspired by reform movements in Western Europe, argued that the serfs should no longer be forced to labor in unfavorable conditions. The Decembrists fought for the abolition of serfdom, a rejection of court life and excess, and an end to the tsar's ability to affect the condition of the people. The Decembrists stopped short, however, of advocating for complete suffrage.

Difficulty Level: Medium

57. **E.** In Russia, the issue of serfdom became a major point of contention for monarchs in the eighteenth and nineteenth centuries. While most monarchs believed that serfdom was justifiable, Catherine the

Great went so far as to publicly support serfdom and increased penalties for serfs attempting to escape their duties. Alexander II abolished serfdom before he was assassinated in 1881.

Difficulty Level: Medium

58. **C.** Charles Darwin's view of evolutionary development and "survival of the fittest" was used to justify the expansion of nations through imperialism. Many imperialists, such as Herbert Spencer, argued that expanding political power over weaker nations was the natural evolutionary result of the strong surviving where the weak had failed.

Difficulty Level: Hard

59. **B.** The Opium Wars (1839–1842 and 1856–1860) resulted from Chinese resistance to the amount of opium imported to China by the British. The British used opium as a trading commodity, leading to an unequal balance of power between China and England. The British were granted most favored nation status, given territorial holdings, and allowed to establish economic ports.

Difficulty Level: Hard

60. **D.** The opening of the Panama Canal substantially impacted international maritime trade, because it replaced French economic interests in South America with American interests, leading to a rapid decline in French maritime authority. Overall, the Canal allowed for easier and more efficient water transport. The Panama Canal did not result in new European port cities, but instead became beneficial to ports already in existence.

Difficulty Level: Hard

61. **B.** *Portrait of Picasso* by Juan Gris is painted in the Cubist style, as evidenced by the sharp planes, multiple angles, and fragmented point of view. Cubism was a form of artistic rebellion that rejected traditional styles in favor of an extreme point of view.

Difficulty Level: Easy

62. **A.** The most immediate cause of the Spanish Civil War was the assassination of Calvo Sotelo by the Assault Guards. This assassination

crystallized many of the objections that the Nationalists had to the existing government and provided impetus to action.

Difficulty Level: Medium

63. **C.** This excerpt reflects the key themes and writing styles of D. H. Lawrence. In terms of social history, D. H. Lawrence faced a landmark obscenity case in London when the publisher of *Lady Chatterley's Lover* was accused of publishing pornographic material. Lawrence's writing was emblematic of the early twentieth-century style that focused on the sensuous expression of high emotion.

Difficulty Level: Medium

64. **C.** The campaign for women's suffrage in the early twentieth century was hindered by cultural assumptions and prejudices about the role of women in society. One of the major arguments used against women was the idea that women and men existed in "separate spheres." A women's sphere was inside the home; as such, she should share her views with her husband, and he could act on them if he thought them wise.

Difficulty Level: Medium

65. **C.** The early twentieth century saw a gradual buildup of military arsenals that, when coupled with the increasingly entangling political alliances of Western Europe, marked it as a very different age. During this time period, countries were prepared to fight for their political and social rights using military rather than diplomatic means. Peacekeeping was not used extensively and armies were frequently conscripted in times of great need.

Difficulty Level: Hard

66. **D.** The Schlieffen Plan was a plan of German aggression intended to defeat enemies via swift and decisive action. When it failed, the German army ended up spread out over a large geographical range, with limited access to resources or military support. The only option was to dig trenches; these would come to define the brutal conditions of wartime on both sides of the German borders.

Difficulty Level: Hard

67. **C.** The Lost Generation was a loose organization of writers whose work focused on themes of aimlessness, a loss of morality, and problems associated with modern consumerism. Writers included Gertrude Stein, Ernest Hemingway, and F. Scott Fitzgerald. They frequently wrote about the failure of traditional religious thought for survivors of World War I.

Difficulty Level: Medium

68. **B.** Fascism, especially in the form popularized by Italy's Benito Mussolini, used warfare as a tool of the state. Warfare was considered the ultimate expression of both citizenship and manliness. None of the other political philosophies listed advocated violence or warfare. Many, in fact, supported the avoidance of violence.

Difficulty Level: Easy

69. **C.** The rigid adherence to the gold standard in many European nations led to a worldwide economic depression in the interwar years. The term *gold standard* deals with the valuation of currency, not jewelry production. While mercantilism relies on hard currency, such as gold and silver, and thus could potentially be a valid answer, the silver standard system had been abandoned as an international trading method prior to the twentieth century. Countries that did not use the gold standard, such as China, avoided the harshest depths of the Great Depression.

Difficulty Level: Medium

70. **E.** Under the Weimar Republic, currency underwent a rapid period of hyperinflation that resulted in exorbitant prices far beyond the reach of the average citizen. Many citizens found it difficult to provide for themselves and faced severe hardship. Despite the economic setbacks, the Weimar republic was an age of increased democratic participation, freedom of the press, and political consolidation of the president's power.

Difficulty Level: Hard

71. **E.** Hitler used his charisma to muster political force and create a dictatorship that required absolute obedience and unquestionable rule.

Difficulty Level: Medium

72. **E.** The Marshall Plan was the U.S. economic plan to provide aid to countries facing the worst devastation from the war under the argument that poorer countries were more susceptible to Communism. This plan provided a great bulk of the aid that went toward rebuilding Europe and creating a free trade, modern industrial economy that limited the reliance on armed forces.

Difficulty Level: Hard

73. **D.** This image reflects the curving lines and natural motifs that are the hallmark of the Art Nouveau movement. The image does not represent either Dadaism or minimalism, because it does not break an image down into its most basic components. The reliance on strong lines and shading suggests Art Nouveau rather than expressionism.

Difficulty Level: Medium

74. **D.** The division of Berlin in 1949 was an expression of the larger Cold War policy of maintaining a balance of power between Communist and non-Communist states. By governing a section of the former capital, the Western nations could ensure that the Soviets never fully controlled the economic and political heartland of Germany.

Difficulty Level: Medium

75. **C.** In Soviet Russia, as well as in most other Communist states, women were encouraged to have as many children as possible via state propaganda that stressed the need to expand the population. These countries provided the social support that mothers required, such as day care, which allowed women to return to their state jobs almost immediately after giving birth.

Difficulty Level: Hard

76. **B.** The term *domino theory* was used to describe the belief that Communism would naturally spread to neighboring countries, who would then "fall like dominos." Closely tied to ideas of containment, domino theory was used as the official rationale for U.S. and Allied actions limiting the spread of Communism, such as the active funding of destroyed states through the Marshall Plan and the Truman Doctrine.

Difficulty Level: Hard

77. **E.** NATO was a collective defense pact, formed in the midst of the Cold War, requiring member nations to come to the defense of other member nations if they were invaded or attacked by Communist forces. In response to this perceived threat, the Soviet states created the Warsaw Pact to provide for mutual defense against Western aggression. These two pacts symbolized the international distrust and uncertainty that characterized the Cold War.

Difficulty Level: Easy

78. **C.** The Vietnam War was an unpopular war that demonstrated a multi-leveled alliance among French colonial interests, U.S. imperialism, and ideas of self-determination. Perhaps the most significant factor leading to the end of this conflict was the use of television to broadcast the conditions faced by soldiers.

Difficulty Level: Medium

79. **B.** The Internet has significantly affected the way people access and process information as well as the way they interact with each other.

Difficulty Level: Easy

80. **A.** The collapse of the Soviet Union resulted from a variety of factors; the most striking of these was the negative effect of democratization on the Soviet state. Gorbachev's policies of *glasnost* and *perestroika* weakened the authority of the Soviet state by allowing competing Western influences into its territories.

Difficulty Level: Medium

Section II, Part A
(SAMPLE ESSAY)

1. A good response may begin with an acknowledgement of the differences between Napoleon's early military career (during the 1790s) and his later political one (after 1810).

> Documents 1–3 show Napoleon as a strong-willed, decisive general, while Documents 5–7, which are based on public perception,

portray him as a weak and ineffectual politician. Although the images in Documents 6–7 are affected by the choices Napoleon made as "Emperor" and the defeats he suffered, they nonetheless show how his twenty-five-year rise to power led to irrevocable changes in France.

During the French Revolution, Napoleon emerged as a charismatic military leader. He was able to motivate soldiers by appealing to their personal sense of ambition and hunger for power, as well as their desire to serve a larger nationalist cause (Document 1). His subsequent military and political success was based on an exploitation of the strong revolutionary forces that arose at this time. When leading a conspiracy to overthrow the government in 1799, Napoleon portrayed himself as noble and humble, a "soldier of liberty, a citizen devoted to the Republic" (Document 2). The opposite was actually true, but the French people were exhausted and disgusted by the many years of turmoil France had endured at that point. Thus, Napoleon became not only a viable option, but also a national hero.

The implementation of the Napoleonic Codes in 1804 represented a huge change from the pre-Revolutionary system, as these laws promoted equality for all men. However, the same was not true for women (Document 4). While the codes changed the foundation of French society, they also served as political tools for Napoleon. "Equality" for Napoleon meant everyone was equal under *his* power. In regard to political and civil liberties, Napoleon was willing to do whatever he thought necessary to protect that power.

During the early 1800s, Napoleon strengthened France and led it to control most of Europe. People who swore loyalty to Napoleon also swore loyalty to their country. However, by the time Napoleon got involved in the long war in Spain (1808–1814) and launched a failed invasion of Russia (1812), perceptions of him began to change. By 1812, he was no longer a fiery young general; instead, he was a pudgy, middle-aged bureaucrat who, despite his military uniform, no longer projected the same intimidating military presence he'd displayed in his prime (Documents 3 and 5). By 1814, Napoleon was frequently ridiculed in political cartoons because his reign of annexing foreign territories (shown in the cartoon as soap bubbles) appeared to be nearly over (Document 6). Following his defeat at Waterloo in 1815, another political cartoon shows how far Napoleon has fallen by depicting him as a little man dancing to the tune of the English (Document 7). This cartoon also encapsulates the change in French stature by the time of his overthrow: France is seen as a weakened country unable to return to its pre-Revolutionary self.

Section II, Part B
SAMPLE ESSAYS

2. The Renaissance was not only a period of great developments in art and thought; it was also a time of significant economic change. During this era, European economies began to recover from the damages caused by disasters such as the Black Death and slowly started to take on more modern forms. Agriculture and commerce were two economic areas that experienced important changes during the Renaissance. Agriculture saw the rise of a monetarily based economy, the implementation of scientific developments, and changes to the status of farmers. Meanwhile, commerce also changed, seeing a growth of wealth, an increase in international trade, and a rise in commercial organizations.

During the Renaissance, agriculture began to take on a more modern form. One major change was the replacement of the barter system with a monetary (money-based) economy. With this new system, farmers could use set currency to buy and sell. They could adjust their crops according to current prices and demand and pay rent with money instead of crops and labor. In addition, this type of economy encouraged farmers to produce fewer food crops and instead focus on more valuable raw materials used in industry. While these changes were taking place, there were also important developments in agricultural science. Improved tools and more sophisticated plows helped farmers increase yields. Additionally, advances in biological knowledge and farm planning led to improvements in both crop rotation and drainage. Finally, the Renaissance saw changes in the perception of the agrarian lifestyle. More people began moving to towns to work in industry, leaving their agricultural roots behind. Although many people began to look down on farmers, those who continued to farm now dealt with less competition and were able to demand better prices and an end to serfdom.

Commerce also underwent great change during the Renaissance, becoming the second most important branch of the economy, just behind agriculture. One of the most significant changes in commerce was a growth of wealth. Many people began working in commerce when they realized they could make more money exchanging goods than in actually producing them. Many individuals, businesses, and families began amassing significant fortunes through commercial activities. This was made possible partly due to an increase in international trade that occurred in the Renaissance era. Many European and other nations sent caravans and ships to meet in major commercial centers, spreading goods, ideas, and wealth.

Yet another development in commerce was a rise in organizations. Business was no longer confined to small shops and guilds; people began developing large merchant companies that worked together for a variety of reasons, such as safety. They even developed the concept of the business partnership, in which members contributed labor or money to a specific goal and then shared the profits.

The Renaissance was more than a time for new art and thought. As Europe emerged from the Black Death era, its economy became more varied and modern. Agriculture changed under the new money economy, scientific developments, and the differences in the perception of farming as a way of life. Meanwhile, commerce experienced growth, an increase in trade between nations, and an explosion of commercially oriented organizations.

3. Many factors contributed to the Industrial Revolution of the eighteenth and nineteenth centuries in Europe. One of the main factors making the Industrial Revolution possible was technology. Technology led to many important innovations in this era, including the creation of the factory system, the usage of new resources and energy sources, and the introduction of new machines, all of which were critical to the Industrial Revolution.

Perhaps the greatest technological development that influenced the Industrial Revolution was the creation of the factory system. Prior to the rise of factories, practically all goods were handcrafted by people in their homes or in small village shops. The idea of the factory, a building where many workers and machines contributed to the production of a specific item, was in itself revolutionary. Factories allowed for the mass production of goods, which meant there were more items available for lower prices. The factory system also created a division of labor and contributed to the rise of cities that began draining workers away from their traditional roles in agriculture.

Meanwhile, new resources and energy sources helped to fuel the Industrial Revolution. Craftspeople of prior eras had been limited by their materials, but now scientists were discovering new resources that were strong, inexpensive, and able to be made into a wide variety of goods. The conversion of iron into steel, for example, made a new and much more durable material. Steel became the basis for many of the machines needed to increase industry. Factories also adopted a wide variety of new energy sources to power their machines. While the earliest factories were powered by water and had to be located by creeks or rivers, technology allowed factories to be built almost anywhere. These factories and their machines could operate on coal or steam power. Later, electrical and gasoline-powered engines and machines led to even greater opportunity.

These energy sources and new resources would not be useful if not for the introduction of powerful new machines. Every improvement in machinery meant that people could accomplish more while doing less actual labor. Early innovations in machinery included the spinning jenny and power loom, which greatly benefited the textile industry. New kinds of smelting furnaces, fueled by coal, allowed workers to melt ore efficiently and safely and create new kinds of metals, which were in turn used to make even more machines. Other mechanical advancements came in transportation and communication: the creation of telegraphs, steamships, locomotives, canals, and railroads made it easier and less expensive to import and export goods and resources across and among nations.

Among the technological factors contributing to the Industrial Revolution were the creation of the factory system, usage of new resources and energy sources, and the invention of new machinery. These innovations allowed industry to become a leading part of the economy and helped to modernize European society.

4. Peter the Great was one of the most influential figures in Russian history. He became emperor, or tsar, to a country that was stuck in the past and suffering from many serious problems. Prior to Peter's reign, Russia was a backward country with a large population of poor serfs. Russia had been isolated from the great developments of the rest of the continent. Peter the Great put forth efforts to modernize Russia and help it evolve. His efforts were largely responsible for the eventual Europeanization and Westernization of Russia.

Peter the Great was able to recognize many problems in Russia and find ways to change them. One of his main efforts was to modernize Russia, or make it more suited to the modern era. He accomplished this in many ways. Peter worked to reduce the power of landowners, which helped the serfs gain more balanced rights and advance beyond their subservient conditions. He also found ways to grant more rights to women, who traditionally enjoyed few rights. In addition, Peter made a few seemingly small but very important changes. For instance, he helped to popularize the potato in Russia. This easy-to-grow crop became a major food source for peasants and contributed positively to public health. Peter also encouraged the publication of newspapers, which helped spread information and literacy across the country.

Shortly after becoming tsar, Peter traveled from Russia to other nations in Europe. Few tsars had interest in other lands, but Peter realized he could learn a great deal from the countries that had flourished during the Renaissance and Age of Discovery. When he returned to Russia, he brought many new ideas about politics, society, and economy. Peter began encouraging Western-style education, opening schools in which students could learn science and art. Schools also taught navigation, which would help a new generation of Russian explorers travel to new lands. Peter promoted European fashions that helped change the mind-set of the people. He made great strides in modeling the Russian army to more closely resemble the most powerful armies of Europe. Finally, Peter the Great extended his country's connection with Europe and the West by moving his capital to a bustling port city of his creation, St. Petersburg.

Peter the Great became tsar in a Russia that needed serious reevaluation and redesign. Prior to Peter's reign, Russia was isolated from the great cultural advances of the rest of Europe and many of its people lived as poor serfs. Peter made many changes in Russia to improve the country and help it become a great modern European nation. His efforts to modernize Russia and to Europeanize and Westernize it had a tremendous effect on its people and the future of the nation.

Section II, Part C
SAMPLE ESSAYS

5. During the Reformation period, religious thought underwent many changes in Europe. The Anglican and Calvinist Churches were two new branches of Christianity that formed during this time period. These churches developed around the same time but in different lands and in different ways. Although the churches both followed the general

doctrines of Protestantism, they differed in the ways in which they performed rituals and viewed life and faith. Anglicans and Calvinists came into serious conflict and even war during the seventeenth century.

Both the Anglican and Calvinist Churches formed around the time of the Reformation. The Reformation was a period in which many Europeans began to question religious ideas that they had once held as permanent and unchangeable. Reformers called Protestants sought radical changes in the Catholic Church, particularly an end to the sale of indulgences and other corrupt policies. Some Protestants proceeded to form their own churches, such as the Anglican and Calvinist churches which both began around the 1530s.

The natures of these churches were quite different, however. The Anglican Church began in England. The king of England, Henry VIII, was a loyal Catholic until he came into conflict with the pope. When the pope refused to grant Henry a divorce, Henry appointed a local archbishop to grant it. Then, he decided to break away completely from Catholicism. With the help of an act of Parliament, Henry VIII created a national religion for England called Anglicanism. Although the Anglicans are considered Protestants and Henry quickly took an anti-Catholic position, Anglicans use many rituals similar to those of the Catholics.

Around the same time, the Calvinist Church originated in Switzerland when a Frenchman named John Calvin decided to establish a faith free of what he saw as the excesses of Catholicism. Unlike Anglicanism, which is based in a single country, Calvin's ideas spread through many lands including France, Scotland, and England. Leaders in these countries created different branches of Calvinism. Unlike Anglicans, Calvinists rejected most of the rituals of the Catholics. Calvinists believed in stricter moral codes and rejected almost all pleasures in life, dedicating themselves to religious devotion and hard work.

Another difference between the Anglicans and Calvinists was in their political power. Anglicans were quite powerful, as they were endorsed by the government and led by the king. Calvinists, on the other hand, were not very powerful, particularly in their early years. Branches of the Calvinist faith, including the Huguenots in France and the Puritans in England, were frequently the victims of harsh discrimination. In fact, the English monarchy's unfair treatment of Puritans partly triggered the English Civil War, or Puritan Revolt.

The Anglican and Calvinist Churches were two branches of Protestantism that formed during the Reformation period. Although they developed around the same time and followed Protestant ideals, they differed in many other ways. They flourished in different lands and promoted distinct views of faith, ritual, and lifestyle. Their differences led many to lose sight of their similarities and contributed to bloody conflicts.

6. After the Age of Exploration and Discovery, Europeans of many nations wanted to become involved with the new lands they were learning about. These people wanted new wealth, resources, and property. A period of intense imperialism in Europe began in the sixteenth and seventeenth centuries as nations tried to colonize the lands that had only recently been discovered. Nations such as Spain, France, Britain, and others quickly sent ships across the Atlantic Ocean in hopes of expanding their empires to the Americas.

During this period, one of the strongest empires was that of Spain. By the end of the sixteenth century, the Spanish had colonized large parts of the Americas. These areas included Mexico, western regions of North America, much of Central America and South America, and many islands in the Caribbean. Spanish colonizers had many goals in mind, including adding land to the Spanish empire, spreading Catholicism, and searching for gold and other treasures.

Another major power during this imperial age was France. France established trading colonies in the Caribbean and near India. It focused its colonial efforts, however, on North America. French colonists took control of lands that are today eastern Canada and the Mississippi Valley. The French were primarily interested in trade, and all around the French colonial settlements a brisk trade in animal furs began.

The third major colonial power was Britain. By the seventeenth century, the British had established thriving colonies along the east coast of North America. Britain wanted to expand its empire and gain land and resources; in addition, many British colonists had immigrated in search of religious freedom. The British began fighting a series of wars against their French and Spanish competitors and eventually won control of most of North America.

This imperialist activity, including the efforts of smaller nations such as Holland and Portugal, had dramatic effects on the populations of these newly colonized lands as well as on the course of history. Among these was the relocation and frequent oppression of native peoples, the modernization of the Americas, the spread of European technologies, and a string of bloody wars including the French and Indian War, King Philip's War, and (eventually) the American Revolution.

Spurred by explorations and discoveries of new lands, many European nations became strongly imperialist during the sixteenth and seventeenth centuries. Spanish, French, British, and other explorers and colonizers spread out across the globe and particularly to the Americas. They went in search of new land, resources, wealth, and freedom. They brought massive changes that included the subjugation of native groups, the spread of modern European lifestyles and technologies, and a scourge of deadly conflict.

7. One of the most significant changes that took place in Europe during the eighteenth and nineteenth centuries was urbanization, or the increase in the size and importance of cities. Cities have been around for thousands of years, but were historically limited in size and influence. Starting in the 1700s, however, the Industrial Revolution sparked the growth of huge cities. This urbanization led to great changes, both positive and negative.

Although cities have existed in Europe for thousands of years, they were seldom very large, because most people still relied on farms for food and income. The Industrial Revolution changed the rural vs. urban balance dramatically. The factory system turned cities into hubs for workers. Searching for new ways of life and better pay, thousands of former agricultural workers migrated into cities in hopes of getting factory jobs.

Big cities began growing throughout Europe. These cities tended to be located where there was a factory or a new center of industry. Workers would move in and entrepreneurs would begin to develop streets and build houses and shops to accommodate the workers. In this way, cities grew swiftly in many nations. In some cases, cities that were already prominent, such as London and Paris, grew to enormous proportions. In other cases, formerly tiny villages and towns boomed.

The urbanization of Europe brought about changes in culture and perceptions. For example, cities attracted new, ambitious people from different parts of the country. These people brought a sense of energy as well as new ideas stemming from their liberation from traditional ways of life. On the other hand, there were negatives as well. While previous cultures had revered agriculture, the people of urbanized societies often frowned upon farmers, stereotyping them as "backward." Others longed for the serenity of the countryside and characterized cities as places of greed, filth, and immorality.

Serious problems can be tied to urbanization. The logistics of fitting large masses of people together in relatively small, crowded environments presented difficulties and dangers. Early cities experienced significant problems with sanitation, transportation, and public health. Education was often overlooked and sometimes children were made to work long hours in factories under horrifying conditions. In addition, industrialized cities emphasized distinctions in class, magnifying the clear gap between the rich and the poor. The upper classes became richer; they owned businesses and lived in plush homes. Meanwhile, the lower classes became poorer; they frequently lived in slums or ghettos, and faced poverty and hunger on a daily basis.

Urbanization, or the rise of cities, was one of the most significant forces in Europe in the eighteenth and nineteenth centuries. Sparked by the Industrial Revolution, urbanization brought cities and industries ahead of rural communities and agriculture. It brought vast changes, both positive and negative, to European cultures and societies.

Using the Diagnostic Test

Calculating Your Score

When you take the actual AP European History Exam, your test is scored as follows:

- The multiple-choice questions in Section A count for 50 percent of the total exam score. This part of your score is based on the number of questions answered correctly. Because you will not lose points for answering any question incorrectly, it is in your best interest to answer as many questions as possible, even if you are not entirely sure of the answer. This part of the exam is objective and will be scored by machine.

- The essay portions of the exam, Sections B and C, count as 50 percent of the total exam score. Within this section, the DBQ counts for 45 percent of the score, while the two FRQs count for 55 percent of the score. Essays are subjective and will be scored by teams designated by the College Board.

The two parts of your score are then combined and converted to a scale of 1–5. The process used by the College Board to determine the score range is labor-intensive and complex; for more information on how this works, you can review the College Board website (www.college board.com) for details.

5 = Extremely well qualified

4 = Well qualified

3 = Qualified

2 = Possibly qualified

1 = No recommendation

Improving Your Score

The diagnostic examination in this book is meant to help you understand where you may need to improve in terms of either the material you are studying or your actual test-taking habits. The diagnostic test varies slightly from the real AP exam because the questions in the multiple-choice section are presented in roughly chronological order. This is intentional, as it will help you more easily determine if your studies should be focused more specifically on particular periods of time, cultural ideas, historical figures, and so on.

To determine roughly how you performed on the multiple-choice section of this test, count the number of items you answered correctly, divide that number by 80, and then multiply by 100. For example, if you correctly answered 45 out of 80 items, you achieved a raw score of about 56% on this part of the exam. Even though the AP examination is scored in a more complex manner, this should still give you a general sense of how you are likely to perform on the actual test.

Go back through Section A to review the questions you answered correctly and those you answered incorrectly. What kinds of patterns do you see? Remember, this part of the test was presented in a roughly chronological manner so that you would be able to determine if there are particular periods of time, cultural ideas, or historical figures on which you should focus your study. Also review the vocabulary terms you highlighted. Are these similar in nature or related to particular time periods or ideas? Take the time to look up the definitions for these terms. Figure out how they apply in the context of the question. Close this gap in your knowledge so that it is not a problem when you get to your actual test.

To determine how you performed on Sections B and C, review your essays as carefully and objectively as possible. (You might also ask a friend, teacher, or parent/caregiver to review your essays for feedback.) Ask yourself: did you answer the question as it was asked? If the question called for a comparison between two historical figures or cultural events or time periods, for example, did you remember to answer both parts of the question?

Review the sample essays provided for key points related to the content of each question. Although the substance of your answer may vary, did you remember to summarize your point of view with a thesis statement? Did you substantiate the thesis statement in a point-by-point manner? Did you write your essays in a relevant and logical manner? Is your argument clear? Is your reasoning sound? Does your response make sense in the context of the question?

Additionally, remember that the DBQ is worth nearly 25 percent of your grade. Did you use the source documentation to the best of your ability? Remember, the DBQ does not require you to use any sources beyond those provided, so it is critical to spend the time to carefully read the source material provided, and to utilize it to the fullest extent possible. The result should be the crafting of a logical, well-reasoned, well-substantiated argument that supports your point of view with evidence.

Finally, how did you do with time? Did you stay within the stated parameters of the exam? Did you spend too much time on one section or another? Or did you fail to spend *enough* time on each section? Remember, successful test-taking is as much about managing your time as it about understanding the content.

A Final Word about the Diagnostic Test

Finally, don't feel too badly if you didn't do well on the examination this first time through. After all, the whole point of this book is to give you ample opportunities to test and retest, so that you will feel thoroughly comfortable with both the setup and the content of the examination by the time you're ready to sit for it.

Now that you've had an opportunity to test and see all the different question types, familiarize yourself with the test-taking strategies in the following chapters. As you move forward, you'll be able to see more specifically how you can apply these strategies to your advantage.

Multiple-Choice Strategies

You have just 55 minutes to answer the 80 multiple-choice questions, so that gives you less than one minute per question. Make the most of the time that's available to you.

Don't be afraid to mark up your test booklet. While your answer sheet needs to be kept clean and free from any stray markings, the test booklet can be marked up as much as you want. Don't be afraid to flag the questions you want to return to, or underline or otherwise mark any part of the question or answer option that you think needs to be reviewed more carefully.

First, mentally answer the question. Read the full question, and then mentally answer it *before* you look at the answer choices. Sometimes answer options are intentionally distracting. (That's why they're called "distracters.") If you already have an idea of the answer you're looking for, you'll be less confused by the answer options.

Pay attention to the wording. Some questions include the words NOT or EXCEPT. For those questions, you're looking for the answer that is NOT true or does NOT apply. These can be tricky, so make sure you're aware.

Apply what you know. Some questions will ask you to place a quote you've never read before or interpret an illustration you've never seen before, such as a map, graph, chart, or cartoon. Some of these may be completely new to you. What you're really looking to do is "place" the quote or illustration based on your knowledge of the author, the artist, or the time period. Consider the language, the point of view, and/or the time period.

Review all answer options before making a selection. Make sure you review *all* of the answer options before making your answer choice. Sometimes, more than one answer is correct; one choice might be "more correct" than another.

Does your answer choice completely *address the question? Is it qualified in some way?* If an answer is only partially true, or if it's qualified with narrow conditions (look for words like *never, always, only*), it's probably not the right answer.

Use elimination strategies. If you don't know an answer, start by eliminating answer choices. See if you can eliminate one or two of the choices. Look for clueing words like *always, only, never,* and so on. Once you've eliminated answer choices you believe are wrong, guess from those that remain. The more answer choices you eliminate, the better your chances of getting the correct answer.

Take a guess! If you're lost on a question or don't feel like you have enough time to analyze it as deeply as you'd like, take a wild guess. Fill in an oval at random if you must. There's no penalty for guessing, and you just might get lucky.

Flag difficult questions. Answer them on the answer sheet, but flag them on the test. Come back to them after you've gone through the entire test.

Be careful on the answer sheet! Don't make mistakes. Make sure your question and answer numbers correspond. Also, be sure you have penciled in the answer space completely and have no stray pencil marks in other spaces.

Essay Strategies

Section II of the exam contains three essay questions, including the document-based question. You're given 15 minutes to read the documents for the DBQ and 45 minutes to write the DBQ essay. You're given 70 minutes total to write the remaining essay questions.

Start with a laundry list. Once you've read the question, take a few minutes to jot down whatever comes to mind about the topic. Don't worry about structuring the essay first, just get those juices flowing.

Analyze and categorize the DBQ. Before reading each document for the DBQ, first consider the author/source. What is that person's general point of view? Consider the time period in which the document was produced, as well as its purpose. As you read, mark any part of the document that sheds light on the author's purpose or that somehow relates to the prompt. Once you've read all the documents, organize or group them by the viewpoint or idea they support.

Go beyond the DBQ documents. The AP readers don't want you to regurgitate what the documents say. That's really important, so let's repeat: *Do not regurgitate the source material.* Instead, what you want to do is analyze the material, evaluate the evidence within, and bolster it with your own knowledge. The documents are fodder for your analysis, but the analysis should be yours alone.

Create a coherent thesis. All of your essays should start with a thesis statement. Your thesis statement is important. It should be clear and focused. It should cogently present your position and clearly state the central idea of your essay. Most importantly, it should directly address *all* parts of the prompt. Many prompts are essentially two-part questions asking you to compare and contrast historical figures, time periods, ideas, points of view, etc. All parts of the prompt should be addressed. If you can't sum up your argument in a single thesis, then you probably don't have a clear argument.

Outline your argument. Organization is critical to a well-written essay. Each of the ideas in your essay should support your thesis. Follow good essay-writing practices by outlining your essay before you actually write it. Organize your ideas so that they flow into each other smoothly and with appropriate transitions. Use time wisely.

Develop strong paragraphs. Once you have your thesis statement and an organized outline, write your body text. Your body text should provide specific evidence in support of your thesis. The end result should be specific, clear, and analytical in nature.

Provide a conclusion. Don't just end your essay; bring it home by providing a conclusion that ties it all together.

For DBQs, make sure ALL source material is used. You're expected to utilize all of the source material that's provided, so make sure each document is referenced logically within your essay. You'll lose points if you fail to use material.

Write legibly and coherently. While the exam is not a test of penmanship, if the AP readers can't read what you've written, you may lose points needlessly. So, even if it slows you down, write clearly enough that your material can be read without difficulty.

Review Chapter 1: The Renaissance, the Reformation, and European Conquest

The Renaissance

The Renaissance began around 1050 and lasted until about 1600, bridging the period from the later Middle Ages to more modern times. As a cultural movement, the Renaissance involved a resurgence of classical learning as well as a surge in the development of literature, the arts, the sciences, religion, and politics. The Renaissance wrought great changes in European economics, politics, and culture. Although the Renaissance is generally associated with Italy, where it originated before later spreading throughout much of Europe, historians view the Italian Renaissance as distinct from the Northern Renaissance.

- The *Italian Renaissance* originated in Italy around 1050. At this time, Italy was not a single united nation; instead, it operated as a series of independent city-states, which included Florence, Genoa, Venice, and the Papal States. The city-states were run by families, despots, or religious leaders and were mostly politically unstable. The Italian Renaissance was characterized by a focus on philosophical study and the creation of poetry, paintings, and other types of artwork, most of which were secular rather than religious and drawn from classical inspirations.

- The *Northern Renaissance* began around 1475 and involved other

European nations. Although it shared many of the artistic and philosophical themes as the Italian Renaissance, the Northern Renaissance was generally more religious in nature. Reformers during this time sought social changes based on Christian beliefs.

Politics

During the Renaissance period, Italy was unstable due to its fragmentation into city-states. However, in other parts of Europe, nations became stronger due to the centralization of power and the rise of dynasties. Some nations in which this occurred were Spain, France, and England.

- Leaders in Spain united that nation and converted it to a major European power.
- Although French leaders centralized their power during this time period, France was weakened by conflict.
- In England, the Tudor family ended the bloody War of the Roses and launched their dynasty.

Philosophy

The Renaissance was marked by major developments in philosophy, many of which were derived from ancient Greek thinkers. In general, philosophers during this period focused on the ideas of individualism and humanism. In Italy, a philosophy of secularism also thrived.

- *Individualism* was grounded in the belief that all rights, values, and duties originated in and with individuals. For the first time since classical times, a spirit of individuality arose; people affirmed their belief in the power and worth of the individual person.
- *Humanism* centered on human interests or values and stressed the individual's dignity, worth, and capacity for self-realization through reason. Humanism was related to individualism and inspired by classical texts and work. Humanistic philosophers studied human nature and touted the abilities of individuals.

- *Secularism* involved a focus on secular matters such as pleasure and wealth along with indifference to or rejection of religious considerations. During the Italian Renaissance, many citizens stepped back from religion and instead concerned themselves with more secular pursuits.

Artwork

The Renaissance is perhaps best known for its awe-inspiring art. During the early Italian Renaissance, many cities commissioned artists to create works celebrating religious themes. Later, patrons began supporting more secular artistic pursuits, including paintings and sculptures that glorified individuals or families.

Similarly, early Renaissance painting focused on classical ideals such as realism and symmetry. These artists mastered perspective, proportionality, and color contrast to make their works photorealistic. Artists later in the period rejected this movement and subscribed to *mannerism*, a style from late sixteenth-century Europe that was characterized by spatial incongruity and excessive elongation of the human figure. Mannerism emphasized the importance of self-expression over more realism-based approaches.

During this period, artists were well respected and their talents widely recognized. Some of the great Renaissance artists included

- Donatello (1386–1466), an Italian sculptor known for works such as *David* (1425–1430);
- Leonardo da Vinci (1452–1519), a multitalented Italian genius known for paintings such as the *Mona Lisa* (1507);
- Michelangelo (1475–1564), an Italian artist famous for, among other pieces, his religious fresco paintings on Rome's Sistine Chapel (1508–1512);
- Albrecht Dürer (1471–1528), a German artist known for highly realistic paintings and engravings.

Literature

Just as the visual arts thrived during the Renaissance, so too did literary pursuits. Humanists promoted literature as a way to educate people, often about social and moral behavior. Importantly, the invention of the printing press by Johann Gutenberg around 1450 meant that books could be mass produced and distributed more widely than ever before. This relative abundance of books encouraged the spread of literacy and education throughout many nations.

Some of the most noteworthy Renaissance writers included Niccolò Machiavelli, Thomas More, and Baldassare Castiglione.

- Niccolò Machiavelli (1469–1527) wrote *The Prince* (1513), a handbook advocating ruthlessness for politicians.
- Sir Thomas More (1478–1535) wrote *Utopia* (1516), a Christian critique of contemporary society.
- Baldassare Castiglione (1478–1529) wrote *The Courtier* (1528), which encouraged artistic and intellectual pursuits for the nobility.

The Reformation

The Reformation (1500–1600) brought drastic change to religious thought and practices throughout Europe. During this time, many Christians expressed displeasure with the actions of the Catholic Church and protested for change. The Christian faith eventually splintered into a variety of branches broadly classified as *Catholic* and *Protestant*. This change contributed to many social and political developments as well as conflict and war in several countries.

Causes of the Reformation

The Reformation started as a call for change in the Catholic Church. Reformers were inspired by *humanist* philosophies of the Renaissance, and believed they had the right and responsibility to demand moral behavior from religious leaders.

Reformers were concerned with events and attitudes they believed tarnished the image of the Catholic Church and disenfranchised common churchgoers. Some of these concerns included

- the *Great Schism*, a period during the fourteenth and fifteenth centuries in which the credibility of the pontiff was seriously damaged;
- *indulgences*, or transactions in which an individual could pay money to the Church to "buy" salvation;
- immoral behavior and lavish lifestyles of the clergy, including the pope.

The Protestant Reformation

The reform movement came to be known as *Protestantism*. The leading figure in the Protestant movement was Martin Luther (1483–1546), a German monk and professor. Luther publicized his Protestant ideals in 1517 in a document called *Ninety-Five Theses* and founded a branch of Protestantism known as *Lutheranism*. Lutheranism was based on several principles, including

- rejection of the pope as the leader of the Christian Church;
- belief that faith is the most important path to salvation;
- advocacy for individual Bible study and the use of vernacular texts.

Effects of Protestantism

The introduction of Lutheranism had a drastic impact on many levels. In 1521, Luther was excommunicated by the pope and condemned by Holy Roman Emperor Charles V's *Edict of Worms*. Even as Luther faced personal sufferings, however, the spirit and ideals of Protestantism quickly spread throughout Europe. Luther finalized his split with the Catholic Church via his *Augsburg Confession* (1530).

Thousands of discontented Catholics joined the Protestant movement. Some supporters felt Luther's teachings brought greater dignity to peasants and women. Others were attracted by its democratization of religion, its rejection of strict organizational hierarchy, and its reliance on vernacular texts. Luther's teachings also fostered a spirit of patriotism within the German states.

Spread of Protestantism

Protestantism expanded through the German states, the Holy Roman Empire, and eventually to the rest of Europe. As it spread, it fragmented into different branches, each with its own system of beliefs and practices.

Some of the major figures in this time period included the following:

- Ulrich Zwingli (1484–1531), a Swiss reformer who promoted Luther's belief in literal scripture readings;

- John Calvin (1509–1564), a Frenchman who founded the Protestant sect of *Calvinism*. Calvinists believed people must live godly lives to earn salvation. Calvin also promoted the idea of *predestination* as well as the importance of a strong work ethic. Calvinists were based in Geneva and spread throughout Switzerland, the Netherlands, and France in the mid-1500s. Calvinism was later carried to Scotland by John Knox (1514–1572);

- England's King Henry VIII (1491–1547), who rejected papal authority and broke from the Catholic Church after the pope refused to annul his marriage to Catherine of Aragon in the 1530s. Henry founded the Anglican Church and made it the official Church of England with himself as supreme head. Although protected and promoted by the government, the Anglican Church was opposed by many critics, including Henry's Catholic daughter, Mary Tudor. A group called the *Puritans* began calling for the Anglican Church to simplify its practices and reduce its decadences.

In addition, other Protestant branches—including the pacifistic *Anabaptists* (the basis for later Quakers, Baptists, and Congregationalists) and the *Huguenots* (French Protestants influenced by Calvinism)—arose during the Reformation period.

Catholic Counter-Reformation

During the age of Reformation, many Catholics felt compelled to defend their religion against Protestantism. Many of these Catholics also pushed for reforms within their own religion. The actions of these Catholics have come to be known as the *Catholic Reformation* or the *Counter-Reformation*. Some of the main events of this period involved

- the founding of new religious orders, such as the Society of Jesus (Jesuits) founded by Ignatius of Loyola to promote Catholicism around the world;
- the *Council of Trent* (1545–1563), which reformed Catholic policies pertaining to indulgences, celibacy, papal authority, and the number of sacraments;
- repressive measures, such as banning books and the confinement of Jewish citizens to ghettos;
- the *Peace of Augsburg* (1555), which allowed the princes of the Holy Roman Empire to choose either Catholicism and Protantism as the religion of their territory, with citizens expected to follow their lead.

Wars of Religion

Religious tension brought on by the Reformation frequently mixed with political disagreement and led to war. From around 1560 to 1650, Europeans fought several major conflicts based at least partly upon religion. The most important of these included conflicts in France, revolts in the Netherlands, Spanish attacks on England, and the Thirty Years' War. The wars of religion were finally ended by the Treaty of Westphalia in 1648.

- In France, the tension between French Huguenots and Catholics was further aggravated by feuds between political dynasties. In 1572, supporters of Catholic factions killed thousands of Huguenots across the nation in the St. Bartholomew's Day Massacre. The fighting finally ended with the *Edict of Nantes*, a truce signed by King Henry IV. Henry declared France officially Catholic but tolerant of Protestantism.

- In the Netherlands in 1572, Protestant revolutionaries revolted against their Catholic rulers and attempted to secede from the nation. In 1609, the warring factions reached a peace agreement.

- The Catholic rulers of Spain hoped to win a military and religious victory over Anglican England when they dispatched the *Spanish Armada*, a massive fleet of warships, against Britain. The English navy defeated the Armada, however, ruining Spain's plans for invasion and seriously weakening the international power of the Spanish.

- The *Thirty Years' War* raged from 1618 to 1648. This war of religion in the Holy Roman Empire pitted Catholics, Protestants, Lutherans, and Calvinists against each other for supremacy. The conflict began as a Protestant religious revolt and quickly escalated. Soon, most of the major powers of Europe were participating.

- After generations of war, European leaders signed the *Treaty of Westphalia* in 1648 to restore peace among the nations. The treaty not only pacified religious disagreements but also altered the borders of Europe and emphasized the weakening Holy Roman Empire. In addition, it acknowledged the permanency of the rift between Catholics and Protestants.

European Conquest

During the Renaissance and Reformation periods, Europeans experienced an influx of new ideas, advances in education and technology, feelings of patriotism and expansionism, and religious fervor. All of these factors contributed to the European conquest of other lands, part of the *Age of Exploration* that lasted from about 1450 to 1650.

- The Renaissance emphasis on learning created a desire to seek out new lands. With increased knowledge of navigation and new technologies such as the astrolabe, magnetic compass, and cannon, people were more empowered to explore the world.

- Despite the tensions of the Reformation era, most Europeans remained loyal to their Christian roots. They desired to spread their faith to so-called "pagans." In addition, during times of religious war and oppression, many Europeans yearned for new lands where they could practice their faith freely and without interference from others.

- Many Europeans faced limited economic opportunity in their home countries. Many people went into exploration in order to find or follow trade routes to other countries and continents. Spices and precious metals such as silver and gold were among some of the most valuable trade items of the era.

Major Explorers

Europeans have long been known for their explorations and expansions, dating back to the Viking era. In the last half of the 1400s, international exploration once again became a major pursuit. Explorers, primarily those representing Spain and Portugal, began voyaging to Africa and across the Atlantic Ocean. They sought trade routes to India and other parts of Asia as well as new sources of precious metals and goods.

Among the most influential of the early explorers were the following:

- Christopher Columbus (1451–1506), an Italian navigator funded by the Spanish monarchy. In 1492, he set off on a journey to discover new trade routes to Asia. Instead, his ships ended up in the Caribbean. Columbus realized he had not reached Asia but had instead discovered a "New World." He set up a colonial government, introduced Christianity, and laid the groundwork for European expansion into the Americas. These actions started a long trend of subjugation and exploitation of Native Americans.

- Vasco da Gama (1460–1524), a Portuguese explorer who discovered a route for sea trade with India. This route was uncovered when da Gama sailed around Africa in 1498. The new route led to a brisk trade in Asian spices.

- Hernán Cortés (1485–1547), a Spanish explorer and colonizer. Cortés helped strengthen Spain's claims to land in Central and South America by leading a military conquest of the Native American Aztec civilization in Mexico in 1521. He established Mexico City as the capital of New Spain.

- Francisco Pizarro (1474–1541), another Spanish explorer, who traveled to Peru. From 1531 to 1534, he led a military expedition to overthrow the ancient Inca civilization. He was able to open silver mines in Peru and eventually sent thousands of pounds of the precious metal back to Europe.

- Ferdinand Magellan (1480–1521), a Portuguese sailor and navigator, who became the first person to *circumnavigate*, or sail completely around, the world. He accomplished this feat between 1519 and 1522, proving that the planet was not only round, but also much larger than previously estimated.

Effects of Exploration

Early European conquests in Africa and the Americas critically changed the course of world history.

- New trade routes allowed sharing of goods and ideas across nations and cultures.

- Europe expanded its boundaries and pushed Christianity to people across new lands.

- Native Americans were impacted positively via trade, but negatively via the near-destruction of the culture through oppression, war, displacement, and disease.

- The African slave trade was introduced and brought to other nations.

- The stage was set for the eventual ascendancy of Britain and France as colonial powers.

Multiple-Choice Review Questions

1. The primary effect of the Council of Trent (1545–1563) was to

   A. spread the doctrines of Lutheranism internationally.
   B. compile a list of unacceptable books to be banned.
   C. force Germans to accept the faith of their leaders.
   D. compel Jewish citizens to live in closed ghettos.
   E. reform many traditional principles of Catholicism.

2. Which of the following European explorers led a Spanish conquest of the Aztec civilization in Mexico?

   A. Hernán Cortés
   B. Francisco Pizarro
   C. Ferdinand Magellan
   D. Vasco da Gama
   E. Christopher Columbus

3. Which of the following statements best represents the philosophical movement of secularism?

   A. Classical texts, such as those of the ancient Greeks and Romans, are the best source of modern inspiration.
   B. The study of human nature is the truest means of understanding nature, society, and philosophy.
   C. Religion provides fundamental principles that underlay all laws of human government.
   D. The individual is more important than the government, society, nation, or empire.
   E. Pleasure on earth, rather than earning a place in heaven, is of central importance to humans.

4. In which way did the Italian Renaissance and the Northern Renaissance differ?

    A. Only the works of Northern Renaissance artists were heavily influenced by humanistic philosophies.
    B. Only the Italian Renaissance spread widely and influenced the art and thought of other nations in Europe.
    C. The Northern Renaissance flourished more strongly in city-states such as Genoa, Venice, and Florence.
    D. The art and thought of the Northern Renaissance tended to involve stronger religious themes.
    E. The Italian Renaissance took place more than four centuries after the Northern Renaissance.

5. All of the following are basic tenets of Lutheranism EXCEPT

    A. the need to reform the policies of Catholicism.
    B. the purchasing of indulgences to reduce sinfulness.
    C. the rejection of the supreme power of the pope.
    D. the dissemination of vernacular religious texts.
    E. the encouragement of personal faith and private study.

Answer Explanations

1. E. The Council of Trent was an important milestone in the Catholic Reformation. At the Council, religious authorities agreed to revise many of the old traditions of the Catholic Church relating to papal authority, indulgences, and other important issues.

2. A. The European explorer who led the conquest of the Aztecs was Hernán Cortés. The campaigns of Cortés led to the Spanish colonial domination of Central and South America and the establishment of Mexico City.

3. E. Secularism was a movement that brought great change to civilization during the Renaissance. This movement encouraged people to

distance themselves from religious devotion and focus on the pleasures of earthly living.

4.   **D**. The Italian Renaissance and the Northern Renaissance were similar in many ways, including their overall artistic styles and philosophical standpoints. One major difference between them, however, was that the Northern Renaissance was generally more influenced by religion.

5.   **B**. Lutheranism revised many of the existing practices of the Catholic Church into a new form of religion. This new faith accepted all of the above principles except the purchase of indulgences, a traditional Catholic practice that Lutherans found abhorrent.

Review Chapter 2: Absolutism and a New World View

Absolutism

Before the era of revolutions and the spread of democracy, Europe was ruled by absolutism. *Absolutism* is a philosophy of government in which all power and authority is centrally vested in one leader, usually a monarch. Monarchs of many nations established absolute rule in their territories and controlled most aspects of daily life, including religion, the military, and the taxation and governing of citizens. Absolutist rulers maintained their power through the strength of customs, the support of the princes and nobles, and the belief that God selected and empowered them to rule the people.

Theory of Absolutism

By the sixteenth century, Europe had a long tradition of absolutism. Kings, not legislatures or nobles, ruled the nations. These kings had the power to create armies, regulate the government, and set up bureaucratic organizations. They were supported by the personal loyalty and consent of nobles and princes, who saw absolutism as a way of maintaining their own power and wealth while fostering stability throughout the land.

Few dared to question a king because of the widespread belief in the

Divine Right of Kings—the belief that kings are granted their power by God and are therefore answerable only to God, not to other people.

Absolutist Rulers in Europe

Most major powers in Europe were ruled by absolutist governments, with mixed results. Chief among these were the following:

- The *tsars*, or emperors, who were in power in Russia. In 1613, the Romanov family became the ruling dynasty in Russia. The greatest ruler among the early Romanovs was Peter I (1672–1725), also known as Peter the Great. He expanded and modernized Russia and founded the powerful new capital city of St. Petersburg.

- Prussia, originally a German state that came to be ruled by the Hohenzollern family. This family fostered the support of local princes and nobles in uniting German territories into a stronger union. Under their efficient, ambitious leadership, Prussia quickly became a major power in central Europe.

- The Holy Roman Empire, composed of a group of Germanic and Slavic nations in central Europe and led by the Hapsburg family of Austria. Due to the weak sense of unity among these nations, along with the vastly different ethnicities and cultures within them, the Holy Roman Empire eventually declined in power and importance.

- France, ruled by a series of monarchs whose powers were reduced via parliament. Among the ruling monarchs of France was Louis XIV (1638–1715), who was known for his ongoing wars, his lack of support among nobles, and his 1685 revocation of the Edict of Nantes that had served to protect the Protestant population of France.

A New World View

Disillusionment with the traditional absolutist approach eventually led to a rise in constitutionalism in some parts of Europe during the 1600s. *Republican* states, in which legislatures were established and vested with some of the powers normally reserved for kings, were on the rise. These states were not strictly democratic, since many legislatures were dominated by the nobility, but they were a step toward democracy and significant in Europe's changing world view.

A revolution in scientific knowledge, new philosophical movements, and cultural advances in music, art, and literature all contributed to the changes in European societies and perspectives. These led to a period of revolution and reform in the eighteenth century that ultimately brought about the modern continent.

Constitutionalism

In the seventeenth century, European states such as England, the Netherlands, and Poland-Lithuania found ways to curtail the power of rulers and reform the government. They did this in part via *constitutionalism*, the process by which the power of a state is limited by laws that are recorded in constitutions. Constitutions can be written or unwritten.

- In England, royal power was reduced during the English Civil War (1642 to 1649) and the Glorious Revolution (1688). In the decades leading to the English Civil War, James I (1566–1625) and Charles I (1600–1649) had centralized government authority, weakened the English parliament, and alienated most Puritans (who were influential in the legislature). The result was conflict between the *Royalists* (or Cavaliers), who supported the monarchy, and the *Roundheads*, who supported Parliament and the interests of Puritans.

  ○ In 1649, Roundhead commander Oliver Cromwell (1599–1658) defeated the Royalist forces. King Charles was beheaded.

  ○ Cromwell took control of England, Ireland, and Scotland and ruled as a harsh Puritan dictator.

  ○ After Cromwell's reign, England returned to a monarchical system under Kings Charles II (1630–1685) and James II (1633–1701).

  ○ In 1688, in the Glorious Revolution, monarchs William (1650–1702) and Mary (1662–1694) took power peacefully and allowed the *Bill of Rights* to be written and enacted. This document limited the powers of the monarchy and ensured that authority was divided fairly between the Crown and Parliament.

- In the Netherlands, the independent Dutch Republic prospered under the leadership of prominent families rather than monarchs. Trade and industry flourished, expanding the middle class; agricultural development occurred in the countryside; and a sense of religious tolerance spread. The Dutch briefly became a major power in trade in Latin America, East Asia, and Africa. It was also the Golden Age for Dutch arts, science, and literature.

- In the Poland-Lithuania region, a commonwealth formed in 1569 and successfully divided power between the king and parliament. For a time, religious tolerance was also present in the commonwealth.

The Scientific Revolution

Beginning around the 1500s, a slow process of development took place in different fields of scientific inquiry. Known as the *Scientific Revolution*, this gradual increase in scientific knowledge and achievement lasted until around 1700 and had a profound influence on many European nations. The Scientific Revolution was brought on by factors such as

- a sense of curiosity and love of learning based on Renaissance ideals;
- the motivation of individual scientists to discover, study, and share new knowledge;
- Protestantism's generally pro-science stance;
- improved scientific methods applied to research;
- availability of improved scientific education.

Great strides were made in various fields of inquiry, such as astronomy, mathematics, and anatomy.

- The field of astronomy flourished in the sixteenth and seventeenth centuries, as scientists used new methods and tools, such as the *telescope*, to reevaluate ancient beliefs about the universe. Classical conceptions about the universe, based more on philosophy and religion than actual science, were disproven. For example, scientists proved that Earth was not the center of the universe.

- Nicolaus Copernicus (1473–1543), a Polish astronomer, publicized findings that showed the *heliocentric* nature of the universe.

- Tycho Brahe (1546–1601) and Johannes Kepler (1571–1630) used an observatory and careful recording practices to note movements of the planets and develop theories based on this research.

- Galileo Galilei (1564–1642) applied new technology as well as mathematics to the study of the planets and the sun. He introduced the *experimental method* to science.

- The study of mathematics also flourished during the Scientific Revolution. Astronomers used and refined math in their study of the planets. Sir Isaac Newton (1643–1727) used mathematical principles to study the pull of *gravity* on the universe. He also developed the mathematical system of *calculus* to calculate motion, volume, and area.

- Knowledge of anatomy increased as scientists Andreas Vesalius (1514–1564) and William Harvey (1578–1657) made new discoveries about the nature of the human circulatory and skeletal systems.

The Scientific Revolution had profound effects on the study of science.

- Traditional sources of "scientific" knowledge, such as theology and philosophy, were rejected in favor of empirically based study.

- Modern scientific methods replaced the old ways. Modern methods used observation, theory, and experiment.

- Results were recorded carefully to ensure that experiments could be repeated and verified.

- The scientific community shared their findings with the world at large via their correspondence with each other as well as via publication and demonstration.

Cultural Advances

Developments in politics and the sciences led to changes in European culture. Renaissance-style humanist education, the Reformation, and insights gained during the Age of Exploration all contributed to new ways of looking at the world.

Cultural advancements during this period took many forms, ranging from new styles of architecture, painting, music, and literature to new philosophical movements that helped modernize Europe.

- Many architects, particularly in Catholic countries, favored the *Baroque* style of architecture. Baroque style involved large-scale, highly ornate, and emotionally charged designs, often based on religious themes. Baroque architecture reflected an awe and respect of leaders and was generally used in the design of palaces and other places that symbolized absolutist authority. Some examples of Baroque design include the Palace of Versailles in France and the Russian capital city of St. Petersburg.

- In this era, painting changed drastically from the strict realism and religious themes of the Renaissance. Although some painters embraced a Baroque style of painting and continued portraying biblical scenes and Christian figures, many others explored alternate directions, such as

  ○ *Secularism*, or the portrayal of regular scenes from daily life, as exemplified by the works of Rembrandt von Rijn (1606–1669), a Dutch artist who often painted commoners and middle class families.

  ○ *Rococo*, a scaled-down version of the Baroque style that employed similarly curved designs but with less ornamentation. An artist known for his work with Rococo was Jean-Antoine Watteau (1684–1721).

  ○ *Classicism*, the realistic and orderly portrayal of nature in the style of the early Renaissance and ancient Greece and Rome. An example classicist artist is French painter Nicolas Poussin (1594–1665).

- During the Baroque period, music was known for its fine ornamentation as well as its heavy use of bass notes. Some musical artists of the era include German composer Johann Sebastian Bach (1685–1750) and Italian composer Antonio Vivaldi (1678–1741).

- Literacy spread widely due to the advent of the printing press and improved education. Writers were eager to examine nature and society and share their feelings about the developments of the age.

  - William Shakespeare (c. 1564–1616), an English playwright, dramatized human psychology and European history in works such as *Hamlet, Othello, Macbeth, Julius Caesar,* and *Henry V.* He was also known for his tragedies, such as *Romeo and Juliet;* comedies, such as *The Two Gentlemen of Verona* and *A Midsummer Night's Dream;* and an extensive collection of poetry.

  - Miguel de Cervantes (1547–1616), a Spanish author, was best known for his novel *Don Quixote,* a parody of Spain's ideals of chivalry and their application to contemporary society.

  - John Milton (1608–1674), an English Puritan author, discussed the sinful nature of pride in his novel *Paradise Lost.*

  - Philosophical works during this period included *Leviathan* by Thomas Hobbes (1588–1679), *Two Treatises of Government* by John Locke (1632–1704), and *Essays* by Michel de Montaigne (1533–1592). These works helped to establish important schools of thought that would affect coming generations in Europe.

  - Religious works included the King James Bible, a Bible translated into the English vernacular, intended to make Christian teachings more accessible to all classes.

- Philosophical changes came alongside the other cultural developments in art and literature. The new and accepted philosophies of the era included humanism, political moderation, and skepticism.

  - Humanism, which had been around since the Renaissance, still held an important role. Humanists stressed the need for moral behavior and education and even attempted to increase literacy among women.

○ Political philosophers such as John Locke called for more moderate government. In his *Two Treatises of Government*, Locke posited that people are generally peaceful and should be guaranteed certain freedoms and protections by governments. These ideas would become crucial in the coming era of the Enlightenment.

○ *Skepticism*, a school of thought that doubts whether it is possible to determine truth or definitive knowledge, developed during this time primarily due to the writings of Michel de Montaigne.

Multiple-Choice Review Questions

1. Which of the following was the most immediate effect of the Glorious Revolution of 1688?

    A. The victory of the Roundheads over the Cavaliers
    B. The return to the monarchical system in England
    C. The establishment of an oppressive Puritan dictatorship
    D. The beheading of King Charles I of England
    E. The peaceful transfer of power to William and Mary

2. A specialist applying the theories of Andreas Vesalius would most likely be a

    A. physician treating an arterial dysfunction.
    B. musician composing a Baroque symphony.
    C. mathematician calculating motion and volume.
    D. astronomer studying the heliocentric model.
    E. theologian carrying out the work of Jesuits.

"This, then, sirs, is to be a knight-errant, and what I have spoken of is the order of his chivalry, of which, as I have already said, I, though a sinner, have made profession, and what the aforesaid knights professed that same do I profess, and so I go through these solitudes and wilds seeking adventures, resolved in soul to oppose my arm and person to the most perilous that fortune may offer me in aid of the weak and needy."

3. The quotation above is from a work by

   A. Thomas Hobbes.
   B. Antonio Vivaldi.
   C. William Shakespeare.
   D. Miguel de Cervantes.
   E. John Milton.

4. All of the following were contributing factors to the Scientific Revolution of the sixteenth and seventeenth centuries EXCEPT

   A. advances in scientific education in universities.
   B. Renaissance celebration of learning and curiosity.
   C. Protestant attitudes toward the importance of science.
   D. developments in Rococo techniques in Europe.
   E. greater means of recording and sharing knowledge.

5. Republican states differ from purely democratic states in that republican states generally

   A. lack the legislative bodies common to democracies.
   B. were not established under constitutionalist principles.
   C. have legislatures swayed by the interests of nobility.
   D. cannot thrive in highly populated regions or nations.
   E. lack centralized leadership and bureaucratic offices.

Answer Explanations

1. **E.** The Glorious Revolution was a major step in the great English political upheavals of the seventeenth century. It led most immediately to the peaceful rise of monarchs William and Mary, who legalized a Bill of Rights establishing constitutionalism in that country.

2. **A.** Andreas Vesalius was an anatomist who made great strides in the study of the human circulatory system. The circulatory system involves the flow of blood through the body. A physician helping a patient with an arterial disorder, or a problem with the arteries, would be most likely to refer to Vesalius' work.

3. **D.** This quotation comes from *Don Quixote*, the most famous novel by Miguel de Cervantes. In this satirical novel, a Spanish man tries to restore the old-fashioned ideals of chivalry in the modern world.

4. **D.** All factors listed facilitated the Scientific Revolution except the development of Rococo. Rococo was an artistic rather than a scientific movement. It involved a more intricate and ornamental vision of the Baroque style, used primarily in painting and architecture.

5. **C.** Republican states are similar in many ways to democratic ones. However, a primary difference is that, in a true democracy, the legislature directly represents the people. In most republics, however, the interests of nobles or monarchs dominate the legislature.

Review Chapter 3:
The Age of Revolution

The eighteenth century in Europe was a time of great revolution. Some were military revolutions, but others took place in philosophy or society. Major features of this period in history include the Enlightenment, European expansion, the Agricultural Revolution, the beginnings of the Industrial Revolution, and the French Revolution.

The Enlightenment

The philosophies of the Age of Absolutism contributed to the *Enlightenment*, a period in intellectual and cultural history during which the world reached a new understanding of both nature and society.

In general, the thinkers of the Enlightenment believed that

- societies and governments are capable of change and improvement;
- people have natural rights that governments should respect;
- religious preferences may differ, but tolerance is needed;
- reason and natural science are the keys to understanding life.

Enlightenment thinkers, often called *philosophes*, attempted to spread their ideas as widely as possible among the public. They wrote pamphlets, dictionaries, and histories, as well as plays and novels (frequently satirical) to demonstrate their principles. The public reacted positively to the philosophes, and publishing, reading, and a freedom of the press thrived.

The philosophes often met in busy *salons*, which were generally operated by women. In this way, women were included in the philosophical debate and education. The philosophes also pursued universal laws and justice that would end discrimination, as well as reforms in government that would promote the rights of all. However, in reality, Enlightenment society remained divided by class, gender, religion, and race.

Some of the major figures of the Enlightenment included

- John Locke, an English philosopher whose ideas for political reform helped spark the Enlightenment; he also promoted the idea that people are all capable of learning and improvement.
- John Toland (1670–1722), an English writer who promoted the *Deist* movement, which holds that the universe has a creator whose existence can be proven through observation and reason.
- Voltaire (1694–1778), a French writer who criticized Catholicism and defended persecuted Protestants in the mid-1700s.
- Mary Wollstonecraft (1759–1797), the English author of *A Vindication of the Rights of Women*, who promoted women's rights.
- Jean-Jacques Rousseau (1712–1778), a Swiss author known for his belief in government as a social contract.
- Adam Smith (1723–1790), a Scottish economist and the author of *The Wealth of Nations*, who advocated for free markets and a specialization of labor.

Enlightened Despotism

The principles of the Enlightenment even influenced some of the absolute rulers of Europe. However, despite minor reforms, the nature of absolutism remained fundamentally unchanged. Despots primarily used Enlightenment ideas to strengthen their nations and military forces, not to benefit individual citizens. Some so-called *enlightened despots* included

Catherine II (Catherine the Great), Frederick II (Frederick the Great), Maria Theresa, and Joseph II.

- Catherine the Great of Russia (reigned 1762–1796) advocated for social reforms in Russia. She funded the construction of printing presses and new educational centers. At the same time, however, she maintained a variety of dictatorial practices including censorship, the oppression of dissidents, and serfdom.

- Frederick the Great of Prussia (reigned 1740–1786) revised laws and the justice system and provided support for agriculture, art, and education. Although his policies led to a rise in taxation, he was ultimately successful in building Prussia into a major European power.

- Both Maria Theresa (reigned 1740–1780) and her son and co-regent Joseph II (1765–1790) of Austria worked to limit the power of the church, diminish the burden on peasants, abolish serfdom, and reduce religious persecution.

European Expansion

Following the Age of Exploration, European nations colonized the Americas and established a brisk trading economy on the Atlantic Ocean. By the 1700s, the balance of world power began shifting, as England and France took the lead over the Spanish, Dutch, and others. All nations maintained colonial possessions and trade networks, however.

- England entered a union with Scotland in 1707 to become Great Britain. Britain had already developed into a primary power in world trade and it used the *Navigation Acts* to create a near-monopoly on colonial commerce. Britain's colonies included territories in North America, India, and the Caribbean. The American colonies in particular held the promise of expansion and riches, until the colonists fought for and won their independence in the American Revolution.

- France maintained colonies in North America based around the Ohio Valley, Louisiana, and parts of Canada. French colonizers used these territories as fur trading hubs with Native Americans. Later, France and Britain engaged in a power struggle ultimately won by Britain, and much of France's colonial influence was erased from the continent.

- A weakening Spain maintained its territorial claims in South America, Central America, southern parts of North America, and the Caribbean.

- The Dutch empire retained small colonies in South Africa, South America, India, and Indonesia.

Major Events in Expansionism

Wars in Europe as well as in overseas colonies helped determine the future of European expansionism. These wars included the War of Austrian Succession, the Seven Years' War, and the American Revolutionary War. Another important event was the introduction of slavery to the colonies.

- During the War of Austrian Succession (1740–1748), Britain, Russia, and Austria joined forces to fight Prussia and France and ensure the survival of the Hapsburg Empire.

- During the Seven Years' War (1756–1763), Britain and Prussia joined forces against France and Austria. The nations fought both in Europe and their foreign possessions; the war extended to India and North America, making it the first true worldwide conflict. The part of the conflict that took place in North America is called the French and Indian War.

- During the American Revolutionary War (1775–1783), Britain's colonies in North America declared independence and fought a war to free themselves from British rule. With significant assistance from the French, the colonists were successful, forming the United States of America. The ideals that prompted the Revolutionary War were profound and had revolutionary effect on Europe in the late eighteenth century.

- Enslaved Africans were first brought to the Americas by Spanish, Dutch, and Portuguese colonizers in the sixteenth century. With the rapid development of agriculture and the easy availability of fertile farming land, slavery quickly became an important feature of economy and society in many parts of the Americas.

Agricultural Revolution

As Europe expanded its knowledge, territory, and capabilities, a revolution was also taking place in agriculture. Throughout Europe, scientists and farmers were developing new ideas and products to increase the productivity of farmers. These innovations included the following:

- Open fields were enclosed (fenced) to aid in crop organization and the management of animals.
- Urban population growth demanded an increase in food and other agricultural products. Agriculture was commercialized to meet this increased demand.
- New technologies, such as the seed drill and horse-drawn hoe invented by Jethro Tull, were applied.
- More arable farming land was created by draining formerly unusable marshes.
- New crops and new methods of crop rotation were implemented in order to create larger and better yields.

However, many problems remained. For example, the enclosure system also ended the medieval practice of communal fields, which meant that the poorest farmers lost the opportunity to use a piece of shared land. In addition, social inequity continued to plague agricultural communities, with abuses against farmers and serfs still rampant, particularly in the East.

The Agricultural Revolution contributed to a number of important changes in European society, such as:

- A rapid growth in population in the 1700s, due in large part to more-abundant food and access to better nutrition as well as a drastic reduction in famine and disease epidemics.
- The rise of the "cottage industry" system, in which poor urban citizens produced crafts and other goods in their homes.

Industrial Revolution

While agriculture was booming in Europe, the industries of many nations were also experiencing rapid growth. The *Industrial Revolution*, a gradual process of industrial development in Europe, began in Britain around the 1780s and spread throughout the European mainland by about 1815. Industrialization continued and increased through the nineteenth and twentieth centuries. It created a more modern social and economic state for most of Europe.

Industrialization spread slowly in nations that were in conflicts or otherwise unstable. However, for the most part, Britain's innovations created a blueprint by which other nations could begin their own industrialization processes.

The Industrial Revolution took hold in Britain for several major reasons.

- Being an island nation and a major colonial power, Britain engaged in a brisk trade market that called for an increase in British-made goods.
- The British government was stable and the economy sound enough to support change and growth.
- The British people were generally prosperous. With a decrease in food prices, they also had enough money to become more of a consumerist society.
- A mobile labor force was available to move into Britain's growing urban areas to work in factories.

Technologies

At this time, major industries in Britain included textile, coal, and steel. Each of these expanding sectors utilized important technologies developed during this period. For example, the first large factories in the world were built in Britain to produce textiles. Coal was used as an energy source for factories as well as for heating homes and other buildings. Innovative technologies included the spinning jenny, the water frame, and the steam engine. Railroads became a major source of transportation during this time.

- The spinning jenny was invented in 1765. It allowed thread to be produced quickly and with relative ease.
- The water frame made thread production more efficient on a factory scale.
- Steam engines originated in the late 1700s with little success. The first truly efficient steam engine was developed in Scotland in the 1760s by James Watt. Steam power revolutionized the textile and iron/steel industries.

Effects of Industrialization

Industrialization had both positive and negative effects.

- Manufactured goods decreased in price and increased in availability, improving quality of life.
- Industrialization led to an increase in urbanization and capitalism and created wealth and a new social class. The population in industrialized nations skyrocketed.
- Working conditions in early factories were frequently poor and workers were often miserable.
- Child labor was a common practice in the early years, and long hours of labor were often required of poor and orphaned youths.

The French Revolution

The French Revolution involved an ideological clash between proponents of absolutism and proponents of Enlightenment ideals. The French Revolution was long and bloody; the conflict itself ran from 1789 to 1791 but it also led to subsequent violent counterrevolutions and regime changes, which were ongoing until 1799. The French Revolution was a reaction to long-standing social, political, and economic problems in the *ancien régime*, or old order, of French government.

Some of the causes of the French Revolution included the following:

- The ancien régime was almost bankrupt due to the costs of many wars, including French aid to the United States in the American Revolutionary War. Because aristocrats in France refused to pay higher taxes, the tax burden fell disproportionately upon the already suffering lower classes.

- Under the ancien régime, French society was divided into three *Estates*. The first two were reserved for clergy and nobility, while the Third Estate was a catchall for the lower classes. The Third Estate was by far the largest, yet received no extra representation and paid the highest taxes.

- The members of the three Estates did not receive equal treatment under French law. Members of the Third Estate typically lived under harsher restrictions and higher penalties. The monarchy also held the right to make arbitrary legal rulings and unexplained arrests.

Major Events of the French Revolution

The major events in the French Revolution included the following:

- King Louis XVI (1754–1793) called the *Estates General* (representatives of the three Estates) to assemble so he could request more funding. The Third Estate revolted and withdrew from the assembly. Calling itself the National Assembly, the Third Estate then demanded major reforms in politics and society.

- Citizens of the Third Estate joined the revolt, storming the *Bastille*, a jail which held many political prisoners.

- Louis XVI, driven from the Palace of Versailles, tried to flee France in 1791. He was captured and later executed along with his wife, Marie Antoinette (1755–1793).

- In 1792, revolutionaries declared France a republic; they adopted a red, white, and blue flag along with the motto Liberty, Equality, Fraternity.

- In 1793, the *Jacobins*, a radical revolutionary faction, and their leader, Maximilien Robespierre (1758–1794), seized power and began a Reign of Terror during which thousands of nobles, royalists, and members of the monarchy were imprisoned and executed.

- The Jacobin movement fell in 1794, leading to the takeover by the *Directory*, an unstable government that ruled France until the end of the century.

Multiple-Choice Review Questions

1. Which event resulted from a conflict over the legitimacy of the heir to the Hapsburg Empire?

   A. Seven Years' War
   B. War of Austrian Succession
   C. Reign of Terror
   D. Industrialization of England
   E. Colonization of the Americas

2. The National Assembly that formed in France in 1789 was made up primarily of

    A. discontented members of the Third Estate.
    B. Jacobin revolutionaries and criminals.
    C. Huguenot princes promoting Protestantism.
    D. disenfranchised members of the Directory.
    E. conservative legislators hoping to quell rebellion.

3. All of the following are true about the salons of the seventeenth and eighteenth centuries EXCEPT

    A. they were meeting places for philosophes.
    B. many were operated by female proprietors.
    C. their members often discussed reform and justice.
    D. many served as hideouts for violent revolutionaries.
    E. their membership extolled Enlightenment principles.

4. A spinning jenny and water frame would most likely be found in a

    A. sawmill.
    B. metal refinery.
    C. textile factory.
    D. farming community.
    E. coal mine.

5. All of the following were events and innovations of the Agricultural Revolution in the eighteenth century EXCEPT

    A. the draining of swampland to create new farms.
    B. new strategies for seasonal rotations of crops.
    C. the universal abolition of agricultural serfdom.
    D. the planting and hoeing machines of Jethro Tull.
    E. a rising demand for food in European cities.

Answer Explanations

1. **B.** The War of Austrian Succession was a conflict pitting Britain, Russia, and Austria against France and Prussia. These nations battled from 1740 to 1748 after disagreeing on the eligibility of Maria Theresa to inherit leadership of the Hapsburg Empire.

2. **A.** The National Assembly formed in 1789 during the beginning stages of the French Revolution. The Assembly was composed primarily of disgruntled members of the legislative body called the *Third Estate*. The Third Estate, which represented France's commoners, faced constant inequality and oppression under the old order.

3. **D.** The salons were important places in the development of the Enlightenment. They served many purposes, but were not typically hideouts for revolutionaries. Rather, their typical clientele were philosophers and artists who participated in discussions and debates.

4. **C.** The spinning jenny and water frame were important inventions of the 1700s. Both were used to make thread, a basic material required for textile production. These inventions helped fuel the growth of the Industrial Revolution.

5. **C.** The Agricultural Revolution was a time of great change in Europe, not only on farms but also in the cities that relied on agricultural production to feed their inhabitants. One event that did NOT occur, however, was the universal abolition of serfdom. In many areas, particularly in Eastern Europe, serfdom was common until well into the 1860s.

Review Chapter 4:
The Age of Isms

The period following the Age of Revolutions, beginning with the Napoleonic Wars and leading to the beginning of the twentieth century, is sometimes known as the Age of Isms. The term *isms* represents the many new social and political ideologies of this period, many of which end in the suffix *ism*.

- Among these ideologies were conservatism, liberalism, socialism, imperialism, and nationalism.
- Artistic movements during the period include Romanticism, realism, Impressionism, and expressionism.
- European civilization also experienced continued urbanization and industrialization.

Napoleonic Wars

France was in disorder in the years following the French Revolution. In 1799, a French general named Napoleon Bonaparte (1769–1821) took control of the troubled French government and, in 1804, declared himself the new emperor. Napoleon brought both order and war to France during his brief and tumultuous reign.

- In 1804, Napoleon implemented the *Napoleonic Code*, a series of reforms which set out new laws for France and solidified traditional ideals of French culture.

- Napoleon granted amnesty to nobles and confirmed the gains made by the lower classes in social status.
- Napoleon centralized the authority and administration of France and established himself as absolute ruler.
- Napoleon promoted the idea of citizenry in service of the state, and supported the arrest and/or censorship of dissenters.

Although he brought stability and progress to France, Napoleon also led France into many conflicts.

- In 1805, French fleets were routed by the British navy at the Battle of Trafalgar.
- In 1805, Napoleon won a major victory over Russia and Austria at the Battle of Austerlitz.
- In 1806, the French began to blockade British trade in Europe. Additionally, Napoleon won a great victory at the Battle of Jena.
- In 1812, Napoleon led a disastrous French invasion of Russia.
- In 1815, Napoleon's forces were decisively beaten by a joint British, Russian, Prussian, and Austrian force at the Battle of Waterloo.

Napoleon's reign collapsed in 1814 and 1815. European leaders dealt with the fallout of his reign via the *Congress of Vienna*. Dominated by Austrian chancellor Klemens von Metternich (1773–1859), the emissaries chose to rebuild the old order and destroy the revolutionary vestiges in war-ravaged Europe. The Congress of Vienna resolved to do the following:

- Restore the Bourbons to the throne, beginning with Louis XVIII (1755–1824).
- Return French national boundaries to those that existed prior to the Napoleonic Wars.
- Establish international cooperation to stifle revolutionary tendencies and maintain a balance of international power.

- Pursue policies of conservatism in Europe in an effort to stifle liberalism.

Political Isms

The cycle of revolution, war, and restoration brought massive change to Europe and new political ideologies began to surface and spread.

- *Conservatism*, as supported by the delegates at Vienna, was a nineteenth-century belief that national traditions, religions, monarchies, and aristocrats were needed to maintain stability in any country. Many conservatives felt that liberals were low-class and prone to revolutionary behaviors.

- *Liberalism* in the nineteenth century was a belief in the importance of freedoms (such as freedom of press, elections, economy, and religion), human dignity, and social equality over national traditions. Many liberals felt that conservatives sought to hold down the middle class and preserve social inequities.

- *Socialism* was a radical political ideology that arose in post-Napoleonic Europe. Socialists wanted an equal distribution of money and property among all citizens of a nation. One branch of socialism was *Marxism*, which held that class struggle was inevitable, and the workers of the world were destined to overthrow capitalism. Marxism was related to *Communism* and was championed by Karl Marx (1818–1883) and Friedrich Engels (1820–1895).

- *Imperialism* involved the building of colonies and empires and subjugating of foreign people. Between 1880 and 1914, a wave of imperialism swept across Europe. Many of Europe's greatest powers struggled to gain influence in faraway lands such as Africa and Asia. Their motives included a desire for economic gain and a sense of racism and nationalism that led to feelings of superiority and entitlement.

- *Nationalism* was another radical idea that took hold in Europe. Spread by Napoleon's armies throughout many nations, nineteenth-century nationalism held that cultural unity was both possible and desirable, and that different cultures of people should constitute their own nations. While promoting unity and pride, nationalism also fostered a sense of rivalry and prejudice among neighbors. Nationalism would play a key role in various revolutionary events in the 1800s as well as the unification of Germany and Italy in the 1870s.

Revolution and Unification

The spirit of nationalism that spread in Europe contributed to a number of revolts and other conflicts, as well as the unifications of previously fragmented states.

- Greece and Serbia won independence from the Ottoman Empire in 1830.
- Belgium gained its independence from the Netherlands in 1830.
- Failed revolutions took place in Russia and Poland in 1825 and 1830, respectively.
- Liberals launched the 1848 Revolutions in Germany, France, and Austria, but were defeated.
- Revolutions in France over a period of almost sixty years caused repeated conflict and resulted in a succession of monarchs and republics.
- The Crimean War (1853–1856) was an international conflict among Britain, France, Russia, and the Ottoman Empire. This war ended the illusion of international cooperation in post-Napoleonic Europe.
- The unification of Italy, which operated as dozens of separate city-states, was achieved around 1859. The effort was planned by *Carbonari*, a secret society, and the unified nation came under the control of King Victor Emmanuel II (1820–1878).
- The unification of Germany, unsuccessfully planned and attempted for generations, finally came to fruition in 1871 after a long series of wars in which Prussia was dominant. Conservative Otto von

Bismarck (1815–1898) planned the unification, and control of the unified Germany went to Emperor William I (1797–1888).

Progress and Reform

The many changes in Europe in the nineteenth century carried along a tide of progress and reform. These developments came in many fields and took many forms.

- Europe began the long process of *industrialization* during previous centuries, but during the 1800s these movements finally brought the continent into a modern state. This era is sometimes termed the *Second Industrial Revolution.*

  - Nations such as Germany and Russia industrialized quickly after years of struggle and hesitation.

  - Factories—large and small, urban and rural—became common sights across the continent. Factory workers continued to deal with low wages, long hours, and dangerous working conditions, which were often worse for women and children.

  - However, workers in all countries learn to cope and form a new social group, the *proletariat*, which sometimes unionized, bargained, and went on strike to gain better benefits and working conditions.

- *Urbanization*, or the growth of cities, went hand in hand with industrialization, due to the influx of workers looking for jobs in urban factories. Early industrial cities tended to be overcrowded, dirty, and poor. In time, however, better city planning and public health procedures led to improved living conditions in larger urban areas.

- The demands of industrialization and urbanization led to growth in energy and transportation technologies in the 1800s.

  - *Steamboats*, ships powered by steam engines, carried people and goods across rivers and oceans.

  - In 1830, the first successful railway in Europe launched. Over the next several decades, *railroads* changed life in Europe by allowing for easier migration and a quicker transport of goods.

- ◦ Scientists introduced the first large-scale *electric power* operations in Britain in 1881. Electric power soon rivaled and then surpassed steam and coal power in industries.

- ◦ The first *automobile* debuted in Germany in the 1880s. In the coming decades, cars and trucks become mainstays of European transportation.

- A succession of important *social reforms* affecting women, workers, serfs, Jews, and enslaved people spanned across many European nations.

  - ◦ *Women's rights* organizations, particularly in Britain, made some headway in the campaign for suffrage and opportunities for education and work for females.

  - ◦ Several nations passed *worker protection laws* to limit excessive working hours, curb unemployment, and help injured laborers.

  - ◦ In Russia, Alexander II (1818–1881) abolished serfdom in 1861. The difficulties for former serfs continued, however.

  - ◦ The treatment of Jews in Europe varied drastically depending on time and place. In some areas, Jewish citizens were protected and enfranchised as much as other citizens.

  - ◦ Slavery was banned in the colonial possessions of Britain, France, the Netherlands, Denmark, Portugal, and Sweden between 1833 and 1863.

- *Immigration*, often to the United States, increased during the 1800s. People from struggling nations of Europe immigrated in the hope of a new life in America. Tragedies such as the Irish potato famine, which led to widespread starvation among already suffering Irish farmers, caused a rapid increase in immigration from Ireland.

- Several scientists, including Sigmund Freud and Charles Darwin, contributed new and revolutionary facets to European thinking during the nineteenth century.

- ° Sigmund Freud (1856–1939) was an Austrian scientist who developed groundbreaking theories about the unconscious human mind. He also founded the field of *psychoanalysis*.
- ° Charles Darwin (1809–1882) was an English naturalist whose treatise *On the Origins of Species* presented a new theory about life as a struggle for survival. Darwin posited that, in nature, only the fittest organisms prospered. Social scientists later applied this theory of natural selection to humans (*Social Darwinism*).

Art and Science

The arts and sciences also thrived during the nineteenth century. New or revived art styles included Romanticism, realism, Impressionism, and expressionism. They all brought new and striking images to life.

- *Romanticism* was a major movement in art and literature. Romantics rejected the classical emphasis on science, order, and balance. Romantic artists and writers believed that art should reflect life and nature and be emotionally engaging, spontaneous, and personally meaningful. Some Romantic writers and artists include William Blake, Samuel Taylor Coleridge, J. M. W. Turner, and Eugene Delacroix.
- *Realism* was an older movement in art that continued to flourish during the nineteenth century. Realistic painters, sculptors, and writers attempted to capture true-to-life details in their work in an effort to reflect the nature of human life. Gustave Courbet's *The Artist's Studio* and Winslow Homer's *The Gulf Stream* are examples of realist paintings. Authors such as Leo Tolstoy, Fyodor Dostoyevsky, Charles Dickens, and George Eliot wrote from the realist perspective.
- *Impressionism* was a style of painting that involved the creation of compositions using small dabs of color. It was more about feeling than realistic representation. Some major Impressionist painters included Claude Monet, Pierre Auguste Renoir, and Edgar Degas.

Monet's painting *Poppies, Near Argenteuil* is highly representative of this method. Later, *Post-Impressionists* reinterpreted the style. Paul Cezanne, Georges Seurat, and Vincent van Gogh were notable Post-Impressionist artists of the later nineteenth century.

- *Expressionism* was a style of painting employing jarring colors and unexpected combinations of images to convey emotional messages to viewers. A good example is Edvard Munch's *The Scream* (1893).

Multiple-Choice Review Questions

1. Which feature do the artistic movements of Romanticism, expressionism, and Impressionism share?

   A. Common application to visual and written artwork
   B. Desire to capture the realistic details of everyday life
   C. Communication of feelings and emotions to viewers
   D. Use of jarring and often clashing color schemes
   E. Application of dabs of color to create larger images

2. Which of the following was a conservative political leader who dominated the proceedings of the Congress of Vienna?

   A. Napoleon Bonaparte
   B. Klemens von Metternich
   C. Friedrich Engels
   D. Victor Emmanuel II
   E. Otto von Bismarck

3. Which of the following would be most representative of the social group known as the proletariat?

    A. An urban laborer
    B. A political appointee
    C. A clergy member
    D. A factory owner
    E. A women's rights activist

4. A nationalist political thinker in the nineteenth century would be most likely to support which of the following ideas?

    A. Nobles and traditional systems of aristocracy are essential for social stability.
    B. Creating overseas colonies allows extensive opportunity for financial gains.
    C. Human dignity and freedom are universal goals that must be achieved at any cost.
    D. Class struggle is inevitable and ultimately forges a new and fairer class system.
    E. Pride among the citizens of a country and unity against foreign powers are essential.

5. Which of the following countries was unified in 1871?

    A. Poland
    B. Italy
    C. Netherlands
    D. Serbia
    E. Germany

Answer Explanations

1.　**C.** Some of the major art movements of the nineteenth century, particularly Romanticism, expressionism, and Impressionism, were based on the idea that portraying and communicating feeling/emotion is a crucially important part of the artistic process.

2.　**B.** Klemens von Metternich, the chancellor of Austria, was the most powerful figure at the Congress of Vienna. He helped influence the decisions of the congress that ultimately led to the restoration of many prerevolutionary orders in Europe.

3.　**A.** *Proletariat* was a term created to describe the world's working class, who increasingly came into conflict with business owners and other wealthier and more powerful citizens. An urban laborer would be strongly representative of the proletariat.

4.　**E.** Nationalism was one the driving forces in Europe during the nineteenth century. This ideology held that pride in one's country, typically paired with rivalry and suspicion of outsiders, was of foremost importance. This mind-set contributed to a long series of conflicts in the 1800s and beyond.

5.　**E.** All of the listed nations experienced upheaval and massive change during the nineteenth century. The Netherlands, Serbia, and Poland also underwent revolutionary war. Italy and Germany were both unified. Germany, however, was the only one of these countries unified in 1871. That year, Otto von Bismarck oversaw the union of the German states into a single nation.

Review Chapter 5: The Twentieth Century and Beyond

The twentieth century was a time of both dramatic advances and tragic destruction. Some of the milestones of the century include World War I, World War II, the Cold War, and the Post-Cold War era. The twentieth century also saw major developments in science, technology, and culture.

World War I

World War I (1914–1918) started for a variety of reasons.

- The *nationalism* and *imperialism* that arose in Europe during the nineteenth century gave nations and empires a sense of superiority and rivalry.

- A spirit of *militarism* meant a focus on military aims and a race for weapons and alliances.

- The *alliance system* contributed to the arms race. Under this system, countries partnered together in the hopes of building military strength. The two main alliances during the World War I era were the *Central Powers* (Germany, Austria-Hungary, and the Ottoman Empire) and the *Triple Entente* (Britain, France, and Russia, later joined by the United States).

- *Multiethnic empires* united diverse groups of people who differed significantly in language, culture, and religious beliefs. Because there was so little to hold these groups together, national unity was difficult. Empires such as Austria-Hungary and the Ottoman Empire experienced serious internal tension, instability, and conflict due to ethnic diversity.

- The assassination of Austro-Hungarian archduke Franz Ferdinand in 1914 was an act of violence brought on by ethnic and political tension within Austria-Hungary. However, due to the alliance system (and other factors), this relatively small, otherwise isolated incident quickly escalated into a worldwide conflict.

Major Events of World War I

- After the assassination of Archduke Ferdinand, a complex series of alliances led more and more countries into war. Soon the Central Powers and Triple Entente were fighting along two main European fronts: (1) the *Western Front* in northern France, where the Germans were fighting the French and British; and (2) the *Eastern Front* in Poland, Russia, and other areas, where the Germans and Austro-Hungarians were fighting the Russians.

- Warfare became incredibly brutal and destructive with the introduction of new military strategies, such as *trench warfare*, and technologies like poison gas, tanks, submarines, and machine guns.

- Due to internal revolution, Russia was forced to withdraw from the war in 1917. During the Russian Revolution, the tsarist government was overthrown and ultimately replaced by the Bolsheviks. Led by Vladimir Lenin (1870–1924), the Bolsheviks quickly altered the Russian government and Russian society in a quest to establish a Marxist state.

- The United States, angered by German submarine warfare practices, joined World War I in 1917 to support Britain and France.

- In 1918, the Central Powers were defeated; Europe was in ruins.

- The *Treaty of Versailles* was an agreement to end the war.

  - The treaty succeeded in temporarily promoting democracy, encouraging the fall of empires, and allowing for the creation of new states such as Czechoslovakia, Austria, Hungary, and Poland.
  - The treaty was designed to incriminate and punish Germany for the war. The real result of the *War Guilt clause*, however, was the breeding of discontent that would later lead to World War II.

The Interwar Years

The years 1919 to 1938 are considered an "interwar" period in Europe because they fall between World Wars I and II. This period in European history was marked by rapidly falling expectations, economic difficulties, and the rise of dictatorships in the countries of Italy, Germany, and Russia.

Expectations

After the devastation of World War I, many believed it inconceivable that another world war could occur. Europeans felt more secure due to the establishment of the *League of Nations*, an international organization designed to negotiate future conflicts and avoid wars, and the placing of military restrictions on Germany. However, all of these safeguards soon proved false. The League of Nations floundered, unable to enforce its rulings. Consequently, Germany and other nations were able to stockpile weapons shortly after the end of the war.

Economic Hardships

Despite the brisk economy of World War I, downturns and economic suffering set in shortly after the war.

- Consumption, productivity, and industrial strength all weakened.
- Germany was unable to pay its war reparations and fell into depression.
- Rampant inflation spread throughout Europe.

- The Great Depression spread across the globe, starting in 1929.
- Economic problems reduced the credibility of capitalism and made Communism and dictatorships seem more appealing.

Rise of Dictatorships

The discontent and disenchantment of many Europeans made them desperate for change. The arrival of dictators in the 1920s and 1930s seemed to offer struggling nations a chance for new glory and prosperity.

Three main dictatorships took hold in Europe.

- In 1922, a fascist dictatorship led by Benito Mussolini (1883–1945) took control of the Italian government. *Fascism* is an autocratic political system hostile to democracy and Communism. Mussolini and his followers gained power over most aspects of life in Italy and began spreading propaganda and building military power.
- In 1920s Germany, Adolf Hitler and the Nazi party rose to power. Hitler used growing military might, oppressive secret police, propaganda, and racism (primarily targeting Jews) to install a Nazi dictatorship over Germany.
- In 1922, the Communist Soviet Union (USSR) was formed from several nations in Eastern Europe. After the death of Bolshevik leader Lenin, Joseph Stalin took power. He used oppression and terror tactics, including deadly famines, to consolidate power and expand the Soviet Union.

World War II

The intensifying crises in Europe led the world directly into another, even more destructive war. World War II (1939–1945) began as an attempt to stop German territorial expansion. It ended six years later with tens of millions dead and much of Europe in ruins.

Major World War II Events

- In 1935, both Germany and Italy undertook unprovoked acts of aggression against other countries. Italy attacked Ethiopia, while Germany annexed Austria and parts of Czechoslovakia. Instead of taking action to stop this behavior, leaders of Europe's major powers adopted a strategy of *appeasement*. That is, they made concessions to hostile nations in the hopes of diverting a war.

- In 1939, German forces invaded Poland, finally prompting a military response from Britain and France. The countries of Europe declared war. The primary members of the alliances in conflict with each other were the Axis (Germany, Italy, Japan) and the Allied (Britain, France [until its defeat], and the USSR and the United States [after 1941]). The Axis invaded or annexed numerous lands including Austria, Czechoslovakia, Poland, Norway, Denmark, Greece, and Yugoslavia.

- In 1940, German forces occupied a defeated France.

- In 1940, the Germans launched repeated air attacks on Britain only to be ultimately repelled in the Battle of Britain.

- In 1941, the Germans broke a nonaggression pact with the USSR and invaded Russia.

- In 1941, German's ally, Japan, launched a surprise attack on United States naval forces at Pearl Harbor, causing the United States to enter World War II on the Allied side.

- In 1943, Soviet forces defeated the Nazis at the Battle of Stalingrad, forcing a bloody retreat to Germany.

- In 1943, the rule of Mussolini in Italy collapsed.

- In 1944, after years of strategic landings and bombings, the Allies invaded Europe on *D-Day* and sent the Germans into retreat.

- In 1945, Allied armies captured Berlin, destroying the Nazi regime. Hitler committed suicide. World War II ended in Europe.

Results of the War

- During World War II, the Nazis and their allies killed millions of perceived enemies, particularly Jews, in an event known as the *Holocaust*. Nazis (and Soviets) also persecuted many other groups in Europe.

- The United States ended World War II globally by dropping two *atomic bombs* on Japan in 1945. The use of weapons of mass destruction in war was unprecedented and drove fears of nuclear war in the coming decades.

- With the fall of fascism in Europe and the victory of the USSR, Communism became stronger than ever. Europe immediately entered a tense period known as the *Cold War*, during which Communist and democratic nations teetered constantly at the brink of conflict.

The Cold War

Immediately following World War II, an armed standoff began between the Communist and democratic countries in Europe. (Aiding and leading the democratic faction was the United States.) During this era, the United States and USSR, with their respective allies, coexisted in a state of great unease, gathering weapons and undergoing several crises that heightened fears of a global nuclear war. The Cold War ended in the 1990s with the collapse of European Communism.

The United States and the USSR adopted policies to limit the power of the other. Leaders in the United States enacted a strategy of *containment* meant to stop the spread of Communism. They also pursued the *Marshall Plan*, an economic recovery program meant to assist European nations so they could withstand potential Communist takeovers. Meanwhile, Soviet leaders expanded their holdings in Europe, ostensibly to gain "buffer states" to protect them from democratic encroachment. Both factions built alliances and organizations during this time.

- The *United Nations*, formed in 1945, was established to oversee and mediate international problems.
- The *North Atlantic Treaty Organization* (NATO) of 1949 began a partnership between democratic nations, led by the United States.
- The *Warsaw Pact*, established in 1955, was a partnership in Eastern Europe among states allied with or dominated by the USSR, including East Germany, Poland, Czechoslovakia, Hungary, Romania, and Bulgaria.

Major Events in the Cold War

- In 1945, Germany was split into two parts: democratic West Germany and Communist East Germany. The capital, Berlin, was similarly divided.
- In 1948, the USSR began isolating East Germany, prompting a United States airlift of food and supplies to West Berlin in the *Berlin Airlift*.
- In 1953, Joseph Stalin died and the USSR came under the control of Nikita Khrushchev, who denounced the policies and crimes of his predecessor.
- In 1956 and 1968, Soviet forces crushed pro-democracy protests in Eastern Europe.
- In 1961, the Soviets constructed a concrete barrier known as the *Berlin Wall* to separate the two parts of Berlin.
- In the 1980s, Soviet repression lightened under the rule of Mikhail Gorbachev, who brought changes to the USSR and the Warsaw Pact countries including policies of *perestroika* (economic reforms) and *glasnost* (greater freedom of expression).
- In 1980, reformers from the Polish worker's union *Solidarity*, led by Lech Walesa, resisted Communist rule and won some democratic concessions. By the end of the 1980s, Solidarity had gained great support and was elected to government power in Poland's first free elections.

- In 1989, Communism in Europe began to collapse for a number of important reasons.

  - Nationalism in Eastern Europe led to discontent with Soviet authority and rule.

  - Economic shortfalls suggested serious weak points in the Communist financial strategy and worldview.

  - Increasing numbers of reformers in many nations demanded change.

  - Soviet leaders chose to reduce the constant threat of war and opt out of the arms race with the United States.

- In the 1990s, numerous Eastern European nations abandoned Communism and adopted independent, democratic forms of government. At that time, Communism and the Cold War ended in Europe.

Post-Cold War Europe

Among the notable events in Europe in the aftermath of the Cold War were changes in politics, society and economy, and culture and art.

Politics

After the fall of Communism, many nations in Europe underwent massive political redesign. In Eastern Europe, countries suffered from recession, unemployment, and various other difficulties due to the problematic transition between forms of government.

The other main political change of the Post-Cold War era was the formation of the *European Union*, a partnership of nations in Europe that had its roots in economic cooperatives in the 1950s.

- In 1951, an economic partnership, the *European Coal and Steel Community*, promoted trade and cooperation among Western European nations. The idea that economic interaction was a deterrent to war would contribute to the creation of other, similar organizations.

- In 1957, the *European Economic Community (EEC)* was formed with France, Italy, West Germany, Belgium, Luxembourg, and the Netherlands. Other nations joining later included the United Kingdom, Ireland, Denmark, Spain, Greece, and Portugal. The EEC believed in removing tariffs and barriers to trade among member nations.

- In 1975, Spain, the last dictatorship in Europe, converted to democracy under King Juan Carlos I.

- In 1993, the EEC was renamed the *European Union (EU)* under the *Maastricht Treaty*. In addition, the treaty laid out plans for a single currency, the *euro*, to be established throughout Europe. The euro was introduced in 1999 and put into circulation in 2002.

- In 1995, Austria, Finland, and Sweden joined the EU.

- In the 2000s, the EU continued to expand and build economic and political unity among the nations of Europe. Among the innovations of the EU were an open-border policy, allowing citizens of member nations to travel freely and easily among all nations.

Society and Economy

Among the changes to take place in European society and economy in the latter part of the twentieth century were the following.

- The worldwide *baby boom*, beginning around 1945, contributed to a sharp increase in world population.

- Standards of living, mass production, and industrial and agricultural productivity increased in most areas of Europe beginning in the 1950s.

- The United Kingdom introduced the *welfare state*, a style of government that guarantees social security, housing, and healthcare for citizens, between 1945 and the 1970s.

- Rapid gains in *feminism* beginning in the 1960s led to women gaining generally equal rights in most European nations.

- The decline of imperialism in the later twentieth century led to *decolonization*, or the reduction in colonial holdings. Nations such as the United Kingdom, France, and the Netherlands struggled with and eventually gave up many of their colonies, including India, Pakistan, Vietnam, Indonesia, Algeria, and sub-Saharan Africa.

- *Globalization* became a major topic during the 1990s, with some Europeans supporting it and others protesting against it.

- *Terrorism* became a serious concern in Europe after the terrorist attacks of September 11, 2001 in the United States as well as other attacks in Europe itself.

Culture and Art

The twentieth century included many developments in culture and art.

- With the increase in *globalization*, many Europeans were strongly influenced by other cultures, such as those of America and Asia. Cultural influences included music, cuisine, dress, literature, and film.

- Organized religion weakened significantly, although it remained an influential force in society.

- *Modernism* took hold. In this art and literature movement, artists break traditional boundaries, explore the minds, and challenge common expectations. Some modernist writers and sample works include James Joyce (*Ulysses*, 1922), Virginia Woolf (*To the Lighthouse*, 1927), and Marcel Proust (*In Search of Lost Time*, 1913–1927).

- Another philosophy which became popular was *existentialism*, or the examination of life and its absurdities.

- Advances in technology like television, air transportation, space travel, personal computers, and the Internet revolutionized the ways in which Europeans traveled, learned, and communicated with each other.

Multiple-Choice Review Questions

1. In what way were the Austro-Hungarian and Ottoman Empires alike?

    A. Both sided with the Triple Entente during World War I.
    B. Both boasted a strong sense of national unity.
    C. Both were allied with Russia during World War I.
    D. Both experienced serious ethnic tension and instability.
    E. Both avoided joining the arms race or alliance system.

2. Which of the following characterizes the acceptance of organized religion in Europe during the twentieth century?

    A. It increased significantly.
    B. It decreased significantly.
    C. It stayed about the same.
    D. It decreased in Western Europe only.
    E. It increased in Eastern Europe only.

3. The baby boom that began in Europe and other parts of the world around 1945 was most directly the result of

    A. nations surrendering their colonies.
    B. demobilized veterans returning home.
    C. the modernization of medical care.
    D. feminists gaining women's rights.
    E. the establishment of the welfare state.

4.   Which pair of countries best represents an imperial nation and the colony it had to surrender during the decolonization movement of the post-World War II era?

   A.   France and Vietnam
   B.   Germany and Czechoslovakia
   C.   Russia and Estonia
   D.   England and the United States
   E.   Spain and Venezuela

5.   Which of the following best describes perestroika and glasnost?

   A.   Plans for the economic recovery of Europe
   B.   Strategies for the confinement of Communism
   C.   Periods of international tension in the Cold War
   D.   Workers' unions that defied Soviet domination
   E.   Soviet policies allowing reforms and freedoms

Answer Explanations

1.   **D.** The Austro-Hungarian and Ottoman Empires were alike in that they included a wide variety of ethnic groups. Their multiethnic design led to tension and instability that ultimately helped to bring both empires down. Many ethnic groups within the empires leapt at the opportunity to create their own nations.

2.   **B.** One of the major changes to take place in Europe during the twentieth century was a marked weakening of organized religion. Although religion remained important to society as a whole, fewer Europeans found organized religion to be a driving force in their lives.

3.   **B.** The baby boom, a drastic increase in population in many parts of the world, began around 1945, the year World War II ended. Millions of veterans returned to their homes to begin families during that time, causing a later population explosion.

4. **A.** Decolonization was the process by which imperial nations gave up the lands they had claimed as colonies. Among the listed nations, France and Vietnam are the most directly affected in the period after World War II. During the colonial era, France had claimed Vietnam, but surrendered this claim in 1954.

5. **E.** In the 1980s, the Soviet Union began to weaken; its leaders loosened many of the most oppressive Communist laws. The policies of perestroika and glasnost granted the people of Soviet states economic reforms and expanded freedom of expression.

THE BIG PICTURE: HOW TO PREPARE YEAR-ROUND

No matter how far in the future you plan to take the AP European History Exam, the time to start preparing is *now*. And this part of your book is here to help. Here you will learn how to register for the test, how to make the most of your preparation time both in the classroom and outside of it, and how to manage the stress a test of this magnitude may bring. As you get closer to your test date, make sure you are using all of the materials provided in this book. That way, when the day of the exam arrives, you'll be ready to earn your max score!

Strategies for Long-Term Preparation

Step 1: Get Registered

The AP European History test is offered once a year, generally early in the month of May (to coincide with the end of the school year). If you're enrolled in an AP European History course at your high school, you'll probably take the test there, or at another local institution. Even if the test is offered at another school in your district, your teacher or the AP coordinator in your district usually handles testing arrangements and supervises the registration process. So, you just need to make sure you're talking to the right people and getting the right information. It's never too early to ask when you'll be registering and when you'll be testing!

If unusual circumstances make it impossible for you to test on the official testing date, you *may* be able to test during a late-testing period offered late in the month. However, don't wait until the last minute to determine if you'll be able to do so. If you know the scheduled test date is going to be problematic, be proactive! Contact your guidance counselor or AP coordinator for assistance.

What if you're not enrolled in an AP European History course at school? Can you still take this examination? The answer to that question is a resounding yes! Each year hundreds of home-schooled and independent-study students take this examination. To learn where you can take the test, when it is offered, and how to register, contact the administrators of the test, the College Board (www.collegeboard. com). The College Board can direct you to local institutions offering the examination. You can then contact that school to make arrangements. (TIP: When you call, ask to speak to the AP coordinator. If no one in the school is so designated, ask to speak to the guidance counselor, who can usually direct you.)

Here are some important points to keep in mind as you get started.

- *Do you know what you need to know?* We can't emphasize enough how important it is to make sure you have accurate information about this test. Refer to the College Board's official website (www.collegeboard.com) for current information about the test, including eligibility, late testing, special accommodations for students with disabilities, and reduced testing fees for low-income students. This site also provides information on how your score is reported to the colleges and universities you're interested in attending. Don't depend on getting this information from anyone else! Since you purchased this book, obviously you're interested in doing well on the examination. So, don't risk losing points by not knowing what you need to know. Time spent on early research can pay off for you down the road.

- *It's never too early to get started.* The tricky thing about an examination like the AP European History Exam is that you really only get *one* opportunity each year to take this test. If you're enrolled in an AP course, ask your teacher no later than January or February as to how you will go about registering for the test (if that hasn't already been explained and discussed in class, of course).

- *Make sure you register for the correct test.* As silly as it may sound, some testers have found out the hard way that it's entirely possible to go through the whole preparation process only to discover you've registered for the *wrong* AP test. During the registration process, check and double-check that you're registering for **AP**

European History, not AP U.S. History or AP World History (or anything else!).

- *Remember, it's worth it!* You might be worried about your anxiety level for this exam. You might be thinking that in the overall scheme of senior year and college prep, this test is less important than others you need to worry about. You may be concerned about not doing well. If your thought process is running in this direction, slow down for a minute! Consider how little you have to lose if you score poorly on the test, and how much you have to gain if you do well. Plus, you may do better than you expect if you make the best use of study time and material at your disposal. (Consider especially the resources in this book.) Even if, after all is said and done, you *don't* do well, remember, a low score only means you won't get college credit for the course. It usually doesn't impact your ability to get into the college of your choice. Plus, if you're concerned, you can cancel your score so that it won't appear on the report the College Board sends to colleges. Finally, many colleges value the fact that students chose to challenge themselves with AP coursework, even if those students don't ultimately get college credit for the class. The only thing you'll really be out is your time and the testing fee.

Step 2: Become an Expert Student

To do well on the exam, you must retain a ton of information both in and out of the classroom. You will have to work hard and study. Did you know that studying is a discipline in and of itself that many people just don't know how to do well? It's true. Even the smartest people need to learn *how* to study in order to maximize their ability to learn.

One of the most critical study skills involves notes. More specifically, it involves taking effective notes rather than just writing down everything your teacher says. Don't underestimate how important good note-taking is both during class *and* while you're studying alone or with a partner. Good note-taking serves several purposes. First (and most obviously), note-taking is important for making sure you have recorded the key points being made by your instructor (or your study partner). Since this person is very familiar with the material and the test, he or she knows where you should focus your time, so you should glean as much knowledge from him or her as possible. Second, effective note-taking is important because the process of working on notes can actually help you in your retention of the material. For example, the deceptively simple act of writing and rewriting your notes reinforces your memory just from doing the activity. Additionally, writing in conjunction with listening or reading forces your brain to fire up additional cognition skills, making it a lot more likely that you'll remember what you're recording.

Here are some tips for taking great notes.

- *Listen actively.* The first key to taking good notes is to practice *active listening*—that is, listening in a structured way to understand and evaluate what's being said. Active listeners are not distracted, thinking about other things, nor considering what they will say next. (In the classroom, this means opening up your mind rather than thinking about some question you might ask your teacher.) Active listening also does not involve writing down every single thing the teacher says. Rather, it means listening in a structured way so that you hear the main ideas, pay attention to cues that impart meaning, and keep your eyes on the speaker (not on your notebook).

  ○ Listen for main ideas. Before you even begin the note-taking process, consider the topic under discussion and be ready to organize your notes around that topic. Is it a person, place, movement? Is it a particular era or concept? Do some pre-thinking about the topic and work from that angle. Also listen for transitions into new topics as the teacher works his or way through the material.

  ○ Pay attention to cues. If you're taking notes in class, certain words and phrases tend to reflect the way the discussion is organized. For example, the teacher usually starts with an introduction, and this introduction generally provides the framework around how the topic will be treated. For example, "Today we will trace the origins of the industrial revolution. We will follow it from Britain to the rest of the world." Listen for transition words such as "next," "the following," and numbered/bulleted lists.

○ Don't just stare at your notebook. Information is conveyed by speakers in a number of ways, many of them nonverbal. Keep an eye on the instructor's body language and expressions. These are the type of nonverbal cues that will help you to determine what's important and what's not.

• *What do good notes look like?* Good notes are not just a jumbled mass of everything. It's unrealistic and ineffective to try to write down everything there is to say about a topic. Instead, you should learn to focus on key words and main ideas. Here are some tips on how to proceed.

○ Start with a clean sheet. Indicate today's date and the main/primary topic. This will jog your memory later on when you study these notes.

○ If the instructor is using slides, don't just copy word for word what's on the slide. Instead, jot down the title of the slide and the key idea, concept, or overall topic under discussion (this should be apparent from either the title of the slide deck, the title of the slide itself, of the instructor's introduction).

○ Listen actively to your instructor's treatment of the material and his or her points of emphasis. Try to *really listen* to what is being said. Then, as your teacher makes important points, write them down in bullet-point/summarized fashion. Don't worry too much about organization in the moment. Just do your best to capture the discussion in a way that makes sense to you.

○ If you're confused about something, ask for clarification. Many students make the mistake of not asking for help when the teacher makes a statement that is confusing or unclear. Sometimes even the best teachers go too fast or fail to transition you through the material plainly. It's much better to ask for help than to write down a bunch of information that makes no sense to you later.

○ This is an important and often-overlooked point: once class is over, *rewrite* or *retype* your notes, using the opportunity to also fold in information from your textbook or other resources. This is your opportunity to bring real organization, clarity, and understanding to the material. You should rewrite or retype your notes regularly (preferably daily, but if that's not possible, at least weekly). You'll be amazed at how much more sense the material makes if you take the time to look at it critically and rework it in a way that makes sense to you on a regular basis.

○ Take notes from your books and other resources as well as your class notes—see the section below on "reading to understand." AP European History covers *a lot* of material. Paying attention to what gets attention in resources can help you focus.

○ Review your notes before class every day. Doing so serves as a reminder of where you are chronologically, and also helps you to transition from concept to concept and era to era. Work mindfully to make connections among the material that you're learning. Those connections will serve you well later.

• *How do you read to understand?* Material such as this book and your class textbook can make the difference between a passing and failing grade, or between a so-so and an excellent score. However, you need to understand what you're reading so that you can supplement your class notes.

○ Do a complete read through. Start with the objectives of the chapter. Review the questions at the end.

○ Map out the main ideas. Once you've read through the material and have an overall understanding, write down the main ideas and leave space to fill in details. Wherever possible, find your own words. Avoid copying text exactly from the book. Paraphrasing the material in your own words helps you engage with the material and facilitates your learning.

- Reread the material. Once you have the main ideas mapped out, you should reread the material with an eye toward filling in details under each of the main ideas.

- Fill in the details. Now that you've reread, write details under each main idea—again, do not copy the words exactly from the book, but use your own words so that you retain the information. Use details from the book or other resource *and* from your class notes.

- Put the book aside, and read through your notes. Do you understand what you've written? Have you accurately represented the main ideas? Did you fill in the appropriate level of detail?

- Review, review, review. Read them over and over again. That's how you get the information to stick.

Step 3: Create a Realistic Study Plan

If you're like many students with challenging classes, extracurricular activities, and other priorities, you may have only a limited amount of time to review for this exam. This section will help you get the most out of your limited test preparation time and make it really count. You need a plan specifically for you—one that addresses *your* needs and considers the time you have available. No two people will have exactly the same plan or use this book in exactly the same way. To develop a personalized test prep plan, you'll need to identify your weak points and then allocate time to address them efficiently and effectively.

Here are the three basic steps to creating a personalized test prep plan.

1. Identify your weak points. Start by taking the AP European History Diagnostic Test in this book (see page 17). This will show you what you're up against. It will also help you get a feel for the exam and identify the subject areas where you need to focus.

Based on your performance, you can prioritize the subjects to review, starting with the areas in which you are weakest. If your time is limited or if you feel you're not ready to take a complete practice test, focus your review by skimming the diagnostic test and identifying those areas where you have the most difficulty with understanding.

2.　Develop a review plan and a schedule. Figure out how much time you can devote each week to test preparation and reserve specific blocks of time for this purpose. Create a written schedule that includes specific time slots and activities or content areas for review. This will help you pace yourself to get through all of the material you want to review. You'll likely find there are content areas or question types you want to focus on more than others. Also make sure your plan includes time to master test-taking strategies and actually take the practice tests.

3.　Marshal your self-discipline. The hard part about a plan for test prep is making yourself stick to it. Schedule your test prep time actively in your calendar. Don't let it get pushed aside by more seemingly urgent activities. You've come a long way; don't blow the test by failing to prepare for it. Develop a plan for your needs in the time you have available and then stick with it.

For some people, it helps to have a study partner. A partner may make it easier to hold to the schedule and it may also help you to study more effectively. You and your partner can quiz each other, share information, and exchange ideas. However, for other people, having a study partner makes it harder to stay on topic and focus on studying. Try to figure out, based on past experience, how you can best enforce your study plan and most effectively use your time.

Step 4: Use All the Resources at Your Disposal

This book is an excellent way to prepare for this test. It includes not only the diagnostic test but two *full* practice tests. Each test has unique questions so you get the opportunity to address all different areas of the content in all different ways.

Additionally, another practice exam is available to you free of charge at mymaxscore.com. Detailed answers and explanations are provided for both the multiple-choice and essay sections.

Check out the website for the College Board (www.collegeboard. com). At this site, you can find actual released tests that are no longer in circulation along with general information about the exam and testing advice. You'll find it particularly useful to review the last several years' worth of essay prompts, especially.

You'll also find lots of other test resources in your library, at the local bookstore, or online. Look around to see what's available and figure out ways to work that material into your study time if you can.

Good luck! Happy studying!

Taking the Practice Tests

This part of your book includes two complete practice tests, with a third practice test available for you on our website. Taking the test multiple times allows you to confirm your knowledge of the material *and* increase your comfort with the format and design of the examination itself. To get the most out of your practice material, you should try to mimic the testing environment as closely as possible. That means you should have *only* the examination open as you work. It also means you should carefully time yourself to make sure you stay within the parameters of the examination. Ask a friend to time you, or use a timer to make sure you do not spend more time than allowed on each section of the test. And, as you complete each section of the test, remember to apply all of the strategies you learned about in this book.

Just like the real AP examination, each practice test includes two sections. Section I is multiple choice. Here you will find 80 multiple-choice questions/incomplete statements, each of which is followed by five suggested answer options. Read the question and the answer options *carefully* before selecting your response. Remember, sometimes more than one answer may be correct; you are looking for the *best* response to each question. It may be best to plan to use your practice tests more than one time, so you may wish to write your answers on a separate sheet of paper.

You will have 55 minutes to complete all 80 questions in Section I.

Take a five-minute break before moving on to Section II, the essay portion of this test. For Section II, you will create three essays in total; one document-based question (DBQ) and two free-response questions (FRQs). Begin with the mandatory 15-minute reading period. During this time, you will carefully review all of the source material for the Part A essay (the DBQ). If you have time left over, review the topic choices for Parts B and C. Choose one essay from Part B and one from Part C.

Once you begin writing, take no more than 45 minutes to complete Part A and no more than 70 minutes to complete Parts B and C. For each essay, spend about five minutes planning what you will write and about 30 minutes crafting the actual essay.

After you have completed the practice test, use the key provided to check your answers. Suggested essay responses are given.

Good luck!

This book contains two practice exams. Visit mymaxscore.com to download your free third practice test with answers and explanations.

AP European History
Practice Exam 1

EUROPEAN HISTORY
SECTION I
Time—55 minutes
80 Questions

Directions: Each of the questions or incomplete statements below is followed by five suggested answers or completions. Select the answer that is best in each case. *Take no more than 55 minutes to complete this part of your test.*

"All the citizens, being equal in the eyes of the law, are equally admissible to all public dignities, places, and employments, according to their capacity and without distinction other than that of their virtues and of their talents…"

1. This passage from *Declaration of the Rights of Man and of the Citizen* is most closely connected to which of the following political concepts?

    A. Divine Right of Kings
    B. Universal suffrage
    C. Popular sovereignty
    D. Constitutional monarchy
    E. Republican democracy

2.   Which of the following represents a strategic purpose for French support of Italian unification?

  A.   Italian unification gave France access to Mediterranean ports.
  B.   Italian unification was connected to a reduced interest in republicanism.
  C.   Italian unification would increase the power of nobles over their states.
  D.   Italian unification would add more land to the Papal States and increase the influence of the Catholic Church.
  E.   Italian unification would reduce the influence of Austria in European politics.

3.   Why was the emancipation of Jewish people incomplete within many German states?

  A.   German rulers often worked against intended reforms.
  B.   German states followed a Federalist model and preferred divergent policies.
  C.   Napoleon had very little influence within German states.
  D.   Emancipation began in Russia, but took several decades to reach the German states.
  E.   The Jewish population in German states preferred migration to reform.

4.   Catherine the Great wished to be known as a great European monarch. What political role did she take on to reach this end?

  A.   International mediator
  B.   Literary translator
  C.   Religious apologist
  D.   Humanist writer
  E.   Artistic patron

5. Which of the following was the principal challenge faced by the Weimar Republic after World War I?

    A. Most citizens were complacent and accepting of the status quo.
    B. A decay in social values led to much personal corruption and despair.
    C. The arts, including literature and cinema, went into steep decline.
    D. Excessive debt led to both depression and inflation.
    E. New territories in Alsace and Lorraine proved too difficult to govern.

6. Which of the following was a principal outcome of the Napoleonic Wars?

    A. An increase in British power in European and world affairs
    B. An increase in the holdings of the Holy Roman Empire
    C. A decrease in the powers of the Russian tsar
    D. A decrease in American involvement in European affairs
    E. An increase in French involvement in the Western Hemisphere

7. Christine de Pizan's *The City of Ladies* is most noted as

    A. a literary sequel to *Romance of the Rose*.
    B. a rebuttal to the ideas of Boccaccio's *Decameron*.
    C. a description of the leadership and intelligence of women.
    D. a portrayal of mores and customs in a progressive nunnery.
    E. a denouncement of the witch hunts of the late Middle Ages.

8. Which of the following was the primary purpose of Auschwitz-Birkenau and other, similar camps?

     A. They were used to build artillery and aircraft for the Nazi cause.

     B. They were used to house European prisoners of war.

     C. They were used to extinguish Europe's Jewish population.

     D. They were used to murder purged members of the Nazi party.

     E. They were used to imprison political dissenters.

9. Why did the bourgeoisie seek tax reform immediately prior to the French Revolution?

     A. They had little money and were often unable to pay taxes.

     B. They believed their share of the tax load was too high.

     C. They felt the clergy should not have to pay taxes on income.

     D. They were concerned about the waning influence of the nobility.

     E. They wished to speed the pace of democratization.

10. By the late nineteenth century, which of the following monarchies continued to uphold the Divine Right of Kings?

     A. Russia

     B. Poland

     C. Ottoman Empire

     D. Spain

     E. Portugal

11. Which of the following was an immediate cause of the English civil war?

     A. The rise of absolutism

     B. The coronation of Charles I

     C. The debate in Parliament over the American colonies

     D. The rise of the Puritan movement

     E. The attempted arrests of Parliament members

12. How did Galileo radically change the field of astronomy?

    A.   He refined current methods of celestial navigation.

    B.   He made the first sighting of the planet Mars.

    C.   He reclassified many former planets as moons.

    D.   He introduced techniques of direct observation of space.

    E.   He eliminated common errors of experimentation.

13. Following World War II, Charles de Gaulle argued that France should see herself as

    A.   a defeated nation.

    B.   a colonial state.

    C.   a world power.

    D.   a minor force.

    E.   a NATO dependent.

14. One of the main purposes behind Denis Diderot's *Encyclopédie* was

    A.   to improve public education.

    B.   to help the lower classes educate themselves.

    C.   to promote the major ideas of the Enlightenment.

    D.   to discourage the ongoing spread of Deism.

    E.   to develop new means of social interaction.

15. As a result of the Berlin Conference of 1884, European powers could maintain legal rights over a portion of African territory provided they

    A.   established a colonial presence in the region.

    B.   offered payment to other European nations.

    C.   participated in a fair tribute system with local leaders.

    D.   developed an effective administrative system.

    E.   pledged to Christianize at least 50 percent of inhabitants.

16. When did the Bolsheviks assume control over Russia?

    A. Revolution of 1905
    B. February Revolution of 1917
    C. October Revolution of 1917
    D. Quiet Revolution
    E. Cultural Revolution

17. Which of the following best explains why the Renaissance originated in the region that is now Italy?

    A. The region did not have a strong centralized government.
    B. The region was close to Arabic states that had kept classical learning alive.
    C. The region was divided into small states or principalities.
    D. The region was home to the Vatican and the Papal States.
    E. The region had never given up on its Roman ideals.

18. Which of the following best explains the immediate influence of the Reformation on the role of women in European society?

    A. The Reformation allowed women to take on minor administrative roles in the Church.
    B. The Reformation allowed women to serve as lay readers in the Church.
    C. The Reformation allowed women to divorce under certain circumstances.
    D. The Reformation encouraged women to seek work outside the home.
    E. The Reformation encouraged women to form Bible reading groups.

19. Which of the following best describes how D-Day is generally regarded?

    A. The start of U.S. and British land victory over Germany

    B. The closing event of World War II

    C. The last large-scale battle of World War II

    D. An example of human cost outweighing the benefits of victory

    E. A solid victory for the French underground against the occupied government

20. The North Atlantic Treaty Organization existed primarily to

    A. provide security for the United States.

    B. guarantee the security of North Atlantic shipping lanes.

    C. promote European unification.

    D. prevent Soviet aggression in Western Europe.

    E. check Soviet aggression in Eastern Europe.

21. Which of the following helped bring about the Golden Age of Spain?

    A. The acquisition of colonies in the New World

    B. The rise in secular, anti-Catholic legislation

    C. The benefits of living under Islamic rule

    D. The combination of art and science

    E. The combination of noble and religious patronage

22. Which of the following best explains how the Peace of Augsburg influenced the development of religion in the Holy Roman Empire?

    A. The Peace of Augsburg made Lutheranism the official religion of the Holy Roman Empire.
    B. The Peace of Augsburg made Catholicism the official religion of the Holy Roman Empire.
    C. The Peace of Augsburg allowed nobles to choose between Catholicism and Lutheranism.
    D. The Peace of Augsburg allowed nobles to choose among most major Western religions.
    E. The Peace of Augsburg allowed common people to choose between Catholicism and Protestantism.

23. *Don Quixote de La Mancha* is often noted as

    A. the first major literary Spanish work.
    B. the first book of such length.
    C. the last book to be inscribed on vellum or parchment.
    D. the first modern novel.
    E. the last literary work of Spain's Golden Age.

24. What kind of role did marriages play in the rise of the Hapsburg Empire?

    A. Major
    B. Minor
    C. Intermittent
    D. All-important
    E. Emotive

25. Which of the following best describes the main goals of the "Big Four" at the negotiations leading up to the Treaty of Versailles?

    A. They shared a desire for peace, but each country also wanted additional territory.
    B. They agreed on the fundamental treaty aspects, but disagreed over the specifics.
    C. Their principal concern was the creation of long-lasting peace in Europe.
    D. They sought to make the U.S. a primary member of the League of Nations.
    E. They desired to break Germany into administrative zones.

26. During the Eighty Years' War (1568–1648), which of the following changes occurred in the Netherlands?

    A. The northern regions developed as a center of commerce.
    B. The southern regions developed as a center of commerce.
    C. The northern regions were damaged by Spanish control.
    D. The western regions developed stronger ties to the Papal States.
    E. The southern regions remained sympathetic to Spanish rule.

27. Which of the following policies would be most favored by a bullionist?

    A. A country attempts to maintain as many gemstones as possible.
    B. A country attempts to acquire as many precious metals as possible.
    C. A country relies on overseas colonies to fuel its growth.
    D. A country refuses to trade with its neighbors.
    E. A country attempts to export as many spices as possible.

28. The Edict of Nantes contributed to the growth of modern individual freedoms by

    A. recognizing that individuals should have some choice in religious practices.
    B. changing the requirements for membership in the priesthood.
    C. creating the concept of freedom of religion.
    D. acknowledging the value of all Western religions.
    E. promoting the similarities between Christianity and Protestantism.

29. Many of the actions of Catherine de' Medici during the French Wars of Religion (1562–1598) were intended

    A. to maintain de' Medici family power.
    B. to sponsor and support the arts.
    C. to boost the prestige of the French.
    D. to establish a government of efficiency.
    E. to promote compromise between warring factions.

30. Which of the following background factors played a role in the St. Bartholomew's Day Massacre?

    A. An escalation in British and German migration to France
    B. A large number of Huguenots residing in Paris
    C. An increase in Protestation migration to the New World
    D. The marriage of Henry of Navarre to Princess Margaret
    E. The marriage of Queen Mary to Philip II

31. How did England stand apart from other regions of Reformation Europe?

    A. The role of its princes in the political development of the Reformation
    B. The high number of social problems in its cities
    C. The experience of its civil war
    D. The early development of a national church
    E. The influence of ideas from the American colonies

32. Why was the murder of Admiral Gaspard de Coligny of special significance?

    A. The murder eliminated a central leader of the Huguenot cause.
    B. The murder demonstrated the French king's lack of control over his country.
    C. The murder illustrated the impact of other nations on French religious wars.
    D. The murder brought a period of intense religious conflict to a close.
    E. The murder resulted in stronger ties between France and Germany.

33. The Peace of Westphalia introduced which of the following political concepts?

    A. Social contract
    B. Sovereign state
    C. Absolute monarchy
    D. Central administration
    E. Trustee representation

34. Why did the government established by Oliver Cromwell fall soon after his death?

    A. Cromwell had been overly tolerant when dealing with local rebels.
    B. The regime passed to Cromwell's politically incompetent son.
    C. Cromwell's military defeat resulted in posthumous dishonor.
    D. The public expressed widespread dissatisfaction with Cromwell's leadership.
    E. After Cromwell's death, power passed to those who favored a monarchy.

35. Which of the following Roman Catholic practices contributed to the rise of the Reformation?

    A. Tithing
    B. Communion
    C. Baptism
    D. Indulgences
    E. Sacraments

36. What form of government would a *politique* support?

    A. Weakened monarchy
    B. Strengthened monarchy
    C. Direct democracy
    D. Parliamentary democracy
    E. Feudal oligarchy

37. In regard to professional astronomy, the theories of Copernicus replaced many of the ideas developed by

   A. Plato.
   B. Newton.
   C. Koepler.
   D. Brahe.
   E. Ptolemy.

38. Which of the following events was an immediate cause of the Glorious Revolution?

   A. The conversion of James II
   B. The birth of Prince James
   C. The political intrigues of William and Mary
   D. The popular resurgence of English Catholicism
   E. The rise of Calvinist groups in Europe

39. Which of the following describes a major outcome of the Fronde of the Princes (1650–1653)?

   A. A reorganization of the French military
   B. A renewed period of war with Germany
   C. A decrease in the power of the French king
   D. A revival of feudal policies
   E. A period of liberal reform

40. During the War of Spanish Succession, which of the following political themes was at stake?

    A. European balance of power

    B. Balance of power in New World

    C. French prosperity

    D. Spanish stability

    E. English independence

41. Which of the following best explains the relationship between the Schleiffen Plan (Germany) and Plan 17 (France)?

    A. Both plans were intended to achieve victory in a two-front war.

    B. Both plans called for prolonged trench warfare.

    C. Both plans urged the use of air power.

    D. Both plans attempted to narrow the scope of battle.

    E. Both plans solicited aid from the United States.

42. As a result of the Treaty of Utrecht, King Phillip V of Spain

    A. solidified Spanish ties to France.

    B. renounced claims to the French throne.

    C. undermined the traditional power system.

    D. acquired portions of Sardinia.

    E. acquired portions of Sicily.

43. Which of the following best defines the genre of baroque art?

    A. A mosaic that shows subjects in a two-dimensional perspective

    B. A painting that uses detail and motion to create affect

    C. A sculpture that incorporates classical mythology

    D. A sculpture that utilizes basic shapes to attain affect

    E. A painting that illustrates royal accomplishments

44. Which of the following best describes the historical relationship between Poland and Prussia?

    A.   Poland and Prussia shared a common language and religion.
    B.   Prussian influence left many parts of Poland underdeveloped.
    C.   Poland and Prussia frequently allied against other great powers.
    D.   Prussia often attempted to gain lands in Poland.
    E.   Prussia was generally fearful of Polish aggression.

45. Which of the following was established by the Council of Trent?

    A.   Revision to religious practices regarding the role of the priest in the liturgy
    B.   System to promote compromise between Catholic and Protestant sects
    C.   New set of regulations regarding converts to the Catholic Church
    D.   Change to many structures in the Catholic Church
    E.   New method of selecting regional Catholic bishops

46. The reforms of Peter the Great were principally intended to

    A.   develop a centralized economic planning board.
    B.   increase Mongolian influence on Russia's elite.
    C.   diminish the flow of finished goods from Russia.
    D.   decrease the power of middle class landholders.
    E.   increase similarities between Russia and Western Europe.

47. Which of the following kings was most closely associated with the Stuart Restoration?

   A.   Henry VIII
   B.   Charles I
   C.   Charles II
   D.   William III
   E.   Edward IV

48. Why did leaders of the Holy Roman Empire experience special difficulties controlling their lands?

   A.   The Holy Roman Empire remained closely tied to the Catholic Church.
   B.   The Holy Roman Empire maintained close ties to Byzantium.
   C.   The Holy Roman Empire overextended itself in Atlantic exploration.
   D.   The Holy Roman Empire failed to solidify its English/Irish holdings.
   E.   The Holy Roman Empire was not territorially contiguous.

49. "Tulip Mania" and the South Sea Company are both examples of

   A.   the disruptive effects of European exploration.
   B.   the pressure of trade on macroeconomics.
   C.   the negative effects of an imbalance in trade.
   D.   the influence of financial bubbles on macroeconomics.
   E.   the problems associated with overconsumption of goods.

50. Which of the following is an example of a mercantile policy?

    A.   A lord extracts tribute from his lands.

    B.   A country limits the trade of its colonies.

    C.   A free trade zone is created in a border area.

    D.   A country lowers its taxes and tariffs.

    E.   A corporation outsources its production services.

51. Which of the following events was an immediate cause of the formation of the Committee on Public Safety?

    A.   The execution of Louis XVI

    B.   The betrayal of a former minister of war

    C.   The conflict between liberal assemblies and French nobility

    D.   The passage of the Law of the Maximum

    E.   The removal of the Dantonists and Hebertists

52. During the nineteenth century, a nationalist would be the most likely to favor the policies of which region?

    A.   Russia

    B.   England

    C.   Spain

    D.   Portugal

    E.   Germany

53. Which of the following best explains the role of the Bourbon-Hapsburg rivalry during the Thirty Years' War (1618–1648)?

    A. The Bourbon-Hapsburg rivalry was an immediate cause of the war.
    B. The Bourbon-Hapsburg rivalry ended as a result of the war.
    C. The Bourbon-Hapsburg rivalry decreased as a result of the war.
    D. The Bourbon-Hapsburg rivalry took on more importance during the war.
    E. The Bourbon-Hapsburg rivalry limited the scope of the war.

54. Which of the following describes the governmental structure of the United Provinces of the Netherlands?

    A. Monarchy
    B. Republic
    C. Union
    D. Confederation
    E. Duchy

55. The Orangists and the Republicans were often in conflict over

    A. the legitimacy of new territories.
    B. the place of commerce in the economy.
    C. the need for a stock exchange.
    D. the balance between heredity and democracy in government.
    E. the trade-off between military and social spending.

56. Which of the following best exemplifies liberal thought?

    A. John Locke
    B. Edmund Burke
    C. Frederick Engels
    D. Charles Dickens
    E. Francis Bacon

57. Which of the following is the best example of realpolitik?

    A. German policies under Hitler

    B. German policies under Bismarck

    C. Austrian policies under Metternich

    D. Austrian policies under Belcredi

    E. Dutch policies under Biesheuvel

58. Napoleon Bonaparte became consul of France through

    A. a series of military invasions and standoffs.

    B. a military coup and political maneuvering.

    C. a general election by the people.

    D. a popular revolt whose leaders demanded ascension.

    E. a referendum led by exiled monarchists.

59. David Ricardo's Law of Comparative Advantage maintained that countries would benefit from trade as long as

    A. economically strong countries traded with other economically strong countries.

    B. economically strong countries traded with economically weak countries.

    C. countries traded only those goods they had a relative advantage in producing.

    D. countries avoided trading with partners with a relative advantage in any area.

    E. countries traded only with countries that followed similar labor practices.

60. Which of the following best describes the role of Cardinal Richelieu in the development of the French state?

    A.　He was responsible for dispersing power within the royal cabinet.
    B.　He helped to centralize authority in the role of the prime minister.
    C.　He empowered the Church at the expense of the state.
    D.　He helped to increase the power of princes and lesser nobles.
    E.　He created the departmental system of the modern French state.

61. The Concert of Europe is sometimes referred to as the European Restoration because many of its members

    A.　worked to restore the dominance of the pre-Reformation Catholic Church.
    B.　sought to eliminate the changes brought on by the French Revolution.
    C.　hoped to avoid any future conflicts and restore peace.
    D.　wished to do away with the new balance of power.
    E.　hoped to restore New World colonies to European control.

62. Which of the following best explains why the Revolutions of 1848 failed to achieve lasting reform?

    A.　Conflicts were not coordinated across international lines.
    B.　Existing class structures were not taken into account.
    C.　Reactionary groups were unable to draw on peasants for support.
    D.　American and British involvement interfered with reforms.
    E.　A popular press had not yet come to fruition in Europe.

63. Frederick William was known as the Great Elector for his contributions to Prussian prestige. Frederick's main contributions to Prussia stemmed from his

   A. efforts to implement both land and civil service reform.
   B. support for general elections and the spread of democracy.
   C. implementation of policies that eventually turned Prussia into a kingdom.
   D. skill at demilitarizing troubled areas in the region.
   E. work on behalf of the emerging working and middle classes.

64. Which of the following best explains Napoleon III's influence on France?

   A. He attempted to reduce French holdings in the Middle East to build a stronger French influence in Western Europe.
   B. He reduced French involvement in European politics to prevent the spread of democracy within France.
   C. He eliminated French involvement in European politics to expand democracy within France.
   D. He sought to honor the Concert of Europe but also to offer the Papal States to Italy.
   E. He expanded French involvement in European politics and presided over increasing democracy within France.

65. With which of the following statements would both James I and Charles I most likely agree?

   A. Monarchs should possess all national power.
   B. Monarchs should represent the interests of all people.
   C. Monarchs should work closely with Parliament.
   D. Monarchs should further the cause of thoughtful patriotism.
   E. Monarchs should engage in constant warfare.

66. Which of the following actions is most in keeping with Otto von Bismarck's policies of kulturkampf?

    A. A migrant center is destroyed.
    B. A church trip is organized.
    C. A monastery is closed.
    D. A study group addresses cultural problems.
    E. A youth camp is built.

67. Which of the following activities was made possible by the ideas of Rene Descartes?

    A. A scientist creates a graph.
    B. A sailor studies the wind.
    C. A philosopher develops a theory.
    D. A technician purifies milk.
    E. A doctor develops a vaccine.

68. Which of the following best describes the relationship between the individual and nature in Romantic literature?

    A. Nature and the individual are in opposition.
    B. Nature is placed over the individual.
    C. The individual is expected to preserve nature.
    D. Nature and the individual are connected.
    E. The individual is a threat to nature.

69. Which of the following explains a principle goal of Russia during the Russo-Japanese War?

    A. Obtaining overseas colonies
    B. Accessing year-round warm water port
    C. Opening emerging Chinese markets
    D. Reducing coal prices
    E. Limiting Japanese tariffs

70. Which of the following best describes Martin Luther and John Calvin?

    A.   Reformation leaders whose lives and actions differed in many ways

    B.   Reformations leaders who avoided political involvement

    C.   Reformation leaders who intended to create entirely new religious societies

    D.   Reformation leaders who preferred to communicate their ideas orally rather than in writing

    E.   Reformation leaders who believed the New World offered the best hope to Protestants

71. Which of the following artistic schools is most closely associated with the fin de siècle?

    A.   Surrealism

    B.   Modernism

    C.   Symbolism

    D.   Pointillism

    E.   Impressionism

72. Which of the following is most similar to the utopian ideal envisioned by Charles Fourier?

    A.   A vegetarian kitchen

    B.   A specialized work/housing center

    C.   A shelter giving aid to the needy

    D.   A farm producing organic foods

    E.   A school for the disadvantaged

73. The rise of absolutism is best explained by the desire of

    A. kings to gain more power over their respective countries.
    B. nobles to gain more power over their respective countries.
    C. popes to consolidate their power over the Catholic Church.
    D. Puritans to hold positions of governmental power through-out Europe.
    E. emperors to solidify power over their holdings.

74. In addition to humanitarian aid to soldiers, which of the following contributions can be attributed to Florence Nightingale?

    A. Improvement in sanitation practices in the British army follow-ing the Crimean War
    B. Sharp reduction in the death rates of injured soldiers during the Crimean War
    C. Increase in the professional and public awareness of the "germ theory" of disease
    D. Publication of a chain of prominent works promoting feminist philosophy and ideals
    E. Creation of systematized medical records for hospital patients

75. One of the political goals of the Stolypin Reforms was to decrease peasant radicalism. To attain this goal, what kind of farms did the reforms attempt to create?

    A. Export-oriented farms
    B. Larger, more communal farms
    C. Multi-crop, sustainable farms
    D. Dairy-based cooperative farms
    E. Smaller, more profitable farms

76. The first Battle of the Marne also marked the beginning of

    A. lightning attacks.
    B. marine defense.
    C. trench warfare.
    D. chemical warfare.
    E. urban bombing.

77. The Great Purge can be best explained as an attempt by Stalin to

    A. consolidate power within the government.
    B. expand Communism across the world.
    C. eliminate numerous foreign threats.
    D. gain access to new markets.
    E. combat American propaganda.

78. Why did the British policy of appeasement fail?

    A. It was unpopular with the British people.
    B. It prevented the U.S. from entering the war until later on.
    C. It provoked a strong response from the Soviet Union.
    D. It led Czechoslovakia to become more sympathetic to Germany.
    E. It encouraged Hitler to pursue further aggression.

79. Which of the following was a background cause of the Franco-Dutch War (1672–1678)?

    A. The desire of France to ally with Spain
    B. The Dutch fear of the growing land power of the French
    C. The English fear of the growing naval power of the Netherlands
    D. The desire of France to conquer territory in the Netherlands
    E. The new alliance between Sweden and France

80. The Treaty of Maastricht led to the creation of today's European Union. As part of this process, the treaty created a common European

    A. language.
    B. currency.
    C. culture.
    D. parliamentary procedure.
    E. university system.

END OF SECTION I
TAKE A FIVE-MINUTE BREAK

EUROPEAN HISTORY
SECTION II
Part A
Planning time—15 minutes

Writing time—45 minutes

Directions: The following question is based on the accompanying Documents 1–6. The documents have been edited for the purpose of this exercise. Write your answer on lined notebook paper. *(During the actual examination, you will be given lined answer sheets for this exercise.)*

This question is designed to test your ability to work with and understand historical documents. Write an essay that:

- Provides an appropriate, explicitly stated thesis that directly addresses all parts of the question and does NOT simply restate the question.
- Discusses a majority of the documents individually and specifically.
- Demonstrates understanding of the basic meaning of a majority of the documents.
- Analyzes point of view or bias in at least three documents.
- Analyzes the documents by explicitly grouping them in at least three appropriate ways.

You may refer to relevant historical information not mentioned in the documents.

1. Compare the effects of nationalism on twentieth-century Russia with the effects of nationalism on twentieth-century Germany.

DOCUMENT 1

Source: Vladimir Lenin, leader of the Bolsheviks, from a speech, 1917
    If we seize power today, we seize it not in opposition to the Soviets but on their behalf.

The seizure of power is the business of the uprising; its political purpose will become clear after the seizure....

...It would be an infinite crime on the part of the revolutionaries were they to let the chance slip, knowing that the salvation of the revolution, the offer of peace, the salvation of Petrograd, salvation from famine, the transfer of the land to the peasants depend upon them.

DOCUMENT 2

Source: Josef Stalin, leader of the Soviet Union, from a radio broadcast on the eve of World War II, 1941

The Soviet people must realize this and abandon all heedlessness, they must mobilize themselves and reorganize all their work on new, wartime bases, when there can be no mercy to the enemy.

Further, there must be no room in our ranks for whimperers and cowards, for panic-mongers and deserters. Our people must know no fear in fight and must selflessly join our patriotic war of liberation, our war against the fascist enslavers.

Lenin, the great founder of our State, used to say that the chief virtue of the Bolshevik must be courage, valor, fearlessness in struggle, readiness to fight, together with the people, against the enemies of our country.

This splendid virtue of the Bolshevik must become the virtue of the millions of the Red Army, of the Red Navy, of all peoples of the Soviet Union.

DOCUMENT 3

Source: Lyrics, from the Soviet national anthem, 1944

United Forever in Friendship and Labor,
Our mighty Republics will ever endure.
The Great Soviet Union will Live through the Ages.
The Dream of a People their fortress secure.

Long Live our Soviet Motherland,
Built by the People's mighty hand.
Long Live our People, United and Free.
Strong in our Friendship tried by fire.
Long may our Crimson Flag Inspire,
Shining in Glory for all Men to see.

DOCUMENT 4

Source: Adolf Hitler, from a speech at a Nazi rally, 1927

A movement today in Germany that fights for the renewal of the people must give its own symbol to this effort, and that is why we have chosen a new flag that is the symbol of the coming new German Reich: a symbol of national strength and power joined with the purity of the blood.

Our goal is for this flag to increasingly lose its character as a party flag and grow to be the German flag of the future. We see this flag is inextricably bound to the renewal of the nation. May these colors be a witness of how the German people broke its chains of slavery and won freedom. On that day this flag will be the German national flag.

DOCUMENT 5

Source: Joseph Goebbels, German Minister of Propaganda, from a New Year's Eve speech in 1934

The German people overwhelmingly has affirmed one man and one idea. A movement fully aware of its responsibility governs the Reich.

The people itself, however, could not support the new regime any more strongly than it does. People, state and nation have become one, and the strong will of the Führer is over us all. The eternal quarreling particularism that threatened the Reich has been overthrown. Germany once more stands before the world as an unshakable unity, and no one inside or outside of our borders is able to damage the interests of the German nation by using some kind of group within the Reich.

DOCUMENT 6

Source: Nazi pamphlet on racial purity, 1943

Each of Europe's peoples must return to the source of its existence and affirm its racial uniqueness if it is to be renewed in the way the German people has been under National Socialism.... The Jews are increasingly excluded from economic life, and marriages with Jews are forbidden. Examples are Slovakia, Rumania, Hungary, Croatia, and Bulgaria. Halfway solutions always prove useless. When any kind of back door is left open, the Jew gets around the intentions of the lawmakers. European nations are increasingly coming to the realization that the Jewish question can be solved only as a racial question, and that only racial thinking consistent with natural laws can guarantee the life and characteristics of the individual peoples. Adolf Hitler introduced a new era in the history of Europe and the world. A new world is rising....The Second World War is a struggle between two worldviews and two ways of life. Our enemy hates us because we have recognized that the single raw material that cannot be replaced is the raw material that the German people have more of than any other people on earth, our good blood, which is our Nordic inheritance. They hate us because they know that we hold the key to victory, to our future, and to the eternal Reich of all Germans.

END OF SECTION II, PART A
IMMEDIATELY BEGIN NEXT SECTION

EUROPEAN HISTORY
SECTION II
Part B
Time—35 minutes

Directions: You are to answer ONE question from the three questions below. Make your selection carefully, choosing the question that you are best prepared to answer thoroughly in the time permitted. You should spend five minutes organizing or outlining your answer. Write your answer on lined notebook pages. *(During the actual examination, you will be given lined answer sheets for this exercise.)*

Write an essay that:

- Has a relevant thesis.
- Addresses all parts of the question.
- Supports a thesis with specific evidence.
- Is well organized.

2.   Assess the use of social commentary in the writings of TWO of the following British authors:

- Sir Thomas More
- Charles Dickens
- George Orwell

3.   Compare and contrast the features and philosophies of TWO of the following artistic movements:

- Romanticism
- Classicism
- Realism
- Impressionism

4.   Compare and contrast the social and political philosophies of John Locke, Thomas Hobbes, and Jean-Jacques Rousseau.

END OF SECTION II, PART B
IMMEDIATELY BEGIN NEXT SECTION

EUROPEAN HISTORY
SECTION II
Part C
Time—35 minutes

Directions: You are to answer ONE question from the three questions below. Make your selection carefully, choosing the question that you are best prepared to answer thoroughly in the time permitted. You should spend five minutes organizing or outlining your answer. Write your answer on the lined notebook pages. *(During the actual examination, you will be given lined answer sheets for this exercise.)*

Write an essay that:

- Has a relevant thesis.
- Addresses all parts of the question.
- Supports a thesis with specific evidence.
- Is well organized.

5. Analyze the reasons nationalism thrived in the Austro-Hungarian Empire and discuss how it contributed to the collapse of the empire.

6. Analyze the causes and effects of political and cultural instability in the Balkans in the early twentieth century.

7. Compare and contrast the political tactics used by Adolf Hitler and Joseph Stalin to hold power in the period from 1935 to 1945.

END OF EXAM

Practice Exam 1 Answers and Explanations

Section I: Multiple-Choice Questions

ANSWER KEY

1.	C	24.	A
2.	E	25.	A
3.	A	26.	A
4.	A	27.	B
5.	D	28.	A
6.	A	29.	A
7.	C	30.	D
8.	C	31.	D
9.	B	32.	A
10.	A	33.	B
11.	E	34.	E
12.	D	35.	D
13.	C	36.	B
14.	C	37.	E
15.	A	38.	B
16.	C	39.	A
17.	B	40.	A
18.	C	41.	A
19.	A	42.	B
20.	D	43.	B
21.	E	44.	D
22.	C	45.	D
23.	D	46.	E

47. C	64. E
48. E	65. A
49. D	66. C
50. B	67. A
51. B	68. D
52. E	69. B
53. D	70. A
54. D	71. C
55. D	72. B
56. A	73. A
57. B	74. A
58. B	75. E
59. C	76. C
60. B	77. A
61. B	78. E
62. A	79. C
63. C	80. B

ANSWER EXPLANATIONS

1. **C.** Popular sovereignty is intertwined closely with the *Declaration*. A is incorrect; the *Declaration* opposed this idea. B is incorrect; the *Declaration* does not broach universal suffrage. D and E are incorrect. However, both are tempting choices, because they are associated with the idea of mixed government.

2. **E.** Northern Italian gains came at the expense of Austria, a rival of France. A is incorrect; France already had access to these ports. B is incorrect; unification was strongly connected to republicanism. C is incorrect; it seemed likely to decrease this power. D is incorrect; it seemed likely to reduce Church holdings.

3.   **A.** As Germany slowly unified, many local rulers were slow to implement the reforms that the inchoate central government had issued. B is incorrect; it is far too charitable in its description of local motivations. C is incorrect. This is an especially tempting option, because Napoleon had significant influence in Germany and he favored Jewish emancipation. However, reforms were still slow. D is incorrect; Russia was among the last to recognize Jewish people as full citizens. E is incorrect; migration was not really an option.

4.   **A.** Because of her own desire and Russia's position on the outside of European politics, Catherine used diplomacy to add to her claim of greatness. B and E are incorrect; they relate to Catherine's attempts to build a personal legacy. C and D are incorrect; while they are tempting options, they do not accurately describe Catherine's behavior.

5.   **D.** The Weimar Republic inherited a huge debt from the war and a second debt pursuant to the reparations clauses of the Treaty of Versailles. A is incorrect; few citizens were accepting of the status quo represented by the new republic. B is incorrect; however, this reasoning was used by the Nazi Party in its bid for power. C is incorrect; the arts were one of the few areas in which Germany remained productive. E is incorrect; Alsace and Lorraine were ceded to France.

6.   **A.** The Napoleonic Wars exhausted the resources of France and other European powers, leaving England to assume power and authority. B is incorrect; the Napoleonic Wars helped eliminate the last vestiges of the Holy Roman Empire. C is incorrect; the Napoleonic Wars may have added to the power of the tsars. D is incorrect; the Napoleonic Wars did not induce America to become involved in European affairs. E is incorrect; the Napoleonic Wars put an end to New France.

7.   **C.** *The City of Ladies* is a description of the contributions of women in a mythical city. In this work, de Pizan confronts the misogynistic sexism which characterized much of the literature of the fourteenth and fifteenth centuries. A is incorrect; Pizan wished to rebut the *Romance of the Rose*. B is incorrect; Pizan was influenced by Boccaccio. D and E are incorrect, as neither explains the significance of the work in question.

8. **C.** The primary purpose of the death camps was to eliminate Europe's Jewish population. A is incorrect; these weapons were built in nearby facilities, but not in the camps themselves. B, D, and E are incorrect, as these do not represent the primary purpose of the camps.

9. **B.** The bourgeoisie paid a huge share of France's tax burden. A is incorrect; the bourgeoisie had money to pay taxes, but wished for the nobles and the church to pay a greater share. C is incorrect; the bourgeoisie wanted the clergy to pay a greater share of taxes. D is incorrect; although the bourgeoisie were concerned about the balance of power among estates, this factor is not at the core of their concerns over taxes. E is incorrect; although the demands of the bourgeoisie echo democratic sentiment, they were not, at heart, demands for increased democracy.

10. **A.** Tsarist Russia was the last country to renounce this policy. B is incorrect; the Polish monarchy had lost considerable prestige during its wars with Prussia. C is incorrect; the Ottoman Empire maintained despotic rule until well into the twentieth century, but did not do so under the aegis of the Divine Right of Kings. D and E are incorrect; such claims in Spain and Portugal were eroded during the Napoleonic Wars.

11. **E.** The attempted arrest of five MPs by Charles I led Parliament to seek armed protection; when royal and parliamentary forces clashed, the sparks of war were ignited. A is incorrect; the rise of absolutism was a background factor. B is incorrect; the ascent of Charles was a background factor. C is incorrect; it was a source of conflict in England, but occurred after the Civil War. D is incorrect; the Puritan movement was a background factor.

12. **D.** Although Galileo made many significant contributions to science, this is considered the greatest, because it opened doors for later astronomers and changed the way that we approach the field of astronomy. The other choices relate to the field of astronomy, but do not describe Galileo's main contribution. A describes advances before Galileo's time. B and C describe later advances. E is the most tempting option; however, Galileo did not engage in extensive experimentation.

Rather, his techniques set the stage for experimentation by the next generation of astronomers.

13. **C.** Choice C represents the underlying philosophy of Gaullism. A is incorrect as it is the opposite of de Gaulle's view. B is incorrect; de Gaulle loosened France's hold on Algeria. D is incorrect; de Gaulle thought that France should resume her role as a great power on the global stage. E is incorrect; although always a key member of NATO, under de Gaulle, France often challenged the edicts of NATO and caused problems for the organization.

14. **C.** The *Encyclopédie* was, in part, politically motivated. A, B, and E are incorrect; they were secondary goals of the *Encyclopédie*. D is incorrect; Enlightenment thinkers tended to be sympathetic and sometimes avidly in favor of Deism.

15. **A.** The goal of the conference was to ensure that European leaders could not claim territory unless they had some actual presence in the region. B is incorrect; European states did not have to pay tribute to one another. C is incorrect; European states were not bound to offer any services to colonists. D is incorrect; European states were not bound to administer their colonies. E is incorrect; the missionary movement grew, in part, from concerns with the harsh treatment of Africans by the great European powers.

16. **C.** The Bolsheviks overthrew the provisional government in October 1917. A is incorrect; it refers to an earlier era of Russian tumult. B is incorrect; the February Revolution overthrew the tsar but did not impose Marxism on Russia. D is incorrect; it refers to Quebecois nationalism. E is incorrect; it refers to Maoist China.

17. **B.** Italy's proximity to Arabic learning centers helped to spark the Renaissance. Italy's place as a center of trade complemented this first factor. A, C, D, and E are incorrect; while each is a true statement about the Italian region, none of them explain why the Renaissance took root there.

18. **C.** Although the Reformation did not have an immediate and profound impact on the lives of women, it did ultimately lead to some significant changes, one of which is described in C. D was brought about by the Industrial Revolution. A, B, and C were brought on in part by the Reformation, but were not immediate.

19. **A.** D-Day marked the beginning of Allied victory in Europe. B is incorrect; V-J Day was the closing event of World War II. C is incorrect; the Battle of the Bulge is considered the last large-scale battle in World War II. D is untrue. While D-Day was costly, almost all sources agree that Allied gains were enormous. E is only partially true; the French underground did contribute to D-Day, but they were not the primary actors.

20. **D.** The main purpose of NATO was to defend the security of U.S. allies in Western Europe. A is incorrect; the U.S. was already fairly secure before the creation of NATO. B is incorrect; if the lanes were blocked, NATO would have taken action, but this was not its primary purpose. C is incorrect; NATO may have promoted the EU and attempts at unification, but these were not its main goal. E is incorrect. As part of the deal, the Soviet Union was allowed to develop a sphere of influence in Eastern Europe. The Soviets often used brutal aggression in this sphere, so E cannot be correct.

21. **E.** The nobles and the Catholic church sought to buttress their power through the creation of sympathetic art. This art, and the injection of capital, helped fuel the Golden Age. A is incorrect; it occurred during the latter part of the Golden Age. B is incorrect; it occurred during the English Renaissance, which coincided with the Spanish Renaissance. Spain remained staunchly Catholic. C is incorrect; this occurred just prior to the Golden Age. D is incorrect; it describes an effect of the Golden Age rather than a cause.

22. **C.** As part of the peace accords, nobles were allowed to choose between these two Christian denominations. A, B, and D are incorrect; the Council gave nobles a very limited choice. E is incorrect; the Peace of

Augsburg applied to nobles only; commoners were expected to follow their liege.

23. **D**. *Don Quixote*, with its focus on a sympathetic protagonist caught between ideals and changing times, captures much of the modern novel. A is incorrect; Spain had a long literary tradition both before and after *Don Quixote*. B is incorrect; although *Don Quixote* is quite long, many books of similar length preceded it. C is incorrect; *Don Quixote* was among the first books to be printed on a printing press, so it cannot have been one of the last to be inscribed on vellum. E is incorrect; *Don Quixote* was one of the earlier works of the Golden Age.

24. **A**. The Hapsburgs used marriages to build their dynasty. B is incorrect; it is the opposite of A. C and E are incorrect; while they are tempting responses, they do not correctly address the question. D is incorrect, as war, conquest, trade, and diplomacy also helped the Hapsburgs build their dynasty.

25. **A**. The Big Four wanted peace, but they also wanted territories and concessions. B is incorrect; the Big Four were unable to agree on basic premises. C is incorrect; the Big Four were more concerned about territory than peace. D is incorrect; although President Wilson favored the League, the U.S. did not join and the European powers were not especially concerned. E is incorrect; this describes post-World War II policies toward Germany.

26. **A**. During the course of this war, the northern regions grew commercially. B is incorrect; the southern regions remained dominated by Spain. C is incorrect; although Spain maintained nominal control, the region prospered. D is incorrect; as a whole, the Netherlands were unsympathetic to the Papal States. E is incorrect; the southern regions were unsympathetic to Spanish rule.

27. **B**. Bullionism argued that the economic health of a given country was determined by the amount of precious metals in its possession. A is incorrect; it describes a policy similar to bullionism, but using gems instead

of metal. C is incorrect; it describes a policy that might add to a bullionist economy but that is not directly bullionist. D is incorrect; it describes an isolationist policy, not a bullionist policy. E is incorrect; it describes a policy that *might* be favored but is not at the core of bullionism.

28. **A.** This is probably the strongest modern legacy of the edict. B is incorrect; this is tempting because it relates to the religious disputes of the time, but does not adequately address the question. C and D are incorrect as they both overstate the case. E is incorrect; it is the most tempting of the responses since it is almost correct. However, the Edict did not actually promote similarities; it merely allowed a modicum of choice.

29. **A.** Catherine de' Medici often stoked conflict to ensure that the interests of her family were preserved. B is incorrect; it describes an action of Catherine de' Medici that does not directly relate to the Wars of Religion. C is incorrect; while Catherine did try to increase France's prestige, this did not influence her actions during the Wars of Religion. D is incorrect; Catherine was more concerned with power than with efficiency. E is incorrect; Catherine, on the whole, did not promote compromise.

30. **D.** The marriage of Henry of Navarre to Princess Margaret would have greatly increased Protestant proximity to the throne. A is incorrect; while this response is tempting because it implies that a Protestant migration was underway, in reality most French Protestants were native to the region. B is incorrect; Catholics made up the vast majority of the Parisian population. C is incorrect; Protestants left in droves after the massacre. E is incorrect; it relates to the problems of Hapsburg proximity to the British throne.

31. **D.** The relationship between Henry VIII and the Church of England was unusual. A is incorrect; while it describes the Reformation, this feature was unique to Germany. B and E do not set England apart from the rest of Europe in regard to the Reformation. C is incorrect; almost all nations have experienced civil war.

32. **A.** Coligny was central to the Huguenot cause. B is incorrect, as the

king of France supported the murder. C is incorrect; other nations had little to do with the murder. D is incorrect; this act did not bring religious conflict to a close. E is incorrect; France and Germany remained at odds.

33. **B.** Sovereign states were a key part of the Westphalian system. A is incorrect; it relates to John Locke. C is incorrect; it relates to Charles I and Louis XIV. D is incorrect; it relates to Royalist and Napoleonic France. E is incorrect; it relates to Edmund Burke.

34. **E.** After Cromwell's death, his son ruled briefly but was quickly supplanted by the return of Charles II. A is incorrect; Cromwell has been accused of genocide rather than tolerance. B is incorrect; although Cromwell's son did inherit the throne, he was not particularly incompetent. C is incorrect; Cromwell did not face military defeat. D is incorrect. The public was divided on Cromwell; "widespread" implies a majority.

35. **D.** The buying and selling of forgiveness via indulgences angered everyone from Chaucer to Luther. This practice enriched the Church but infuriated its critics and sparked early widespread demands for reform. A, B, C, and E are pre-Reformation practices that continued in both the Catholic and some Protestant denominations. Each denomination had a different view of the meaning of the practices, but the practices themselves did not lead to the Reformation.

36. **B.** The *politiques* supported a strong, centralist monarchy. A is incorrect; the *politiques* wanted a strong king, not a weak one. C and D are incorrect; they imply that *politiques* supported democracy. These answers are tempting because they call to mind Enlightenment principles. E is incorrect; this is the type of government that *politiques*, in part, worked to change.

37. **E.** Copernicus argued that the sun was the center of the solar system (heliocentric), while Ptolemy developed the earlier geocentric theory in which the Earth was the center of motion. A is incorrect; Plato might have agreed with Ptolemy, but his ideas were not central to astronomy.

B is incorrect; Newton contributed to physics and the scientific method, not astronomy. C is incorrect; Johannes Kepler extended the ideas of Copernicus. D is incorrect; Brahe extended the works of Copernicus.

38. **B.** The birth of Prince James, son of the Catholic James II, set the stage for Catholic control of the British throne and led to the deposition of James II. A is incorrect; James II was not a convert. C is incorrect; William and Mary did seek power, but it was not the main cause of the Glorious Revolution. D is incorrect; the ongoing strength of Catholicism figured into the Glorious Revolution, but the era was not marked by a true resurgence. E is incorrect; Calvinism was on the rise but it was not an immediate cause of the Revolution.

39. **A.** Many of the rebelling bands were members of the military, which was loosely structured at that time. After the Fronde, the military was re-organized and placed under control of the king. B is incorrect; many of the rebelling bands were seasoned from wars with Germany. C is incorrect; one outcome of the Fronde was an increase in the power of the king. D is incorrect; the reorganization of the military further eroded the vestiges of feudalism. E is incorrect, as the Fronde did not increase liberalism.

40. **A.** A principal issues in the war was the potential unification of Spain and France under one monarch. Such unification would have radically changed the balance of power on the continent. B is incorrect; the balance of power in the New World did change as a result of the war but it was not a principal source of conflict. C is incorrect; almost all parties believed that France would continue to prosper regardless of the war. D is incorrect; Spain was predicted to remain a stable power regardless of the outcome of the war. E is incorrect; England's share of power was at stake, not its independence.

41. **A.** Both plans called for and predicted speedy victories in a two-front war. B is incorrect; neither side anticipated the advent of trench warfare. C is incorrect; air power does not emerge as a major factor in war until World War II. D is incorrect; neither plan called for a narrower scope of battle. E is incorrect; neither plan anticipated U.S. involvement.

42. **B**. As part of this treaty, King Phillip renounced his claims to the throne of France. A is incorrect; the result of the treaty was the opposite. C is incorrect; the treaty upheld the system. D is incorrect; if anything, the treaty added to the system, C is incorrect; Austria received Sardinia. E is incorrect; Savoy received Sicily.

43. **B**. Choice B describes baroque artwork. A is incorrect; it describes an icon. C is incorrect; it describes classical or neoclassical art. D is incorrect; it describes modern art. Although E is a tempting option because baroque painting did address royal subject matter, it is incorrect. Royal accomplishments do not define the baroque genre.

44. **D**. It describes the predatory practices of Prussia against Poland. A is incorrect; Prussia sought to eliminate Polish culture whenever possible. B is incorrect; Prussia tended to economically advance its Polish acquisitions. C is incorrect; these countries have historically been at odds with each other. D is incorrect; Prussia was the aggressor.

45. **D**. The council codified many key ideas of the Counter-Reformation that are still with us today. B is incorrect; the council offered no mercy to Protestants. A and C are incorrect; the Council mostly reified existing practices. E is incorrect; the selection of loyal bishops was an important issue but was not the primary subject of the council.

46. **E**. Peter attempted to turn Russia into a Western-style empire. A is incorrect, as it relates to Soviet Russia. B is incorrect; Peter resented the lingering influence of Mongol domination. C is incorrect; if possible, Peter would have increased the flow of finished goods. Although tempting, D is incorrect. Some of Peter's reforms increased similarities between Russian and Western Europe.

47. **C**. King Charles II, a Cavalier, led the Restoration. A is incorrect; Henry VIII was a Tudor. B is incorrect; Charles I was the last Stuart king before the civil war. D is tempting but incorrect; William III was connected to the Glorious Revolution. E is incorrect; Edward IV was the first Yorkist king of England.

48. **E.** A lack of territorial contiguity was the paradox of Hapsburg power. A is incorrect, as the Holy Roman Empire was secular. B is incorrect; the Holy Roman Empire did not have ties to Byzantium. However, this is an especially tempting option because both empires laid claim to the legacy of Rome. C is incorrect; the Holy Roman Empire was not especially overextended in the Atlantic. D is incorrect. The Holy Roman Empire had failed in its attempts to gain power in England and Ireland; thus, it was not extended in those regions.

49. **D.** Both are classic examples of speculative bubbles. A is incorrect; it describes some aspects of the South Sea Company but does not describe Tulip Mania. B is incorrect; it describes some aspects of the South Sea Company but does not describe Tulip Mania. C and D are incorrect; they describe some aspects of the South Sea Company, but do not describe Tulip Mania.

50. **B.** It describes a mercantile policy. Supporters of the mercantile theory believed that colonies existed for the economic benefit of the mother country. A is incorrect, as it describes a feudal policy. C is incorrect, as it describes a modern, globalized policy. D is incorrect. It is connected to mercantilism, but describes a policy that a mercantilist would find objectionable. E is incorrect; it describes a practice of modern globalization.

51. **B.** The defection of General Charles François Dumouriez to Austria set the stage for the wave of paranoia that allowed Robespierre and others to seize power. A is incorrect; this execution marked the beginning of the Reign of Terror. C is incorrect; it is a background cause. D is incorrect; it occurred after the formation of the Committee on Public Safety. E is incorrect; the Dantonists and Hebertists were removed after the formation of the Committee on Public Safety.

52. **E.** German unification and nationalism were tied together. A is incorrect; Russia was primarily concerned with empire and modernization. B is incorrect; England was primarily concerned with empire and liberal trade. C is incorrect; Spain was mainly concerned with maintaining royal

power over a declining empire. D is incorrect; Portugal was mainly concerned with maintaining royal power.

53. **D.** As the Thirty Years' War progressed, competition between the two families deepened. A is incorrect; the rivalry was a background cause of the war. B is incorrect; the rivalry continued after the war. E is incorrect; the rivalry added to the war. C is incorrect; the rivalry increased during the war.

54. **D.** The United Province is perhaps the most successful historical confederation and helped to pave the way for future democratic experiments. A is incorrect; although it had inherited titles, the Netherlands was not a traditional monarchy. B is incorrect; the Netherlands did share elements of republican government (such as separation of some powers), but it did not place the emphasis on voting or public participation. C is incorrect; the Provinces were united but not into a single body politic. E is incorrect; although some of the Provinces resembled duchies, they featured more complex governmental structure.

55. **D.** The Orangists favored heredity and the Republicans favored assemblies and elections. A is incorrect. To varying degrees, both groups tended to view new territories as legitimate. B is incorrect. To varying degrees, both groups saw trade and finances as helpful to the Dutch economy. C is incorrect. To varying degrees, both groups favored such an exchange. E is incorrect. To varying degrees, both groups favored military spending.

56. **A.** John Locke was one of the founders of liberal thought. B is incorrect, as Burke was conservative. C is incorrect, as Engels was a socialist. D is incorrect, as Dickens was a progressive who drew on liberal thought but applied it to progressive works. E is incorrect, as Bacon was a scientist and essayist but not a true liberal.

57. **B.** Bismarck is closely associated with realpolitik, or the belief that politics should be based primarily on power and practical considerations rather than ideological notions. With the exception of the Biesheuvel,

the other leaders practiced realpolitik, but the term is not closely linked to their identities.

58. **B**. Napoleon ascended through government through a military coup and political maneuvering. A is incorrect; although Napoleon invaded other countries, he did not invade France. C is incorrect; Napoleon, the champion of the plebiscite, was not an elected official. D is incorrect; Napoleon often enlisted the support of the masses but they were not central participants in his original ascent. E is incorrect; Napoleon was generally opposed by monarchists.

59. **C**. This stipulation is what sets Ricardo's law apart from its competitors. A is incorrect; it does not describe a comparative advantage. B is incorrect; it merely describes an exploitative relationship. D is incorrect; it describes the type of situation Ricardo hoped to avoid. E is incorrect; it describes a modern form of protectionism.

60. **B**. As the first French prime minister, Richelieu took on an increasing number of responsibilities, centralizing the power structure. A is incorrect; Richelieu concentrated power rather than decentralizing it. D is incorrect; ultimately, Richelieu's actions decreased the power of these groups. C is incorrect; Richelieu worked with both the Church and the state. E is incorrect; it describes a development of the Napoleonic era.

61. **B**. The Concert of Europe was led by royalist conservatives who wished to undo the changes brought about by the French Revolution. A is incorrect, as it ignores the influence of Protestant leaders on the Concert. C is incorrect; it describes a goal of some of the members of the Concert but not the whole group. D is incorrect; the Concert wished to modify the current balance of power. E is incorrect; the Concert was primarily concerned with events within Europe itself.

62. **A**. As the revolutions were somewhat spontaneous in each country and were not coordinated across national lines. B is incorrect; the revolutions explicitly addressed class. C is incorrect; the peasants sided with the reactionaries. D is incorrect; America and England did not become

involved in continental reform until later on. E is incorrect; a popular press had developed but it does not explain the failure of reform.

63. **C.** Frederick laid the groundwork for Prussian expansion and change from a duchy to a kingdom. A is incorrect; Frederick did not promote civil service reform. Although tempting, B is incorrect. D is incorrect; Frederick was a militarist. E is incorrect; Frederick was neutral on the topic of the middle classes.

64. **E.** These two policies are closely connected with the reign of Napoleon III. A is incorrect; Napoleon III expanded France's ties to the Middle East and proclaimed France the protector of Marionite Christians. B is incorrect; Napoleon III expanded the French role in Europe as well as democracy at home. C is incorrect; Napoleon III expanded the French role in European politics and democracy at home. D is incorrect; Napoleon III opposed the Concert of Europe because of its monarchical leanings.

65. **A.** As absolutists, both James I and Charles I believed that monarchs should be in possession of all national power. B is incorrect; it describes a populist view of the monarchy. C is incorrect; it describes a constitutional monarchy. D is incorrect; it describes a modern monarchy. E is incorrect; it is tempting to think that absolute kings were warmongers, but at times both of these monarchs chose to stay out of war to avoid Parliament.

66. **C.** Bismarck attempted to drive out Catholicism and impose Protestantism on new territories. A is incorrect; kulturkampf encouraged German migration into new territories. B is incorrect; kulturkampf elevated Protestantism over Catholicism but did not especially favor religion. D is incorrect; kulturkampf did not promote study or citizen participation. E is incorrect; German youth camps were influenced by kulturkampf, but do not represent a true example of it.

67. **A.** Descartes developed the Cartesian graph. B and E are incorrect; the sailor and the doctor may use graphs, but these are not essential to their work. C is incorrect; philosophers theorized before Descartes. D is

incorrect; it refers to the discoveries of a different great French intellect (Pasteur), who came after Descartes.

68. **D**. The Romantics placed an emphasis on the connection between people (often poets) and nature. A is incorrect, as it describes a literary theme that emerged after Romanticism and as a theme of medieval folk wisdom. B is incorrect; it describes a theme of contemporary "deep ecology." C and E are incorrect; they describe modern environmental concerns.

69. **B**. Russia's Pacific ports froze during the long winter, so access to a warm water port would be advantageous. A is incorrect; Russian preferred contiguous colonies. C is incorrect, as this comment described England rather than Russia. D is incorrect; the conflict had more to do with coaling stations than coal prices. E is incorrect; Russia was more concerned with port access (to allow wider Pacific trade) than with Japanese trade.

70. **A**. Luther and Calvin were key players in the Reformation but differed both philosophically and personally. B is incorrect, as Luther and Calvin were both caught up in the politics of their times. C is incorrect. Both Calvin and Luther created new religious sects, but Luther did not intend to do so. D is incorrect, as both men were prolific writers. E is incorrect, as Luther was focused solely on Europe. Protestant migrations to the New World did not begin in earnest until after Calvin's time.

71. **C**. The fin de siècle refers to the artistic climate of sophistication, escapism, and world-weariness, or a strong sense of angst. A is incorrect; surrealism followed symbolism. B is incorrect; modernism preceded symbolism. D is incorrect; pointillism preceded symbolism. E is incorrect; impressionism preceded symbolism.

72. **B**. Fourier expounded upon the many benefits of "phalanges," which were cooperative housing and work units. All other choices contain utopian elements, but do not directly relate to Fourier. A relates to British vegetarianism. C relates to charitable works and the Progressive

movement. D relates to the modern "slow food" movement. E relates to the goals of the Progressive movement.

73. **A.** Absolutism greatly empowered kings. B is incorrect; absolutism empowered kings at the expense of the nobility. C is incorrect; although popes similarly attempted to wrest power from their bishops through "infallibility," this is not the same as absolutism. D is incorrect; the Puritan desire to gain power coincided with absolutism. E is incorrect; although this practice has some similarities to absolutism, it is not the same thing.

74. **A.** Following the Crimean War, Florence Nightingale worked with the British Army to improve sanitation in hospitals and fighting units. B is incorrect; Nightingale's work did not improve the survival rates of injured soldiers although it did improve the quality of life during their final days. C is incorrect; as a result of her work in the Crimean War, Nightingale believed in sanitation, but "germ theory" had yet to take hold, even among experts. D is incorrect; Nightingale wrote one feminist work (*Cassandra*), but it was not widely published during her lifetime. E is incorrect; the creation of systematized medical records can be attributed to Linda Richards, an American student of Nightingale's.

75. **E.** Stolypin was a conservative who hoped his policies would allow small farmers to distance themselves from revolutionaries. A is incorrect; Stolypin was more concerned with subsistence and stability than with exports and the macro economy. B is incorrect; these were the type of farms that Stolypin hoped to reform. C is incorrect, although it is a tempting option, as it describes the goals of almost any working farm. However, it is not related to Stolypin. D is incorrect; this describes a type of agriculture that was practiced before and during Stolypin's time but it was not a goal of his reforms.

76. **C.** The Battle of Marne was expected to be short and decisive but instead devolved into lengthy, difficult trench warfare. A is incorrect; it connects to German air power in World War II. B is incorrect; it relates to the embargos and submarine warfare that came later in the war. D

is incorrect; chemical warfare emerged after the Battle of the Marne, in part as an attempt to break the stalemates associated with the trenches. E is incorrect; this pattern does not emerge until World War II.

77. **A.** During the Great Purge, Stalin purged the party and the government of any potential opposition. B and C are incorrect; they describe goals of Stalin but do not describe his purges. D is incorrect; it contradicts the core tenets of the Marxist state. E is incorrect; it describes a goal of Stalin but does not describe his purges.

78. **E.** Hitler realized the British policy of appeasement would allow his aggressions to go unchecked. A is incorrect; appeasement was a popular policy in England. B is incorrect; appeasement did not influence U.S. involvement in the war one way or another. C is incorrect; the Soviet Union did not become involved in this question. D is incorrect, as the policy resulted in the dissolution of Czechoslovakia.

79. **C.** France sought to build favor with England, and England was anxious about the growing Dutch fleet. A is incorrect; France and Spain were often at odds. B is incorrect; the Dutch did not fear the land power of the French. D is incorrect as it does not accurately describe French motivations in this case. E is incorrect; Sweden was not aligned with France.

80. **B.** This treaty brought us the euro. A is incorrect; although the English language is generally considered the common language of Europe, it was not stipulated as so in the treaty C is incorrect; a shared European culture existed before the treaty. D is incorrect; the governing bodies of the EU have emerged through administrative decrees over popular referenda. E is incorrect; almost all European countries maintain distinct university systems.

Section II, Part A
SAMPLE ESSAY

1. A good response may begin with a discussion of the documents containing excerpts from speeches by Russian and German leaders, as

well as those containing propaganda aimed directly at the Russian and German peoples.

All of the documents appeal to the idea of national unity and a higher national calling, sometimes in the face of great odds or enemies (Documents 1, 2, 6). However, the rise of nationalism in both countries ultimately led to the totalitarianism that was a strong contributor to World War II.

In twentieth-century Russia, extreme nationalism had its roots in the Russian Revolution of 1917. Although Bolshevik ideology was not distinctly nationalistic, Vladimir Lenin used it to appeal to nationalistic impulses and gain power. He promised to restore Russia's greatness by ending the famine and giving peasants more land, which were two major needs (Document 1). By the time Joseph Stalin rose in the 1930s and 1940s, Lenin had emerged as a nationalist hero to whom Stalin could refer in speeches and also use as a reminder of what the people were fighting for (Document 2). As a nationalist leader, Stalin made totalitarianism seem viable by providing a strong and vivid sense of direction for the future. Propaganda such as nationalist songs (Document 3) reinforced the idea of Soviet unity, as long as people aspired to the shared goals of the Bolsheviks.

Meanwhile, in twentieth-century Germany, nationalism played a prominent role in the rise of the Nazi party and Adolf Hitler. Hitler was skilled at manipulating nationalistic impulses by connecting them to symbols of Germany's resolve and racial purity, such as the German flag (Document 4). By the time he became the leader of Germany in 1934, Hitler's nationalism was strongly mixed with anti-Semitism. In his estimation, Germany was too crowded with Jews, driving a need for more space in Eastern Europe and Russia.

As Minister of Propaganda, Joseph Goebbels reinforced the idea of German purity by referring to a unified German "people, state, and nation" that, presumably, did not include Jews (Document 5). The propaganda pamphlet on racial purity, written almost 10 years later during World War II (Document 6), takes this idea even further. It establishes a connection between the purity of German blood and the purity of the German cause, and encourages other European nations to do the same.

Ultimately, unchecked nationalism in twentieth-century Russia and Germany had brutal results. Both Stalin and Hitler developed totalitarian states that used propaganda, political and economic control, and imprisonment and murder to achieve their aims.

By World War II, nationalism served different purposes in both countries. Russia relied on nationalism to defend itself from invaders such as Germany (Document 2), while Germany evoked nationalism to justify its actions in Russia and Eastern Europe (Document 6).

Section II, Part B
SAMPLE ESSAYS

2. Two British authors who made extensive use of social commentary were Charles Dickens and George Orwell. Dickens, the author of novels such as *Oliver Twist* and *Bleak House*, and Orwell, who wrote the novels *1984* and *Animal Farm*, included in their works powerful messages about the nature of society. Dickens dealt with topics such as class stratification, poverty, and urban life. Orwell also commented on stratification, and he addressed other issues such as worker oppression and the abuse of language in society.

Many readers consider Charles Dickens' novels as strong criticisms of social stratification. In the Victorian era in which Dickens lived, the gap between rich and poor citizens was broad. The upper classes lived relatively comfortable lives while the underclass struggled to survive. Dickens is well known for his portrayals of the underprivileged members of society. These characters struggle against and try to overcome major socioeconomic restrictions. Characters such as Oliver Twist faced poverty, crime, and poor treatment on a daily basis.

In addition, many of Dickens' less-fortunate characters are city dwellers. Dickens portrays the cities of Victorian England to be largely squalid and immoral places. His urban characters include street urchins, pickpockets, and prostitutes. However, by humanizing these "undesirable" characters, Dickens shows how good can exist even in troubled settings and societies.

Although born long after Dickens's time, George Orwell also addressed concerns with the social stratification that existed in his day. In his novel *Animal Farm*, for example, Orwell suggested that stratification is a social instinct, no matter how unfair or damaging. The animals in the novel attempt to create a utopian society in which all animals are treated equally. This works temporarily while the animal citizens are united against their human enemies. However, as soon as the enemies are vanquished, the animals quickly stratify, and dictators and aristocrats begin dominating the workers. Orwell used his commentary on stratification to suggest the ways in which socialism became corrupted in the Soviet Union.

Orwell continued using animal symbolism to represent unfairness in society when he wrote of the oppression of worker animals in *Animal Farm*. Most of the animal citizens were humble and hard-working, but were kept in a state of powerless naivety by the ruling class. The workers were fed lies and slogans and made to work more and harder for the benefit of the increasingly corrupt leadership. In *Animal Farm* as well as *1984*, Orwell showed how leaders can twist language to exploit the working classes. The slogans of Napoleon in *Animal Farm* and Big Brother in *1984* show how easily words can be used to silence dissidence, hold the people's loyalty, and exploit the masses.

The works of British authors such as Charles Dickens and George Orwell are well known for their social commentary. Dickens and Orwell used their characters, settings, and themes to make powerful statements about the state of society, addressing issues such as class stratification, the despair of urban life, the oppression of workers, and the corruption of language.

3. Classicism and Romanticism share a few common features but have many differences. Both forms of art apply to many mediums and acknowledge the importance of nature. However, the skills and approaches favored by Classicists, including formality, reason, reference to the past, and science, were almost completely rejected by the Romanticists, who preferred informality, emotion, focus on the present, and imagination.

One of the few commonalities between Classicism and Romanticism is that both art forms appear in a variety of mediums. Artists from both schools wrote, created paintings, and built architecture all over Europe. Many of these creations express the artists' reverence for nature. However, Classicists tried to represent nature realistically and in the methods of past artists while Romanticists portrayed nature as a wild, uncontrolled force experienced in a unique way by every individual.

Classicism and Romanticism place opposing values on many other facets of art. For instance, Classicism is noted for its formal approach. Classicist artists alluded to ancient works and used lofty and poetic language to appeal to intellectuals and nobility. Romanticists rejected that approach by trying to make their works more universally accessible. Romantic artists painted common themes that could be recognized by princes or peasants alike. They also used vernacular language in writing.

Artists of the Classicist school placed a great deal of faith in reason. They believed that the world could best be understood through careful study and contemplation, and that reason was necessary to capture the true nature of life. Again, Romanticists embarked on an opposite approach to art, embracing strong emotions instead of reason. Romanticist painters and writers felt they were not capturing their subjects accurately if they did not feel emotional about them.

In addition, the appreciation of time also separated the two schools of art. Classicist artists gained their name because they referred back to Classical art—the art of ancient Greece and Rome. They studied ancient paintings, sculptures, and texts for inspiration, feeling that art and expression hit an unsurpassable peak in those ancient civilizations. This approach differed greatly from that of the Romanticists. Romanticists felt that truth and beauty existed in the present and could only be understood through a unique and individual experience of the moment.

Classicists and Romanticists also drew their creative skills from opposite directions. Classicists tended to favor science and mathematics when creating their works. These artists preferred straight lines, careful symmetry, and balanced and closed compositions. The opposite is true of Romantic works, which celebrate imagination and spontaneity. Romantic art often breaks rules, bends lines, and encourages openness and expansiveness of expression.

Although Classicism and Romanticism are both schools of art that greatly impacted European history, the schools have few commonalities and many differences. Artists of these schools created art in many mediums and often worked with natural subjects, but their approaches and philosophies differed dramatically in most other ways.

4. John Locke, Thomas Hobbes, and Jean-Jacques Rousseau were some of the most influential philosophers to consider questions of society and politics. Their ideas about the nature of society, the existence of human freedom, the nature of government, and the representation of people in government helped modernize political thinking and had a great influence on the revolutionary movements of the seventeenth and eighteenth centuries.

The philosophies of Locke, Hobbes, and Rousseau were based on beliefs about the nature of society. Locke believed that people originally existed in a natural state of chaos that was neither good nor bad. Then societies were formed; society took away some freedom but added security. Hobbes had a differing view, believing that people in a natural state are fearful and warlike, and that society is necessary to restrain their savage ways. Rousseau took an opposite viewpoint. He posited that people were naturally free and equal, but are corrupted by society.

With their differing perceptions of society and freedom, Locke, Hobbes, and Rousseau also had different ideas about the nature of government. For Locke, government was a necessity and its role was in protecting the natural rights of the people. The best government would be designed to protect people from the dangers of itself (unrestrained government). Hobbes felt that governments were necessary, but mostly to protect people from each other. He felt that governments could take any actions necessary to thwart the brutal instincts of humankind. Rousseau believed that governments are made and run by the people to promote the "general will," or the best interests of the majority of the people. He felt that governments should be empowered to do almost anything necessary to further the general will.

The representative nature of these governments was also a point of debate among philosophers. Locke believed that governments must represent people in order to promote their best interests and protect their rights. Hobbes did not feel that representative government was essential; he thought that governments should control society, but should not be required to directly represent the people. Rousseau had an opposing view. He expressed the idea that representation was essential for government and that direct democracy, in which all people are active in the government, was the ideal form.

Philosophers such as John Locke, Thomas Hobbes, and Jean-Jacques Rousseau expressed a range of ideas about the nature of society, human freedom, government, and government representation of people. Their ideas helped to inspire major changes to world governments that altered the course of history.

Section II, Part C
SAMPLE ESSAYS

5. The Austro-Hungarian Empire experienced strong nationalism that eventually played a role in its collapse in 1918. The nationalism stemmed from many sources, including the ineffective political design of Austria-Hungary, the diversity of the peoples within the empire, internal hostilities, and external sympathies. These factors caused nationalism that helped to shatter the empire at the end of World War I.

Austria-Hungary was an empire of many states and ethnic groups, and its politics and policies were complex and often inconsistent. Austrian leaders tended to be more liberal with the ethnic groups under their rule, although Austria sometimes deferred to the judgment of its ally, Germany. Hungarian leaders tended to be harsher, attempting to impose policies that would make various ethnic groups accept Hungarian ways of life. Emperor Francis Joseph attempted to accommodate the many ethnic groups, but the difficulties of running a society with many languages and religions made for inefficiencies. This led to struggles and hard feelings that increased nationalism among different internal groups.

The people within Austria-Hungary encompassed a wide variety of ethnicities and religions. The three major subdivisions were Germanic peoples, including ethnic Germans and Austrians; Hungarians; and Slavs, including Czechs, Slovaks, Serbs, Croats, Ruthenians, and Ukrainians. Each group had its own culture, language, religion, and lifestyle, and each wanted to preserve its ways of life, defying attempts to unify the Empire around a single culture. Many of these groups wanted their own nations rather than to be subjected to imperial rule.

The diversity within the Austro-Hungarian Empire led to both conflict and sympathy, both of which stirred nationalism. The ethnic groups disagreed on many factors and some groups attempted to dominate or assimilate others. Austrians tended to associate more with Germans than with other members of the Austro-Hungarian Empire. Meanwhile, Hungarians began enforcing policies that tried to assimilate various peoples into Hungarian ways of life. Many Slavs, disaffected by these actions, felt greater kinship with outside nations such as nearby Russia. The Russian Empire, also a powerful force in Europe, fostered an attitude of Pan-Slavism, or the connectedness of Slavic people. These conflicts within Austria-Hungary and the sympathies of some citizens to foreign nations increased nationalist sentiments in the Empire.

Ultimately, factors such as the awkward politics of Austria-Hungary, the diversity of ethnic and religious groups within it, and internal conflicts and international sympathies led to the rise of nationalism in the

Empire. This nationalism helped to spark World War I as citizens of the Balkans rebelled against imperial rule. At the end of World War I, nationalists throughout the Empire leapt at the opportunity to gain self-determination and create their own nations, which eventually included Austria, Hungary, Czechoslovakia, Poland, Yugoslavia, and Romania.

6. The Balkans is a region of southern Europe that experienced great instability during the early twentieth century. Events in the Balkans helped trigger many violent incidents, most notably World War I, leading the region to be nicknamed the "powder keg of Europe." The instability in the region came about due to many important factors, including location, the diversity of Balkan peoples, the political tension of neighboring states, and the strong nationalist attitudes that flourished in Southern and Eastern Europe in the 1900s.

First, the location of the Balkans played an important role in its political and social instability. The Balkans is a passageway between Europe and eastern lands such as the Middle East and Asia. This means that many cultural influences have touched upon the Balkans, creating different and sometimes conflicting attitudes and lifestyles. In addition, the location of the Balkans makes the area important for military strategy as well as for politics and trade. Throughout history, larger nations and empires have fought to control the Balkans for those reasons.

The diversity of the Balkans was another prime factor in its political and social instability. Many diverse groups of people lived in the area. They practiced a range of religions, including different kinds of Christianity as well as Islam. Additionally, many of the people identified with differing European and Middle Eastern ethnicities; they tended to view themselves from a cultural rather than a national perspective. As a result, many people felt more loyalty to their particular ethnic or religious group than to any nation or empire. The relatively small size of the Balkans region and its frequently shifting borders meant that these diverse and often hostile people were kept in close proximity, further increasing tensions.

The tension did not exist only within the Balkans, however; it also came from external sources. The Balkans was located in proximity to many powerful nations and empires, including Germany, the Austro-Hungarian Empire, and the Russian Empire. Each of these groups impacted politics in this already troubled region. In particular, Austria-Hungary desired to keep the Balkans as part of its territorial holdings, while Russia shared empathy with the Balkans people who were largely of Slavic background, ethnically related to the Russians. When Austria-Hungary tried to dominate the Balkans, Russia took exception.

Finally, amid the diversity and tension of the region, a strong sense of nationalism arose. The various ethnic and religious groups desired independence and the ability to create their own nations. They did not want to be confined by the arbitrary borders of foreign nations and empires. The nationalism became apparent immediately after World War I, when ethnic groups in the Balkans leapt at the opportunity to form their own nations.

The Balkans played an important and often tragic role in European history. Forces such as location, diversity, international tension, and nationalism contributed to tension and instability in the Balkans that ignited World War I and changed the course of human history.

7. Adolf Hitler and Joseph Stalin created empires and made decisions that impacted the lives and deaths of millions of people. These dictators used many tactics to hold their political power. Some of these tactics were similar, such as fear, violence, nationalism, and censorship. Other tactics differed between the dictators, such as their methods of empire-building and their choice of enemies and scapegoats.

Both Hitler and Stalin relied on fear and violence to maintain power. They thought nothing of condemning thousands to death to advance their political policies. Many of these killings were carried out by powerful secret police organizations. Hitler used the Gestapo to root out political dissidents and spread fear; Stalin used the KGB and other units for similar activities. Citizens learned to live in terror, since they could be arbitrarily arrested or executed by such units at any moment. In addition, Hitler and Stalin both commanded daunting armed forces that were used to impose their will and cement power internationally.

However, Hitler and Stalin did not rely only on terror and brute force. They also used policies of nationalism and censorship to manipulate people and silence dissidence. Both dictators are famous for their animated speeches that touted the strengths and importance of their own nations or empires. Hitler in particular stirred the Germans into a nationalistic fervor by claiming they were a superior race and destined for world domination. Both dictators sanctioned propaganda to praise and elevate themselves and slander their opponents. At the same time, the dictators employed policies of censorship to silence any discontent or disagreement. Stalin was known to even have photographs doctored to erase undesirable people—in effect, using censorship to deny their existence and change the course of history.

Both of the dictators were committed to expanding their empires. Hitler hoped to conquer Europe and turn many parts into *lebensraum*, or "living space," for German people. Stalin wanted to turn the continent into a Communist stronghold. The dictators differed on their expansionist tactics, however. Hitler tended to use military means and was infamous for his style of invading and conquering neighboring nations. Meanwhile, Stalin took a more political approach by using diplomacy, lies, and threats to gain influence over other countries.

Finally, Hitler and Stalin concretized their power by blaming perceived enemies for any misfortunes. They differed in their choice of scapegoats, however. Hitler focused on racial and religious minorities, particularly Jews, that he claimed were detrimental to German goals. Meanwhile, Stalin placed the blame on economic and political scapegoats, such as business owners, fascists, democrats, or anyone else who did not subscribe to his brand of Communism.

Hitler and Stalin were criminal dictators whose actions changed European history and caused the deaths of untold millions. They built their empires and held their power in several similar ways, such as by using fear and violence and employing nationalism and censorship. They differed in some ways as well, such as in their methods of expanding their empires and selecting scapegoats.

This book contains two practice exams. Visit mymaxscore.com to download your free third practice test with answers and explanations.

AP European History Practice Exam 2

EUROPEAN HISTORY
SECTION I
Time—55 minutes
80 Questions

Directions: Each of the questions or incomplete statements below is followed by five suggested answers or completions. Select the answer that is best in each case. *Take no more than 55 minutes to complete this part of your test.*

1. Which of the following statements best describes the Third Estate in France?

   A. It promoted social equality.
   B. It faced the highest tax burden.
   C. It controlled the government.
   D. It enjoyed a high standard of living.
   E. It was loyal to the government.

2. Which of the following enabled the Italian Renaissance to flourish?

    A. A socialist form of government
    B. An avoidance of technology
    C. A limit on contact with the Catholic Church
    D. A wealthy class invested in the arts
    E. An emphasis on ancient Egyptian culture

3. Isaac Newton's theory of motion proposed a

    A. new kind of natural law.
    B. new way to measure distance.
    C. new thinking about space travel.
    D. new kind of chemistry.
    E. new kind of math.

4. Which of the following is an example of Cold War brinkmanship?

    A. Cuban Missile Crisis
    B. Arab-Israeli War
    C. Iran-Iraq War
    D. Cultural Revolution
    E. Korean War

5. Which of the following best describes the views of Martin Luther in his Ninety-Five Theses?

    A. Indulgences can be sold under certain circumstances.
    B. The Church should work to unify German states.
    C. Citizens should revolt against the German emperor.
    D. The Pope should be granted greater authority.
    E. Reforms need to be made within the Church.

6. In its economic relationship with its North American colonies, Great Britain followed the principles of eighteenth-century mercantilism by

    A. outlawing the African slave trade.
    B. limiting colonial trade with other nations.
    C. encouraging manufacturing within the colonies.
    D. establishing laws against business monopolies.
    E. raising taxes to support the military.

7. England became a Protestant country during the Reformation when its

    A. king declared himself head of the Church of England.
    B. people demanded the adoption of Lutheran beliefs.
    C. priests opposed reforms implemented by the Pope.
    D. armies were exposed to Calvinist beliefs in France.
    E. government chose to rely on humanist principles.

8. Both Calvinists and Lutherans condemned Anabaptists for their

    A. willingness to baptize infants.
    B. belief in separating Church and state.
    C. support for the Church.
    D. consideration of a secular worldview.
    E. certainty in superstition.

9. All of the following events occurred during the English Civil War (1640–1660) EXCEPT

    A. the defeat of the royal army by Oliver Cromwell.
    B. the elimination of Presbyterians from Parliament.
    C. the dissolution of the monarchy and the House of Lords.
    D. the execution of King Charles I.
    E. the creation of the English Bill of Rights.

10. Which of the following best explains why Spain was involved in the American Revolution?

    A. To fight against the French as well as the British
    B. To demand the surrender of Spanish territory from the colonists
    C. To regain colonial lands previously lost to the British
    D. To demolish the British navy
    E. To gain financial support from the colonists

11. Which of the following best characterizes the Huguenot population in France during the seventeenth century?

    A. The Huguenots continued to live in France in large numbers.
    B. The Huguenots were driven out of France by the Protestants.
    C. The Huguenots emigrated from France to Russia, helping the Russian economy.
    D. The Huguenots were driven out of France by the Catholics.
    E. The Huguenots emigrated from France to Spain, helping the Spanish economy.

12. Which of the following best represents the main emphasis of nineteenth-century socialism?

    A. Competition and profit
    B. Reason and intellect
    C. Cooperation and service
    D. Production and distribution
    E. Loyalty and duty

13. All of the following describe the early stages of the Scientific Revolution EXCEPT

    A. an emphasis on the value of research.
    B. an attempt to describe Earth's place in the universe.
    C. an ongoing opposition by the Church.
    D. a modeling on Chinese philosophy.
    E. a goal of improving the condition of humanity.

14. Which of the following occurred during Thermidor?

    A. The beginning of the Reign of Terror
    B. The defeat of the French by a European coalition
    C. The restoration of the French monarchy
    D. The decision by the *sans-culottes* to govern France
    E. The end of the Reign of Terror

15. Which of the following best states the position of the Soviet Union at the end of World War II?

    A. It was weaker than Germany.
    B. It controlled most of Eastern Europe.
    C. It controlled most of Asia.
    D. It was ready to rebuild Japan.
    E. It was ready to work with the United States.

16. Which of the following most directly impacted the early Scientific Revolution?

    A. The Enlightenment
    B. The Protestant Reformation
    C. The Renaissance
    D. The Catholic Reformation
    E. The Industrial Revolution

17. Galileo and Newton would have mostly likely favored new scientific thought based on which of the following?

    A.   Continued medieval traditions

    B.   Greek and Roman philosophy

    C.   Church authority

    D.   Hypotheses and testing

    E.   Instinct and emotion

18. Enlightenment philosophers were influenced by the Scientific Revolution to

    A.   believe in the power of human reason.

    B.   reject their beliefs in the Church.

    C.   study the ideas of past civilizations.

    D.   question the results of experimentation.

    E.   oppose individuality in favor of social order.

19. Which of the following describes the effect of the American Revolution on Europe?

    A.   It led to the end of federalism in Europe.

    B.   It brought European countries together in opposition.

    C.   It marked the first time a colony successfully rebelled against a European country.

    D.   It strengthened the position of European leaders who called for traditional order.

    E.   It united Europeans against Alexander Hamilton and Thomas Jefferson.

20. Which of the following is based on Enlightenment teachings of natural rights and separation of powers?

    A. Enlightened despotism
    B. Democratic government
    C. Scientific Revolution
    D. Nationalistic fervor
    E. Industrial Revolution

21. Which of the following is a true statement about the Scientific Revolution and the Enlightenment?

    A. Both used reason to improve humanity.
    B. Both were global movements.
    C. Both broke with classical traditions.
    D. Both supported the Church view of the universe.
    E. Both were spiritual and philosophical.

22. All of the following concepts were based on natural laws EXCEPT

    A. deism.
    B. predestination.
    C. the social contract.
    D. laissez-faire economics.
    E. gravity and motion.

23. Which of the following inventions during the Scientific Revolution led to a better understanding of disease?

    A. The telescope
    B. The thermometer
    C. The microscope
    D. The barometer
    E. The chronometer

24. In the late 1600s, Peter the Great of Russia

    A. prohibited the upper classes of Russia from speaking French.
    B. banned the import of European clothing and goods.
    C. prevented wealthy Russians from educating their children in Europe.
    D. extended Russian influence into Europe.
    E. built a new capital city near Europe.

25. Which of the following statements best illustrates the Enlightenment argument regarding the Divine Right of Kings?

    A. God has chosen all government rulers.
    B. Independence is achieved by military might.
    C. A capitalist economic system is necessary for democracy.
    D. The power of government is derived from the governed.
    E. Government is the only force that keeps society from descending into chaos.

26. Which of the following resulted from the storming of the Bastille by an angry French crowd in 1789?

    A. Access to a greater number of weapons
    B. Change in philosophical direction for the radicals
    C. Escape of important opposition leaders from prison
    D. Leverage for the National Assembly
    E. Increased anger toward the monarchy

27. The Soviet Union formed the Warsaw Pact in 1955

    A. to ease the transition to democracy.
    B. to institute capitalism in Eastern Europe.
    C. to limit the threat of invasion from Western Europe.
    D. to challenge the successes of the Common Market.
    E. to limit the effects of the Cold War.

"We are such stuff as dreams are made on, and our little life is rounded by a sleep."

28. The quotation above describes the Renaissance belief in

    A. humanism.
    B. salvation.
    C. philosophy.
    D. logic.
    E. predestination.

29. Which of the following Enlightenment figures supported absolute monarchy?

    A. Jean-Jacques Rousseau
    B. John Locke
    C. Thomas Hobbes
    D. Baron de Montesquieu
    E. Rene Descartes

30. How did the heliocentric theory of Copernicus impact the early Scientific Revolution?

    A. It was used to revise the Christian calendar.
    B. It contributed to disputes with the Church.
    C. It gave scientists the ability to predict tides more accurately.
    D. It led to a decline in the number of pagan religions.
    E. It emphasized observation and experimentation.

31. The Agricultural Revolution in eighteenth-century England involved the application of new techniques to increase

    A. crop harvests.
    B. factory production.
    C. farm subsidies.
    D. farmland.
    E. grain prices.

32. One of the main tools used by Galileo to solve problems in his research was

    A. the scientific method.
    B. laissez-faire philosophy.
    C. the social contract.
    D. natural law.
    E. the theory of gravity.

33. All of the following were associated with the Agricultural Revolution EXCEPT

    A. the three-field system.
    B. the four-field system.
    C. the Enclosure Movement.
    D. the higher yield of turnips.
    E. the use of nitrogen.

34. Which of the following was directly affected by economic and political changes during the Agricultural Revolution?

    A. The Glorious Revolution
    B. The Scientific Revolution
    C. The Industrial Revolution
    D. The American Revolution
    E. The French Revolution

35. Which of the following factors allowed Napoleon to take control of France?

    A.   Weakness of the French government
    B.   Endorsement of foreign allies
    C.   Support from the French aristocracy
    D.   Promise of strong democratic reforms
    E.   Support of the French king

36. Which of the following statements about the Protestant Reformation is true?

    A.   It strengthened the authority of the Church.
    B.   It spread due to advances in technology.
    C.   It became the basis for Enlightenment thought.
    D.   It did not impact the status of women in society.
    E.   It was carried to the Western Hemisphere by Jesuits.

37. Which of the following best explains the Executive Directory's support of the French military?

    A.   The Executive Directory lost faith in the *sans-culottes*.
    B.   The Executive Directory lost the favor of the nobility.
    C.   The Executive Directory was threatened by Jacobins and Royalists.
    D.   The Executive Directory feared losses in the next election.
    E.   The Executive Directory was anxious about overthrow by Napoleon.

38. The term "Great Fear" would most likely be used in connection with which of the following?

    A. An uprising by urban workers in Paris
    B. The creation of a European coalition against French revolutionaries
    C. An increase in pressure on the National Assembly to enact more radical legislation
    D. The strengthening of the nobility's position
    E. An uprising by overtaxed peasants

39. Which of the following was invented by Johann Gutenberg during the Renaissance?

    A. The bicycle
    B. The printing press
    C. The telescope
    D. The submarine
    E. The pocket watch

40. Leading up to the French Revolution, the Civil Constitution of the Clergy

    A. brought the clergy and National Assembly together.
    B. weakened the power of the clergy.
    C. created greater Assembly support for Catholics.
    D. reaffirmed the place of the Church in the French government.
    E. declared Catholicism illegal in France.

41. All of the following intensified the atmosphere leading up to the French Revolution EXCEPT

    A.   the rise of the *sans-culottes*.

    B.   the escape of the king.

    C.   the factional division of the Assembly.

    D.   the execution of the king.

    E.   the outbreak of war with Austria and Prussia.

42. Compared to the Italian Renaissance, what was the most distinctive feature of the Northern Renaissance?

    A.   Literary works satirizing Greek and Roman cultures

    B.   A democratic form of government

    C.   Art centered around religious themes

    D.   Religious tracts rejecting the study of the natural world

    E.   A system of new math

43. Which of the following best describes the Reign of Terror (1793–1794)?

    A.   It was supported by the government.

    B.   It was openly opposed by the French people.

    C.   It was aimed primarily at the nobility.

    D.   It was not used to execute the clergy.

    E.   It was carried out in the countryside.

44. Which of the following ended the Napoleonic Wars?

    A.   Peace of Utrecht

    B.   Congress of Berlin

    C.   Peace of Westphalia

    D.   Congress of Vienna

    E.   Treaty of Paris

45. Which of the following best characterizes the Dutch Republic during the seventeenth century?

    A. It was centrally governed by its strongest province.

    B. It wielded little economic power in Europe.

    C. It traded in Asia, Africa, North America, and the Caribbean.

    D. It promoted a culture of religious intolerance.

    E. It avoided participation in international free trade.

"The only representatives of the people of these colonies are persons chosen therein by themselves; and that no taxes ever have been, or can be constitutionally imposed on them but by their respective legislatures."

46. The statement above from the Stamp Act Congress (1765) was fundamental to the idea that

    A. colonial legislatures had to be appointed with Parliamentary consent.

    B. only elected representatives had the power to levy taxes on colonists.

    C. colonists were not required to pay taxes on goods.

    D. colonists were required to pay taxes only on certain goods.

    E. colonists were opposed to both Parliament and the king.

47. All of the following were associated with the American and French Revolutions EXCEPT

    A. women's rights.

    B. taxation.

    C. government representation.

    D. natural rights.

    E. Enlightenment thought.

48. In Europe, the end of the American Revolution had an immediate impact on the

    A. practice of slavery.
    B. Anglican Church.
    C. Reign of Terror.
    D. Glorious Revolution.
    E. Enlightenment.

49. Which of the following best describes the Thirty Years' War in Europe (1618–1648)?

    A. War of power
    B. War of economy
    C. War of religion
    D. War of commerce
    E. War of reform

50. The British had all of the following advantages during the American Revolution EXCEPT

    A. military strength.
    B. support from Native Americans.
    C. strong commitment to the conflict.
    D. experienced military commanders.
    E. vast economic resources.

51. All of the following were discovered during the Scientific Revolution or the Enlightenment EXCEPT

    A. planetary motion.
    B. heliocentric theory.
    C. gunpowder.
    D. the circulatory system.
    E. the social contract.

52. The Treaty of Paris in 1783 set forth all of the following EXCEPT

    A.   recognition of American independence.
    B.   new geographical boundaries for the United States.
    C.   procedures for collecting prewar debts from the colonists.
    D.   establishment of fishing rights in New England.
    E.   the meeting of the Second Continental Congress.

53. Which of the following statements is true as regards conservatism during the late nineteenth century?

    A.   It sought to reduce oppression.
    B.   It supported radical governmental change.
    C.   It promoted a strong sense of cultural identity.
    D.   It supported laissez-faire capitalism.
    E.   It rejected a belief in God.

54. Which of the following events led to the start of World War II?

    A.   Germany's annexation of the Sudetenland
    B.   Japan's bombing of Pearl Harbor
    C.   Germany's invasion of Poland
    D.   Germany's bombing of London
    E.   Italy's alliance with Germany and Japan

55. Which of the following best describes the Austro-Hungarian Empire following the Thirty Years' War?

    A.   It shared post-war stability with Prussia.
    B.   Its military might was strengthened.
    C.   It ruled over a large number of Muslims.
    D.   Its people were mostly of a single cultural and political group.
    E.   Its population was primarily from the same religious group.

56. All of the following events occurred during England's Glorious Revolution (1688–1689) EXCEPT

    A. William and Mary were crowned as leaders.

    B. Parliament became more powerful.

    C. Anglican bishops were imprisoned in the Tower of London.

    D. Whigs and Tories opposed each other.

    E. England was invaded by a foreign power.

57. Which of the following best explains why William Shakespeare's writings were so important during the Renaissance?

    A. Shakespeare was both a poet and a playwright.

    B. Shakespeare wrote about human emotions.

    C. Shakespeare wrote about history and philosophy.

    D. Shakespeare used language in a new way to describe human experience.

    E. Shakespeare influenced the works of other artists, such as Leonardo da Vinci.

58. Which of the following is a true statement with regard to liberalism during the early nineteenth century?

    A. It was based on artistic traditions.

    B. It was based on British traditions.

    C. It promoted capitalism at the expense of the individual.

    D. It supported a more restrictive government.

    E. It rejected the natural rights of citizens.

59. Which of the following was a central feature of both the Italian Renaissance and the Protestant Reformation?

    A.   A devotion to religious teachings
    B.   The questioning of political authority
    C.   A confinement to the countries of Italy and France
    D.   A surge in artist creativity
    E.   The refusal to accept Church teachings

60. Which of the following directly influenced the Industrial Revolution in England?

    A.   Urban poverty
    B.   Failure of cottage industries
    C.   New manufacturing methods and inventions
    D.   Foreign trade
    E.   Industrial revolutions in other countries

61. Which of the following best describes the role of nationalism in the nineteenth century?

    A.   It brought about tolerance for diversity.
    B.   It eased tensions between ethnic groups.
    C.   It prevented unification within most European countries.
    D.   It created increased support for monarchies.
    E.   It both unified and divided countries.

62. A central reason the Agricultural Revolution became necessary in England was

    A.   an increase in land ownership.
    B.   a lack of worker productivity.
    C.   a failure of crops.
    D.   an aging population.
    E.   an expanding population.

63. Imperialism in the late nineteenth century was a result of all of the following EXCEPT

    A. nationalism.
    B. militarism.
    C. industrialization.
    D. socialism.
    E. colonialism.

64. All of the following pairs of European nations and their imperial interests are correct EXCEPT

    A. Great Britain and India.
    B. Germany and Africa.
    C. The Netherlands and South Africa.
    D. France and North Africa.
    E. Belgium and South America.

65. Which of the following best describes agricultural changes that took place during the 1700s?

    A. Agricultural changes strengthened the importance of family farms.
    B. Agricultural changes divided large estates into smaller farms.
    C. Agricultural changes encouraged city residents to return to farming.
    D. Agricultural changes led to the production of more food with fewer workers.
    E. Agricultural changes led to mass food production in factories.

66. European imperialism in the nineteenth century was aided by all of the following EXCEPT

    A.   medical improvements.
    B.   abolitionist movements.
    C.   steam engines.
    D.   guns.
    E.   plantations.

67. The important political treaty signed at the conclusion of the religious wars in Europe was the

    A.   Peace of Prague.
    B.   Treaty of London.
    C.   Peace of Augsburg.
    D.   Treaty of Edinburgh.
    E.   Peace of Westphalia.

68. Which of the following political systems unified Germany in the 1870s?

    A.   Realpolitik
    B.   Socialism
    C.   Liberalism
    D.   Marxism
    E.   Conservatism

69. Which of the following best describes a cause of the Russian Revolution?

    A.   The defeat of Germany during World War I
    B.   The marriage of Nicholas II to a German princess
    C.   The economic differences among social classes
    D.   The appeal of Marxism to the Russian nobility
    E.   The defeat of Russia in the Crimean War

70. Which of the following explains the support of Russian peasants for the Bolsheviks during the Russian Revolution?

    A. A promise to increase trade
    B. A promise to maintain the agricultural system
    C. A promise to supply money and gold
    D. A promise to redistribute land owned by the nobility
    E. A promise to support the Russian Orthodox Church

71. The assassination of which of the following leaders led to World War I?

    A. Archduke Ferdinand
    B. Tsar Nicholas II
    C. Chancellor Bismarck
    D. Emperor Franz Joseph
    E. Grigory Rasputin

72. Which of the following best describes the global nature of World War I?

    A. It was fought on every continent.
    B. It was fought in the Pacific and in Europe.
    C. It included involvement by the colonies of the warring countries.
    D. It began in Europe and spread throughout the world.
    E. It involved both Europe and the United States.

73. Which of the following was experienced in England during World War I?

    A. Higher poverty
    B. Higher unemployment
    C. Lower unemployment
    D. Lower status of women
    E. Higher emigration rates

74. Which of the following was a result of the mercantilist relationship between Britain and the American colonies?

    A.   Support for colonial industries
    B.   Prohibition of colonists from fishing and fur trading
    C.   Removal of gold and silver from the colonies
    D.   Purchase of raw materials from the colonies
    E.   Purchase of finished products from the colonies

75. Which of the following contributed the most to France's financial problems prior to the French Revolution?

    A.   Louis XVI's extravagant lifestyle
    B.   Lack of taxation on the Third Estate
    C.   Tax exemptions granted to the nobility and clergy
    D.   Foreign warfare
    E.   Poor economic conditions

76. Which of the following topics would a historian be most interested in researching in relation to the period between World Wars I and II?

    A.   The decisiveness of the League of Nations
    B.   The rise of nationalism
    C.   The creation of the United Nations
    D.   The role of Spain
    E.   The role of the Ottoman Empire

77. Which of the following best describes John Calvin's goal in his book, *Institutes of the Christian Religion?*

    A.   To respond to reforms devised at the Council of Trent
    B.   To defend and explain Protestantism
    C.   To promote dialogue with the Church
    D.   To reject the philosophy of humanism
    E.   To call for civil war between Catholics and Protestants

78. A central reason the French people supported Napoleon Bonaparte was their belief that he would

    A.   adopt the ideas of the Protestant Reformation.

    B.   restore Louis XVI to power.

    C.   provide stability for the nation.

    D.   end British control of France.

    E.   modernize the armed forces.

79. Which of the following intellectual movements is represented in the writings of Jean-Jacques Rousseau?

    A.   Liberalism

    B.   Socialism

    C.   Conservatism

    D.   Romanticism

    E.   Marxism

80. Which of the following best states an important result of the French Revolution?

    A.   France enjoyed a long period of peace and prosperity.

    B.   The French government restored the Church to its former role.

    C.   Political power shifted to the bourgeoisie.

    D.   France lost its spirit of nationalism.

    E.   The monarchy was restored to almost unlimited power.

END OF SECTION I

TAKE A FIVE-MINUTE BREAK

EUROPEAN HISTORY
SECTION II
Part A
Planning time—15 minutes
Writing time—45 minutes

Directions: The following question is based on the accompanying Documents 1–6. The documents have been edited for the purpose of this exercise. Write your answer on lined notebook paper. *(During the actual examination, you will be given lined answer sheets for this exercise.)*

This question is designed to test your ability to work with and understand historical documents.

Write an essay that:

- Provides an appropriate, explicitly stated thesis that directly addresses all parts of the question and does NOT simply restate the question.
- Discusses a majority of the documents individually and specifically.
- Demonstrates understanding of the basic meaning of a majority of the documents.
- Analyzes point of view or bias in at least three documents.
- Analyzes the documents by explicitly grouping them in at least three appropriate ways.

You may refer to relevant historical information not mentioned in the documents.

1. Using the documents below, discuss the problems caused in England by industrialization in the eighteenth and nineteenth centuries.

DOCUMENT 1

Source: An Inquiry into the Nature and Causes of the Wealth of Nations, 1776

The produce of industry is what it adds to the subject or materials upon which it is employed. In proportion as the value of this produce is great or small, so will likewise be the profits of the employer. But it is only for the sake of profit that any man employs a capital in support of industry; and he will always, therefore, endeavor to employ it in support of that industry of which the produce is likely to be of the greatest value, or to exchange for the greatest quantity of money or of other goods.

DOCUMENT 2

Source: Leeds Woolen Workers Petition, excerpt, 1786

...the Scribbling-Machines have thrown thousands of your petitioners out of employ, whereby they are brought into great distress, and are not able to procure a maintenance for their families, and deprived them of the opportunity of bringing up their children to labor: We have therefore to request, that prejudice and self-interest may be laid aside, and that you may pay that attention to the following facts, which the nature of the case requires.

The number of Scribbling-Machines extending about seventeen miles south-west of LEEDS, exceed all belief, being no less than *one hundred and seventy!* and as each machine will do as much work in twelve hours, as ten men can in that time do by hand, (speaking within bounds) and they working night-and day, one machine will do as much work in one day as would otherwise employ twenty men....

DOCUMENT 3

Source: Excerpt of testimony by Peter Smart before the Sadler Committee

You say you were locked up night and day?

—Yes.

Do the children ever attempt to run away?

—Very often.

Were they pursued and brought back again?

—Yes, the overseer pursued them, and brought them back.

Did you ever attempt to run away?

—Yes, I ran away twice.

And you were brought back?

—Yes; and I was sent up to the master's loft, and thrashed with a whip for running away.

Were you bound to this man?

—Yes, for six years.

By whom were you bound?

—My mother got 15s. for the six years.

Do you know whether the children were, in point of fact, compelled to stop during the whole time for which they were engaged?

—Yes, they were.

By law?

—I cannot say by law; but they were compelled by the master; I never saw any law used there but the law of their own hands.

DOCUMENT 4

Source: Excerpt of testimony by John Hall before the Sadler Committee, 1832

Will you describe to the Committee the position in which the children stand to piece in a worsted mill, as it may serve to explain the number and severity of those cases of distortion which occur?

—At the top to the spindle there is a fly goes across, and the child takes hold of the fly by the ball of his left hand, and he throws the left shoulder up and the right knee inward; he has the thread to get with the right hand, and he has to stoop his head down to see what he is doing; they throw the right knee inward in that way, and all the children I have seen, that bend in the right knee. I knew a family, the whole of whom were bent outwards as a family complaint, and one of those boys was sent to a worsted-mill, and first he became straight in his right knee, and then he became crooked in it the other way.

DOCUMENT 5

Source: Great Britain, excerpt from Parliamentary Papers, *1842*

One of the most disgusting sights I have ever seen was that of young females, dressed like boys in trousers, crawling on all fours, with belts round their waists and chains passing between their legs, at day pits at Hunshelf Bank, and in many small [coal mining] pits near Holmfirth and New Mills: it exists also in several other places. I visited the Hunshelf Colliery on the 18th of January: it is a day pit; that is, there is no shaft or descent; the gate or entrance is at the side of a bank, and nearly horizontal. The gate was not more than a yard high, and in some places not above two feet.

When I arrived at the board or workings of the pit I found at one of the sideboards down a narrow passage a girl of fourteen years of age in boy's clothes, picking down the coal with the regular pick used by the men. She was half sitting half lying at her work, and said she found it tired her very much, and 'of course she didn't like it.' The place where she was at work was not two feet high. Further on were men lying on their sides. No less than six girls out of eighteen men and children are employed in this pit.

DOCUMENT 6

Source: Charles Dickens, excerpt from the novel Hard Times, *1854*

It was a town of red brick, or of brick that would have been red if the smoke and ashes had allowed it; but as matters stood, it was a town of unnatural red and black like the painted face of a savage. It was a town of machinery and tall chimneys, out of which interminable serpents of smoke trailed themselves forever and ever, and never got uncoiled. It had a black canal in it, and a river that ran purple with ill-smelling dye, and vast piles of building full of windows where there was a rattling and a trembling all day long, and where the piston of the steam engine worked monotonously up and down, like the head of an elephant in a state of melancholy madness. It contained several large streets all very like one another, and many small streets still more like one another, inhabited by people equally like one another, who all went in and out at the same hours, with the same sound upon the same pavements, to do the same work, and to whom every day was the same as yesterday and tomorrow, and every year the counterpart of the last and the next.

END OF SECTION II, PART A
IMMEDIATELY BEGIN NEXT SECTION

EUROPEAN HISTORY
SECTION II
Part B
Time—35 minutes

Directions: You are to answer ONE question from the three questions below. Make your selection carefully, choosing the question that you are best prepared to answer thoroughly in the time permitted. You should spend five minutes organizing or outlining your answer. Write your answer on lined notebook pages. *(During the actual examination, you will be given lined answer sheets for this exercise.)*

Write an essay that:

- Has a relevant thesis.
- Addresses all parts of the question.
- Supports a thesis with specific evidence.
- Is well organized.

2. Analyze the effects of World War I on art and literature in Europe.

3. Analyze the shortcomings of the ancien régime, also known as the Old Order, in France and their effects on the French Revolution.

4. Analyze the ways in which the religious changes of the Reformation and Counter-Reformation period influenced European military conflicts during the sixteenth and seventeenth centuries. Cite specific examples from at least TWO countries.

END OF SECTION II, PART B
IMMEDIATELY BEGIN NEXT SECTION

EUROPEAN HISTORY
Section II
Part C
Time—35 minutes

Directions: You are to answer ONE question from the three questions below. Make your selection carefully, choosing the question that you are best prepared to answer thoroughly in the time permitted. You should spend five minutes organizing or outlining your answer. Write your answer on the lined notebook pages. *(During the actual examination, you will be given lined answer sheets for this exercise.)*

Write an essay that:

- Has a relevant thesis.
- Addresses all parts of the question.
- Supports a thesis with specific evidence.
- Is well organized.

5. Considering the period from 1965 to 1990, analyze major events leading to the fall of Communism in ONE of the following nations:

- Poland
- Czechoslovakia
- East Germany

6. Analyze the major stages and figures of the English Civil War, also known as the Puritan Revolt, and show how that conflict exemplified the ideals of the Age of Revolution.

7. Analyze the contributions of Galileo and Sir Isaac Newton to the Scientific Revolution and the development of the scientific method.

END OF EXAM

Practice Exam 2 Answers and Explanations

Section I: Multiple-Choice Questions

ANSWER KEY

1. B		24. E	
2. D		25. D	
3. A		26. D	
4. A		27. C	
5. E		28. A	
6. B		29. C	
7. A		30. B	
8. B		31. A	
9. E		32. A	
10. C		33. A	
11. D		34. C	
12. C		35. A	
13. D		36. B	
14. E		37. C	
15. B		38. E	
16. C		39. B	
17. D		40. B	
18. A		41. D	
19. C		42. C	
20. B		43. A	
21. A		44. D	
22. B		45. C	
23. C		46. B	

47. A	64. E
48. B	65. D
49. C	66. B
50. C	67. E
51. C	68. A
52. E	69. C
53. D	70. D
54. C	71. A
55. C	72. C
56. D	73. C
57. D	74. D
58. B	75. C
59. E	76. B
60. C	77. B
61. E	78. C
62. E	79. D
63. D	80. C

ANSWER EXPLANATIONS

1. **B**. Most of the tax burden in France was faced by the Third Estate, the poorest group of French people. The nobility paid no taxes at all. A is incorrect. The Third Estate was made up mostly of peasants, urban workers, and the bourgeoisie. There was no social equality between it and the other two Estates, which were comprised of clergy and nobility. C is incorrect. The Second Estate, not the Third Estate, controlled the government. D is incorrect. Most members of the Third Estate had a low standard of living. E is incorrect. The Third Estate became increasingly disloyal toward the government because of unemployment, poverty, and wage inequalities.

2. **D.** Wealthy families in northern Italy, such as the Medici, support-ed the arts and hired artists such as Michelangelo and Botticelli, whose works encouraged the development of humanism. A is incorrect. Italy's government was not socialist during the Renaissance. It was organized around city-states, each with its own ruler. B is incorrect. Technological advancements such as the printing press helped ideas to spread quickly and contributed to the Renaissance. C is incorrect. Renaissance ideas such humanism and secularism challenged Church teachings, but did not limit contact with the Church. E is incorrect. Ancient Greek and Roman cultures were emphasized during the Renaissance, not ancient Egyptian.

3. **A.** Newton's three laws of motion, which relate to forces acting on bodies in motion, were based on natural law. B is incorrect. Although Newton's laws described how bodies react in response to gravitational forces, they did not specifically measure how far such objects move. C is incorrect. Newton's most famous equation, $E = mc^2$, was used centuries later in space travel. D is incorrect. Newton's theory had more to do with physics than with chemistry. E is incorrect. Although Newton's laws relied heavily on mathematical calculations, they did not specifi-cally propose a new form of math. Newton later coinvented a new form of math, calculus, to help better understand his laws.

4. **A.** The 1962 Cuban Missile Crisis between the Soviet Union and the United States illustrated that the Cold War was fought through diplo-macy that placed the superpowers on the "brink" of constant war. B is incorrect. The Arab-Israeli War in 1948 was a specific conflict between Israelis and Palestinians. It was not part of the Cold War. C is incorrect. The Iran-Iraq War during the 1980s also was not specifically tied to the Cold War. D is incorrect. The Cultural Revolution in China was tied to the repressive policies of leader Mao Zedong. E is incorrect. Although it had some bearing on the Cold War, the Korean War during the 1950s was also a specific conflict between Communist and Western forces that did not involve brinkmanship.

5. **E.** Luther believed the Church was corrupt and that major reforms

were necessary. His views ultimately formed the basis for the Protestant Reformation. A is incorrect. Luther wrote Ninety-Five Theses in 1517 in direct opposition to the sale of indulgences. B is incorrect. Luther believed the Church should have less power, not more, especially in Germany. C is incorrect. While the arguments in Ninety-Five Theses were strong, Luther did not call for open revolt against Emperor Charles V. D is incorrect. Luther viewed Pope Leo X, who was trying to raise money to renovate St. Peter's Basilica in Rome through the sale of indulgences, as an example of everything that was wrong with the Church.

6. **B**. The goal of mercantilism was to maximize wealth for a nation, using its colonies as support. The colonies were restricted in their ability to trade with other nations, because this would compete with Britain's trade rather than support it. A is incorrect. Britain did not outlaw the slave trade. The slave trade helped the mercantilist system prosper by providing low-cost labor that maximized profits. C is incorrect. The colonies were encouraged to provide raw materials for British manufacturing and to purchase Britain's manufactured products. They were not encouraged to create a manufacturing sector that would compete with Britain's. D is incorrect. Business monopolies were encouraged under mercantilism, not discouraged. Monopolies were intended to protect British businesses from foreign competition. E is incorrect. Although mercantilism did emphasize the maintenance of a British military presence, it did not specifically call for particular taxes.

7. **A**. Henry VIII split from the Catholic Church. He declared himself supreme head of the new Church of England, a Protestant institution, in 1534. B is incorrect. Lutheranism originated in Germany and then spread to other European countries and Scandinavia. It did not reach England. C is incorrect. Until the Reformation, English priests were subject to the rules of the Catholic Church, which saw them as divine beings. They would not have opposed the Pope. D is incorrect. The religious wars in France occurred between 1562 and 1598; England became a Protestant country in 1534. E is incorrect. The concept of humanism was part of

the Renaissance. Although it involved challenging Church beliefs, it did not directly lead to England becoming Protestant.

8.   **B.** Anabaptists believed in a separation of Church and state, which strongly conflicted with Calvinist and Lutheran views. A is incorrect. Anabaptists did not believe in baptizing infants to bring them into the Church; they felt only mature adults could make this decision. C is incorrect. Anabaptists were considered radicals by the Church as they did not support many of its practices. D is incorrect. Although Anabaptists had many differences with other religious reformers, they were not strictly secular. They believed in the power of faith. E is incorrect. Although Anabaptist beliefs may have seemed like superstition to some, they were based on close readings of the Bible.

9.   **E.** The English Bill of Rights, which outlined basic provisions of English constitutional law, was created during the Glorious Revolution in 1689. A is incorrect. During the war, the English Parliament made Cromwell the head of the New Model Army, which defeated the army of Charles I. B is incorrect. Puritans removed all Presbyterians from Parliament following the defeat of Charles I. C is incorrect. The remaining members of Parliament; known as the Rump Parliament, dissolved both the monarchy and the House of Lords in 1649. D is incorrect. Charles I was executed in 1649.

10. **C.** Spain lost much of its land in North America following the French and Indian War in 1763. By helping the colonists, Spain hoped to regain some of the land from the British. A is incorrect. Spain and France were allies, not enemies, during the American Revolution. B is incorrect. Spain did not demand any lands from the American colonies. The colonies did, however, offer to restore to Spain much of the land it had lost during the French and Indian War. D is incorrect. Although Spain fought the British navy and engaged British forces elsewhere, it also fought the British on land in Louisiana and Florida. E is incorrect. Spain provided considerable financial support to the colonies during the American Revolution. It did not receive money in return.

11. **D**. Catholics drove Huguenots out of France following the King's revocation of the Edict of Nantes in 1685. A is incorrect. The policies of King Louis XIV forced many Huguenots to leave France or face religious persecution. B is incorrect. Huguenots were French Protestants, not Catholics. C is incorrect. Thousands of Huguenots left France for England, not Russia. Their watch making skills helped start an industry that improved the economy. E is incorrect. Other places where large numbers of Huguenots settled included Prussia, the Netherlands, and North America. They were hard workers whose skills benefited local economies.

12. **C**. Cooperation and social service were hallmarks of socialist philosophy. Although socialist economies could take on different forms, they shared central principles. A is incorrect. Competition and profit were emphasized by capitalism, not socialism. B is incorrect. Reason and intellect were emphasized by rationalism, not socialism. D is incorrect. Although socialist economies cared about production and distribution, these concepts did not represent the main emphasis of socialism. E is incorrect. Loyalty and duty to the state were hallmarks of nationalism, not socialism. Although some socialist governments used nationalism to maintain state control, the concepts were not inherent to socialist philosophy.

13. **D**. Chinese philosophies were different from those of the early Scientific Revolution. Although the Chinese made great advances in science, they were not interested in using these advances to explain unanswered questions about life. A is incorrect. The early Scientific Revolution relied on data and research to explain natural phenomena. B is incorrect. The main goal of the early Revolution was to challenge the long-standing presumption that Earth was the center of the universe. C is incorrect. The early theories of scientists such as Galileo, who used instruments such as the telescope to make observations of the night sky, were strongly opposed by the Church. E is incorrect. During the early Scientific Revolution, participants sought to improve the condition of humanity and lead it out of ignorance and fear.

14. **E**. During Thermidor, bourgeois moderates staged a coup after the

radical leaders of the Revolution were either imprisoned or executed. The coup marked the end of the Reign of Terror. A is incorrect.
Thermidor was the eleventh month of the new calendar adopted during
the Revolution. The beginning of the Reign of Terror, in September
1793, marked the beginning of this calendar. B is incorrect. France was
not defeated by a European coalition until 1815. C is incorrect. The
French monarchy was not restored until Napoleon was defeated at
Waterloo in 1815. D is incorrect. The *sans-culottes* were greatly weakened by the time of Thermidor and were in no position to govern France.

15. **B.** The occupation of Eastern European countries by Soviet armies
helped the Soviet Union establish supporting governments in those countries. This led to the Cold War. A is incorrect. The Soviet Union was
much stronger than Germany following World War II, as its defeat of
Nazi forces allowed it to set up satellite states in other countries. C is
incorrect. Soviet control in Asia, especially Korea and Vietnam, did not
begin until after 1950. D is incorrect. The United States, not the Soviet
Union, worked to rebuild Japan. E is incorrect. The Soviet Union viewed
the United States as an enemy following the war, because the U.S. wanted
it to release its grip on Eastern Europe. When the Soviet Union refused,
the U.S. formed a coalition of nations opposed to Soviet policies.

16. **C.** The spirit of inquiry and the questioning of traditional beliefs about the universe during the Renaissance led to the Scientific
Revolution. Inventions such as the printing press also helped spread
scientific information. A is incorrect. The Enlightenment followed the
Scientific Revolution in the eighteenth century. B is incorrect. Although
the Protestant Reformation changed the political climate in Europe
during the sixteenth century, it did not directly lead to the start of the
Scientific Revolution. D is incorrect. The Catholic Reformation was a response to the Protestant Reformation and not connected to the Scientific
Revolution. E is incorrect. The Industrial Revolution also occurred after
the start of the Scientific Revolution in the eighteenth century.

17. **D.** Both scientists used the scientific method to carry out experiments

based on hypotheses they developed. A is incorrect. Much of medieval tradition was based on the concept of faith over reason, while both Galileo and Newton stressed reason over faith in their work. B is incorrect. Although both scientists were influenced by the ideas of classical philosophers, they most likely would not have favored new science based on classical concepts. Their goal was to use classical thought as a starting point for new discoveries. C is incorrect. Although both scientists were religious, they sought to disprove Church teachings about the nature of the universe. E is incorrect. Reliance on instinct and emotion would not have been favored by the pair in regard to scientific thought.

18. **A.** During the Scientific Revolution, the application of human reason changed the way people thought about the universe. Enlightenment philosophers used human reasoning to change thinking about government and society. B is incorrect. Enlightenment philosophers did not give up their religious beliefs because of the Scientific Revolution. Instead, they focused on concepts of government that were separate from the Church. C is incorrect. Although aware of past civilizations, Enlightenment philosophers did not study them in depth. Instead, they replaced Plato and Aristotle's views on natural law and the nature of man with their own. D is incorrect. Enlightenment philosophers supported experimentation and proposed new experiments about what government should be. E is incorrect. Enlightenment philosophers favored individuality, because they believed most people were reasonable and moral. Social order imposed by a restrictive government imposed on people's natural rights.

19. **C.** The rebellion was the first time a European colony successfully asserted its right to independence and statehood. A is incorrect. Federalism, or a division of government powers among common institutions, was an American invention not found in Europe. B is incorrect. France and Spain supported the Revolution. Along with other European countries, they had already begun to oppose the expanding power and scope of the British. D is incorrect. The Revolution strengthened the position of leaders who questioned the traditional order by promoting

a philosophy of individual rights before the government. E is incorrect. Some Europeans favored Hamilton's vision, which was based on federalism and a strong central government, while others preferred Jefferson's view, which was anti-federalist and centered on power in the states.

20. **B.** Enlightenment ideas helped stimulate a sense of individualism and a basic belief in equal rights. This eventually led to both the American and French Revolutions. A is incorrect. Enlightened despots, such as Catherine the Great, tried unsuccessfully to enact reforms while retaining absolute control. C is incorrect. The Scientific Revolution occurred before the Enlightenment. D is incorrect. Nationalism, or strong feelings for a person's native country, did fuel revolutions inspired by the Enlightenment. However, concepts such as natural rights and the separation of powers had to do with governments in general, not specific governments or countries. E is incorrect. The Industrial Revolution occurred after the Enlightenment.

21. **A.** Both the Scientific Revolution and the Enlightenment found reason to have a practical role in human society. B is incorrect. Neither movement spread to China or Asia. C is incorrect. Although both movements looked forward, they were influenced by classical Greek thought. D is incorrect. Neither movement supported the Church's view of the universe, which relied on faith over reason. E is incorrect. The Enlightenment focused on many spiritual and philosophical issues, while the Scientific Revolution focused on scientific experimentation and invention.

22. **B.** Predestination was John Calvin's belief that God chose the people who would receive salvation; this was not based on natural laws. A is incorrect. Deism was based on the concept that God had left the world to operate according to natural laws. C is incorrect. The social contract theory of Locke and Rousseau involved the preservation of natural rights. D is incorrect. Laissez-faire economics were based on natural laws of supply and demand. E is incorrect. Newton's theories of gravity and motion were based on the natural laws of the universe.

23. **C.** The microscope was invented by Anton Van Leeuwenhoek in the mid-1600s. It allowed scientists to see and describe disease-causing bacteria for the first time. B is incorrect. The thermometer was invented in 1612 and allowed for more accurate temperature readings in chemical and medical studies. It did not specifically alter the understanding of disease. A is incorrect. Galileo's telescope allowed for better viewing of the moon and the planets, but did not affect the study of diseases. D is incorrect. The barometer, invented in Italy in the early 1600s, was used to measure air pressure. E is incorrect. The marine chronometer, invented in 1761, was used to precisely measure time.

24. **E.** Peter built the new capital city of St. Petersburg in western Russia, hoping it would serve as a gateway to Europe. A, B, and C are incorrect; Peter the Great encouraged European influence in Russia. He wanted to make it fashionable for people to speak French, wear Western clothing, and educate their children in Europe. D is incorrect. Peter did not extend Russian influence into Europe. Rather, he sought to increase European influence in Russia.

25. **D.** Enlightenment philosophers argued that government's power was derived from those they served. This idea became implicit in social contract theory. A is incorrect. Enlightenment philosophers opposed the idea that God granted rulers political power. B is incorrect. While many Enlightenment philosophers believed in the theoretical right to revolution, none called for it. C is incorrect. The importance of laissez-faire economics was emphasized during the Enlightenment, but it was not part of the argument philosophers made against the Divine Right of Kings. E is incorrect.

26. **D.** The storming of the Bastille showed the members of the newly created Assembly that French crowds could be used to threaten violence if its demands were not met. A is incorrect. Despite its reputation, the Bastille did not contain many weapons. B is incorrect. Although the storming of the Bastille by a crowd of approximately 80,000 people was surprisingly violent, it continued, as opposed to changing, the direction

of the radicals. C is incorrect. Despite the Bastille's fortress-like appearance, it did not enclose many prisoners. E is incorrect. The storming of the Bastille did not signify additional loss of faith in the king. People had already lost faith.

27. **C.** The Warsaw Pact was formed by the Soviet Union and seven of its satellite countries as a response to NATO. The Warsaw Pact was a defensive military alliance. A is incorrect. The Soviet Union was not interested in transitioning to democracy in 1955. Instead, it tightened its grip on its European satellite countries. B is incorrect. The Soviet government used propaganda to attack capitalism during the 1950s. D is incorrect. The Common Market, based in Western Europe, attempted to unify the region economically and politically. It was not created until 1957. E is incorrect. The Warsaw Pact increased Cold War tensions instead of limiting them.

28. **A.** Humanism was a concept popularized by Shakespeare and other artists during the Renaissance. It stated that the Church should be involved only in spiritual (rather than secular) matters. Europeans needed to determine their own moral and ethical beliefs without influence from the Church. B is incorrect. Salvation was a religious concept that involved saving people from damnation by encouraging them to live a moral life based on Church beliefs. C is incorrect. Although humanism is a kind of philosophy, the term "philosophy" is too general to relate specifically to the quote. D is incorrect. Logic/reasoning was also part of Renaissance beliefs, especially in regards to science. However, it does not relate to the quote. E is incorrect. Predestination was the belief that God chose the people who would be saved. It was popularized by John Calvin, not Shakespeare.

29. **C.** Hobbes felt that government's purpose was to control man's natural impulses. People entered into a social contract in order to exchange their freedom for the safety of organized society. Therefore, he supported absolute monarchy. A is incorrect. Rousseau believed government should be based on the will of the majority, not as an absolute monarchy. B is

incorrect. Locke thought that all people had natural rights to life, liberty, and property, and that it was government's role to protect these rights. D is incorrect. Montesquieu believed in a government divided along the lines of its judicial, legislative, and executive powers. E is incorrect. Descartes believed human reason was capable of discovering and explaining the laws of nature and man and supported revolutionary ideals.

30. **B.** Heliocentric theory proposed that Earth revolved around the sun rather than vice versa. This theory was threatening to the Church and resulted in a major dispute. A is incorrect. The Church did not revise its calendar based on the findings of Copernicus, even though his work challenged how they kept track of time. C is incorrect. Although heliocentric theory began the long process of explaining gravitational forces and their effects on tides, it was not advanced enough to predict tides. D is incorrect. Heliocentric theory did not affect the number of pagan religions, as it was widely discounted by almost everyone. E is incorrect. Reliance on observation and experimentation came much later in the Scientific Revolution under Galileo and Newton. Under Copernicus, both were challenged.

31. **A.** Before the Agricultural Revolution, farmers planted seeds by carrying them in bags and walking through fields. This method was inefficient and wasteful. The invention of the seed drill, a wheeled cart that could be pulled behind a horse, allowed for a more even distribution of grain, resulting in a larger crop. B is incorrect. Increases in factory production occurred during the Industrial Revolution but were not part of the Agricultural Revolution. C is incorrect. Farm subsidies, or government payments to farmers, did not occur during the Agricultural Revolution. D is incorrect. Although more land was cleared for farming, new techniques were not used to clear the land. Trees were simply cut down. E is incorrect. The planting of new crops such as wheat did not result in an increase in grain prices. The additional crops kept prices low.

32. **A.** Galileo used the scientific method, which relied on experimentation and observation, to prove his theories. B is incorrect. Laissez-faire

was a seventeenth-century economic theory, not a scientific one. C is incorrect. Social contract theory was a seventeenth-century philosophical idea pioneered by philosophers such as John Locke. D is incorrect. Natural law was concerned with the laws of nature as well as the social and philosophical implications of those laws. Galileo sought to uncover them through his use of the scientific method, but did not use natural law itself as a "tool" in his work. E is incorrect. Although Galileo conducted many experiments involving gravitational forces, a complete theory of gravity did not emerge until later in the Scientific Revolution.

33. **A.** The three-field farming system was not part of the Agricultural Revolution. It dated back to the Middle Ages and involved the use of nearly all land for crops. It left little room for cattle to produce fertilizer. B is incorrect. The four-field system expanded the amount of available farmland by using clover and turnips to create a "fourth field" from previously unusable land. Both plants helped to maintain the soil's fertility. C is incorrect. The Enclosure Movement involved wealthy landowners. They enclosed large tracts of common land during the Revolution so they could practice the four-field system. D is incorrect. Turnips became an important crop during the Revolution. Higher yields of turnips meant that more land was being made suitable for farming. E is incorrect. Farmers introduced nitrogen as a fertilizer during the Revolution.

34. **C.** Wealthy landowners drove people off common lands through the Enclosure Movement. This forced people to the cities in search of homes and jobs. Additionally, increases in food production led to population growth, which created a workforce for the Industrial Revolution. A is incorrect. The Glorious Revolution occurred in 1688 and 1689, before the Agricultural Revolution. B is incorrect. While discoveries made during the Scientific Revolution led to agricultural improvements, these occurred before the Agricultural Revolution. D is incorrect. Although the American Revolution took place during a similar time frame, it occurred in North America, not Europe. It was not directly affected by the Agricultural Revolution. E is incorrect. The French Revolution was

caused by political struggles in France, including food shortages and ineffective leadership. It was not directly tied to the Agricultural Revolution.

35. **A.** While Napoleon was fighting abroad, the Executive Directory, a five-member Executive Committee that ran the government, was weakened by economic disaster, corruption, and political enemies. When Napoleon returned, he was viewed as a strong leader who could provide a centralized government. B is incorrect. Foreign governments did not endorse Napoleon; his military actions against England, Italy, Austria, and Egypt had earned him many enemies. C is incorrect. Napoleon was supported by the French bourgeoisie, not the French aristocracy. The bourgeoisie were opposed to the aristocracy. D is incorrect. Napoleon expressed support for the democratic ideals of the French Revolution and the interests of the bourgeoisie after he became France's leader, not before. E is incorrect. When Napoleon became Emperor in 1804, King Louis XVI had already been dead for 11 years.

36. **B.** The creation of the printing press and advances in movable type resulted in the availability of books and documents to spread Reformation ideas. A is incorrect. The Protestant Reformation weakened the Church in both religious and political matters. C is incorrect. The Scientific Revolution formed the basis for the Enlightenment, which involved applying reason to improve society. D is incorrect. The Reformation improved the status of women by emphasizing the importance of love within marriage and women's rights. E is incorrect. Jesuits spread Catholicism, not Protestantism, to the Western Hemisphere.

37. **C.** The Directory was primarily composed of moderates from the bourgeoisie. It turned to the military for protection from threats by radical Jacobins and conservative Royalists. A is incorrect. The Executive Directory, which ruled following the Revolution from 1795 until 1799, was not affiliated with the *sans-culottes*. B is incorrect. The Directory was not supported by the nobility. D is incorrect. The Directory was not afraid of elections because the new constitution limited voting rights to the propertied classes, who supported the Directory. E is incorrect.

Although the Directory was eventually overthrown by Napoleon in 1799, it had already been supporting the military for several years.

38. **E.** The Great Fear was a peasant uprising during the summer of 1789. Peasants protested high bread prices and burned records of taxes they could not afford to pay. A is incorrect. During the summer of 1789, the Great Fear was an uprising that took place in rural France, not the urban areas. B is incorrect. The Great Fear was an internal uprising within France and did not affect its foreign relations. C is incorrect. Although the uprising increased pressure on the National Assembly, more pressure was placed on the king, the Church, and the nobility. D is incorrect. The French nobility's inability to deal with the financial crisis weakened its authority.

39. **B.** Gutenberg was a German printer who invented the printing press in 1450. This invention was critical as it led to literacy via the widespread availability of books. A is incorrect. The bicycle was not invented until well after the Renaissance, sometime in the 1860s. C is incorrect. Telescopic lenses were invented in the late 1500s and were popularized by Galileo. D is incorrect. The first illustrations for a submarine were created during the Renaissance, but not by Gutenberg. They were drawn by Leonardo da Vinci. E is incorrect. The pocket watch was invented by Peter Henlein in 1510.

40. **B.** The Civil Constitution was passed in 1789 and required clergy to swear an oath of loyalty to the state, which their faith prohibited them from doing. The action alienated many Catholics, who sided with their priests. A is incorrect. Although the Civil Constitution of the Clergy, in theory, made government employees of the clergy, it caused conflict and alienation. C is incorrect. The Civil Constitution angered most Catholics and created hostility toward the Assembly. D is incorrect. The Civil Constitution sought to weaken the Church and make it less central to the government of France. E is incorrect. It would have been nearly impossible for the Civil Constitution to outlaw Catholicism as it remained the dominant religion in France.

41. **D.** The execution of the King Louis XVI was a result rather than a cause of the revolution. A is incorrect. The rise of the *sans-culottes* ("common people") led to more radical measures during the French Revolution as they sought an economically fair society. B is incorrect. The escape of the king eroded the people's confidence in him and forced them to consider a more radical path. C is incorrect. The development of factions within the Assembly meant that each faction had to compete for support from the crowds and therefore be more willing to listen to demands. E is incorrect. The war with Austria and Prussia in 1792 created an air of crisis in France which made bolder action seem necessary.

42. **C.** The Church retained a much stronger influence during the Northern Renaissance. Paintings by Spanish artists such as El Greco reflected strong religious themes. A is incorrect. Satire during the Northern Renaissance was aimed at targets such as the Church and nobility, not ancient cultures. B is incorrect. Monarchies in northern Europe gained power during the Renaissance; the increase eventually led to nationalism, not a democratic government. D is incorrect. Books by authors such as Thomas More promoted the study of the natural world undertaken by the Greeks and Romans in order to stave off superstition and fear. E is incorrect. New forms of math were not created during the Northern Renaissance, although some artists emphasized math in attempt to create perfectly symmetrical figures in their art.

43. **A.** The Reign of Terror involved the arrest and execution of thousands of people following the French Revolution. Leaders of the French Revolution argued that the Reign of Terror was necessary to eliminate the enemies of the Revolution and create a democratic republic. B is incorrect. The Reign of Terror was supported by crowds in large cities such as Paris. C is incorrect. The Reign of Terror was aimed at large swaths of the French population, including both commoners and the nobility. During this period, anyone could be accused of being an enemy of the Revolution and imprisoned or executed. D is incorrect. Targets

of the Reign of Terror included the clergy. E is incorrect. The Reign of Terror mostly took place in cities as opposed to rural areas.

44. **D.** The Congress of Vienna (1814–1815) ended the Napoleonic wars and adjusted the borders of various European states. A is incorrect. The Peace of Utrecht ended the War of Spanish Succession between England and France. B is incorrect. The Congress of Berlin revised the conditions Russia forced on the former Ottoman Empire at the end of the Russo-Turkish wars. C is incorrect. The Peace of Westphalia ended the Holy Roman Empire and introduced the modern European state system. E is incorrect. The Treaty of Paris was signed in 1778 between the American colonies and France. It formed an alliance against Great Britain.

45. **C.** The Dutch Republic traded all over the world. The government-sponsored Dutch East India Company was formed for trading in Asia. Many Dutch merchants settled and also traded in South Africa, as well as throughout North America and the Caribbean. A is incorrect. The Dutch Republic was not centrally governed during the seventeenth century. B is incorrect. The Dutch Republic was an economic powerhouse. It had tremendous power based on its shipping and trade. D is incorrect. The Dutch Republic was known for its religious tolerance. Many Europeans escaped religious persecution in their home countries by moving there. E is incorrect. The Dutch Republic's largest city, Amsterdam, became a world center for banking during the seventeenth century. Many Dutch philosophers favored free trade.

46. **B.** The idea that only colonial representatives could levy taxes gave rise to the call for "no taxation without representation." The taxing of colonists by English Parliament became a key factor in the American Revolution. A is incorrect. American colonists were opposed to the idea of either the king or the British Parliament influencing their makeup. They showed this most strongly in their stand against the creation of taxes. C and D are incorrect. Colonists were only opposed to "taxation without representation," or taxation by a body in which they had no

elected representative. E is incorrect. The statement does not address the colonists' general attitude toward Parliament and the king.

47. **A.** Although the French Revolution increased women's rights somewhat until the rise of Napoleon, no political rights were gained by women during the American Revolution. B is incorrect. The French Revolution was a revolt against taxes levied against the Third Estate, while the American Revolution was a protest against taxes levied by the British Parliament. C is incorrect. The French Revolution was fueled by a lack of representation of members of the Third Estate, while the American Revolution was motivated by issues of taxation without representation. D is incorrect. Both the American Declaration of Independence and the French Declaration of the Rights of Man and of the Citizen favored natural rights. E is incorrect. Both Revolutions were based on Enlightenment ideas favored by Locke and Rousseau.

48. **B.** The Anglican Church was weakened in Europe since its presence in America could not be sustained (the official head of the Anglican Church was the British king). A is incorrect. European use of slaves continued for over 100 years following the American Revolution. C is incorrect. The Reign of Terror followed the French Revolution, not the American Revolution. D is incorrect. The Glorious Revolution occurred in 1688 and 1689, well before the American Revolution. E is incorrect. The Enlightenment occurred before the America Revolution, influencing its beginning as opposed to its end.

49. **C.** The Thirty Years' War was fought among Catholics, Lutherans, and Calvinists over issues of religious freedom and became known as a war of religion. A is incorrect. Although the war was fought over issues of political and religious power, it was not defined as a war of power. The lack of separation between church and state made the concept of "power" secondary to "religion." B is incorrect. The war did not involve economic issues, so it cannot be termed a war of economy. D is incorrect. The war did not involve commerce or trade issues, so it cannot be termed a war of commerce. E is incorrect. Although the treaty that

ended the war implemented changes to religious practices, the war itself was never called a war of reform.

50. C. The British did not have as a strong commitment to the conflict as the American colonists. The conflict was expensive and far from home. Many in Britain questioned its necessity, and American sympathizers existed in Parliament. A is incorrect. The British military was a dominant and powerful fighting force. It had already defeated France in North America and helped Great Britain emerge as a major world power. B is incorrect. Most Native American tribes supported the British, who promised to protect their tribal lands. D is incorrect. British military commanders were far more experienced than American commanders, having fought many battles against what they considered superior opponents in Spain and France. E is incorrect. Britain's wealth far exceeded that of the American colonies.

51. C. Although gunpowder became more widely used during the sixteenth and seventeenth centuries, its origins date back to China around 850 A.D. A is incorrect. Planetary motion was discovered by Johannes Kepler during the Scientific Revolution. B is incorrect. The heliocentric model was proposed by Copernicus during the Scientific Revolution. D is incorrect. The circulatory system was first described in detail by English anatomist William Harvey during the Scientific Revolution. E is incorrect. The social contract, which proposed an unwritten agreement between people and their rulers, was proposed by philosopher John Locke during the Enlightenment.

52. E. The Second Continental Congress met in 1775, before the start of the Revolution. A is incorrect. The Treaty of Paris officially recognized the United States of America. B is incorrect. The treaty also set new U.S. borders, including all land from the Great Lakes to Florida and from the Atlantic Ocean to the Mississippi River. The borders were significant because they allowed for western expansion. C is incorrect. The treaty stipulated that the United States would pay all existing debts owed to Britain. D is incorrect. The treaty recognized American fishing

rights along banks of Newfoundland, which was important to the New England states.

53. **D.** English conservatives in the late nineteenth century believed in the power of laissez-faire capitalism, or the reduction of government control over economic development. A is incorrect. Liberalism, not conservatism, was centered on the reduction of oppression. It sought to "liberate" mankind from oppressive government and religious and economic institutions. B is incorrect. Conservatism during the late nineteenth century was skeptical about government change, since it believed in the power of proven institutions. C is incorrect. Nationalism, not conservatism, promoted a strong sense of national identity. E is incorrect. As a counterpoint to Marxism, conservatism supported the idea that God oversaw the welfare of the state.

54. **C.** Germany's invasion of Poland in 1939, which followed its invasion of Czechoslovakia, brought declarations of war from France and England. These declarations are considered the start of World War II. A is incorrect. Although Germany wanted to annex the Sudetenland, an area in Czechoslovakia inhabited by German-speaking people, that desire alone was not enough to start the war. B is incorrect. Japan's bombing of Pearl Harbor in 1941 brought the United States into the war, which had begun in Europe in 1939. D is incorrect. Germany's bombing of London, the *blitzkrieg,* happened during the war; it did not start the war. E is incorrect. Although Italy formed an alliance with Germany and Japan, the creation of this alliance did not start the war.

55. **C.** The Austro-Hungarian Empire included many Muslims from Hungary, who arrived after being freed from the Ottoman Empire. A is incorrect. The Austro-Hungarian Empire was not stable following the Thirty Years' War, unlike Prussia. B is incorrect. The Empire's military was weak and often disorganized because of the diversity of its population. D and E are incorrect. The Empire was quite diverse and made up of people of different nationalities, cultural, political, and religious groups.

56. **D.** Although the English Whigs and Tories disagreed at one point, the

groups were united by their desire to prevent the Catholic James II from succeeding to the throne. Once he was on the throne, they united against Britain's reversion to Catholicism. A is incorrect. The English Parliament invited the Dutch Republic's William III and his wife Mary, who was King James II's Protestant daughter, to England. William brought his army with him. They were crowned as leaders in exchange for adhering to an English Bill of Rights. B is incorrect. Parliament gained power over taxation, royal succession, and other issues via the Bill of Rights, which was created in 1689. C is incorrect. Seven leading Anglican bishops were arrested and imprisoned in the Tower of London in 1688 for refusing to follow the king's orders. E is incorrect. The invitation by Parliament to William III technically constituted a foreign invasion, since he was from another European power, the Dutch Republic.

57. **D.** Shakespeare's use of language, with its memorable descriptions and turns of phrase, helped audiences to understand human experience in new ways. A is incorrect. Although Shakespeare wrote poetry and drama, other Renaissance writers, such as Christopher Marlowe, did as well. B is incorrect. Shakespeare's works often summarized the range of human emotions, but his works were not specifically about them. C is incorrect. Shakespeare often referred to history and philosophy, but they were not his main subjects. E is incorrect. Shakespeare's main focus was on literature, while da Vinci's main focus was on art, science, and math.

58. **B.** Despite the defeat of the British during the American Revolution, early nineteenth-century liberal thinkers turned to British philosophers, such as John Locke, in developing their movement. A is incorrect. Romanticism, not liberalism, was based on artistic traditions that went all the way back to Shakespeare. C and D are incorrect. Liberalism was centered on the reduction of oppression and sought to limit government. E is incorrect. Liberalism strongly supported a belief in natural rights.

59. **E.** Thinkers during both the Italian Renaissance and the Protestant Reformation refused to accept Church teachings. Instead, they sought answers based on their own observations and interpretations of the

world. A is incorrect. Both the Italian Renaissance and the Protestant Reformation challenged religious teachings. B is incorrect. The Protestant Reformation questioned the Church's political authority, but the Italian Renaissance did not. It focused more on humanism and the promotion of a secular way of life. C is incorrect. The Italian Renaissance covered a relatively small geographical area in Europe, while the Protestant Reformation spread quickly throughout Europe and eventually into Scandinavia. D is incorrect. The Renaissance was associated with new forms of art and creativity, while the Reformation was more of a political and religious movement.

60. **C.** The Industrial Revolution grew out of numerous technological advances that increased production, allowing greater quantities of goods to be produced at lower cost and dividing the production of goods among larger numbers of workers. These advances included the steam engine, water-powered spinning wheels, and automated textile looms. A is incorrect. Urban poverty, specifically poverty among children, was an effect of the Industrial Revolution, not a cause. B is incorrect. Cottage industries were part of the Industrial Revolution, not a failed system preceding it. Cottage industries were precursors to the modern factory system, dividing production among many different workers and allowing larger quantities of goods to be produced at a lower cost. D is incorrect. Although the Industrial Revolution produced more goods, foreign trade was strong beforehand. E is incorrect. The Industrial Revolution began in England and then spread to other European countries.

61. **E.** Nationalism was a strong unifying and dividing force during the nineteenth century. It brought Germany and Italy together, but divided Russia and Austria. A is incorrect. Nationalism did not increase tolerance; rather, it tended to support a lack of tolerance against other ethnic and cultural groups. B is incorrect. Nationalism tended to create rather than ease tensions. C is incorrect. Nationalism brought some European countries, like Italy and Germany, together. D is incorrect. Nationalism did not increase support for royal rule.

62. **E.** The population reached 16.6 million by 1850 and required more food. Changes in farming systems were necessary to feed the growing population. A is incorrect. Increased land ownership was an effect of the Agricultural Revolution, not the cause. A rising middle class bought up much of the new farmland in England in their ambitious quest for secure investments and noble titles. B is incorrect. Increased worker productivity was another effect of the Revolution. Farmers became more efficient because they had better tools and processes through which to grow and harvest their crops. C is incorrect. Farmers continually looked for new ways to grow crops. No particular crops failed. D is incorrect.

63. **D.** Socialism was a political movement that stressed civic cooperation and social service. It was not connected to imperialism. A is incorrect. Nationalism, or a strong sense of identification with one's country of origin, often led to imperialism. B is incorrect. Militarism, or the maintenance of a large national military, also led to imperialism. C is incorrect. Industrialization created a need for raw materials and markets, some of which were taken by force. E is incorrect. Colonialism, or the domination of one nation by another, occurred a great deal in the late nineteenth century and was connected to imperialism.

64. **E.** Belgium's main imperial interest during the nineteenth century was the Congo in Africa. A is incorrect. The British imperial presence in India originated in the eighteenth century and continued until 1947. B is incorrect. Germany had many imperial interests in Africa, including the Cameroons and New Guinea. C is incorrect. Dutch imperialists took control of South Africa and began to call themselves Afrikaners. British settlers followed. D is incorrect. France also had many imperial interests in North Africa, including Algeria and Tunisia.

65. **D.** As each agricultural worker produced more food thanks to change in farming systems, the proportion of the workers in agriculture fell. This created a workforce for the Industrial Revolution. A is incorrect. Family farms became less important over time. B is incorrect. Farms became larger, not smaller. C is incorrect. People did not leave cities

in large numbers to go into farming. E is incorrect. Although factories were created to increase production of goods following the Agricultural Revolution, they did not mass-produce food.

66. **B.** The abolitionist movement in South Africa, which called for the freeing of slaves, did not help imperialist causes. It created conflict between the Dutch Boers and British settlers. A is incorrect. New treatments for diseases such as malaria helped maintain imperialistic presences in Africa. C is incorrect. The invention of the steam engine allowed Europeans to navigate rivers and travel deeper into the interior of other continents. D is incorrect. Improved weaponry such as guns gave Europeans power over developing societies. E is incorrect. The creation of plantations fueled imperialist interests by allowing them to use native peoples as suppliers of raw materials.

67. **E.** The Peace of Westphalia, signed in 1648, ended the Thirty Years' War. It also marked the end of the Holy Roman Empire. A is incorrect. The Peace of Prague, signed in 1635, was an earlier but unsuccessful attempt to end religious wars. B is incorrect. The Treaty of London was signed between England and Spain in 1604. C is incorrect. The Peace of Augsburg was signed in Germany in 1555 as a temporary settlement between German princes and the Holy Roman Empire over issues stemming from the Reformation. D is incorrect. The Treaty of Edinburgh was signed in 1560 between France and Scotland. It allowed Scotland to become a Protestant country.

68. **A.** Realpolitik, or politics based on practical rather than ideological considerations, was used by Chancellor Otto von Bismarck to unify Germany. B is incorrect. Socialism was primarily an economic philosophy in the nineteenth century; it was not used to unify countries. C is incorrect. Liberalism tended to be a divisive rather than unifying force, as it was used to "liberate" people from oppressive government control. D is incorrect. Although Marxism originated in Germany in the nineteenth century, it was not used to unify the country. E is incorrect. Conservatism developed as a response to liberalism. It was not connected to Germany or realpolitik.

69. **C.** The rigid class system in Russia allowed nobles, priests, and the tsar to live well, while peasants faced poor working conditions, poverty, and food shortages. A is incorrect. Although Russia defeated Germany in a series of battles during World War I, they were not connected to the Russian Revolution. B is incorrect. The marriage of Nicholas to the German princess Alexandra in 1914 was connected to the end of World War I, not the Russian Revolution. D is incorrect. Marxism did not appeal to Russian nobility, since it called for the creation of a classless society. E is incorrect. Russia's defeat in the Crimean War occurred in the mid-1800s, well before the Revolution.

70. **D.** The class system in Russia allowed nobles, priests, and the tsar to live well, while the peasants faced poor working conditions, poverty, and food shortages. A is incorrect. The Bolsheviks outlawed trade, a condition that led to a wide-scale famine in 1921. B is incorrect. Bolsheviks surrendered much agricultural land to Germany at the end of World War I, making it nearly impossible to maintain the system. C is incorrect. The Bolsheviks got rid of money following the Revolution. E is incorrect. The Bolsheviks did not believe in religion and did not support the Church.

71. **A.** The killing of the Austrian-Hungarian Archduke Ferdinand in 1914 was widely seen as the act that led directly to World War I. B is incorrect. Nicholas II, the last Russian tsar, was not assassinated. He left the throne in 1917 during the Russian Revolution. C is incorrect. Bismarck, the Chancellor of Germany, served as German during the mid-1800s, well before the start of World War I. D is incorrect. Emperor Franz Joseph of Austria was not assassinated; he died in 1916. E is incorrect. Although Rasputin was shot in 1916, his death was not connected.

72. **C.** The African and Indian colonies of European nations such as Germany and England took part in World War I, hoping to be granted independence. A is incorrect. World War I was not fought on every continent; no battles were fought in Australia or South America. B is incorrect. World War II, not World War I, was fought in the Pacific as well as

in Europe. D is incorrect. Although the war started in Europe, this does not explain its global status. The war became much bigger than Europe itself. E is incorrect. The war involved many interests besides Europe and the United States.

73. **C.** England experienced little unemployment during World War I, as much of a newly created working class gained status and power. A is incorrect. Poverty rates decreased as England put almost everyone to work as part of the war effort. B is incorrect. Unemployment rates decreased rather than increased. D is incorrect. The status of women rose a great deal during World War I, as they went to work and made money. E is incorrect. Many people stayed in England during World War I, although they left other European countries, such as Italy.

74. **D.** The purchase of raw materials from the colonies was a cornerstone of British mercantilism. The materials supported British manufacturing, increasing the nation's wealth. A is incorrect. Colonial industries were not supported by mercantilism. Instead, the colonies supported British industries by providing raw materials and purchasing finished products. B is incorrect. Fishing and fur trading were not prohibited in the colonies. They were lucrative trades that relied on expansion. C is incorrect. A goal of British mercantilism was to create large reserves of gold, silver, and other precious metals in the colonies, not to remove them. This was seen as a way to create wealth for the nation. E is incorrect. Raw materials were purchased from the colonies rather than finished products. The colonies purchased finished products from Britain.

75. **C.** The tax exempt status of the nobility and the clergy prevented the French government from accessing the majority of wealth in the French economy and, therefore, from solving its financial problems. A is incorrect. Although Louis XVI's lifestyle was a drain on government resources, there was sufficient wealth in France to cover its national debt. B is incorrect. The various classes in the Third Estate, which included almost half the people in France, were already taxed beyond what they could bear. D is incorrect. Although France's foreign wars

also affected its finances, there was sufficient money in the economy to pay for them. E is incorrect. The French economy was not in bad shape before the Revolution. The government simply needed more tax revenue to deal with its financial problems.

76. **B.** Nationalist movements gathered strength during the period between the two wars, specifically in Germany, Italy, and Japan. A is incorrect. The League of Nations was weak and indecisive in the period between World Wars I and II. Although its creation was supposed to guarantee that war never broke out again, its actions had the opposite effect. C is incorrect. The United Nations was not created until the end of World War II in 1945. It took the place of the League of Nations. D is incorrect. Spain did not participate in World War II because it was involved in its own civil war. E is incorrect. The Ottoman Empire was destroyed at the end of World War I and had no effect on World War II.

77. **B.** Calvin used his book to defend French Protestants from attacks by the French king, who was persecuting them. Additionally, he wanted to explain how Protestantism could improve Christianity. A is incorrect. Calvin did argue against the Church reforms devised at the Council of Trent in 1547, which persecuted Protestants, but he did not do it in *Institutes of the Christian Religion*, which was published in 1536. C is incorrect. Calvin was not interested in creating dialogue with the Church; he broke away from it in 1536. D is incorrect. Calvin originally trained as a humanist lawyer, so he did not reject humanism. E is incorrect. Although Calvin had strong beliefs, he never called for civil war.

78. **C.** France became unstable during the Revolution and faced threats from other countries in Europe. Following Napoleon's successful campaign in Italy, people became convinced that he was a great leader and looked to him to end the country's political chaos. A is incorrect. France was a Catholic country, not a Protestant one, and largely rejected the ideas of the Protestant Reformation. B is incorrect. King Louis XVI had already been executed by the Napoleon and became a national hero in

France. D is incorrect. Great Britain was one of many enemies faced by France during the time of the Revolution, but it did not control France. E is incorrect. Napoleon was recognized as a military genius and strategist who did not need to modern the French armed forces. They were already quite advanced.

79. **D.** Rousseau is widely considered one of the chief architects of the Romantic tradition. His writings emphasized the essential goodness of humanity, the need for individual freedom, a mistrust of social institutions, and a desire for a simple life in harmony with nature. A is incorrect. Nineteenth-century liberalism emphasized the concept of "liberating" people from oppressive governments by explaining their natural rights separate from the government. It was John Locke who best expressed the principles of liberalism. B is incorrect. Socialism was primarily an economic philosophy, emphasizing cooperative ownership and management of the means of production. Socialism was represented in the work of such writers as Karl Marx. C is incorrect. Nineteenth-century conservatism was a political philosophy that tended to promote respect for authority and tradition. An excess of individualism was viewed as a threat to the moral and social order. In contrast, Rousseau's writings emphasized the nobility of the individual while criticizing loyalty to established institutions. E is incorrect. Marxism was an economic and political philosophy that promoted the idea of a classless society. It influenced the creation of socialism, not Romanticism.

80. **C.** Before the French Revolution, the bourgeoisie had the highest tax burden and virtually no rights. Following the Revolution, the bourgeoisie gained significant political power via the new constitution for France. A is incorrect. France did not enjoy peace following the French Revolution. Instead, France descended into chaos and became involved in many other conflicts, including the American Revolution. B is incorrect. The French government did not restore the Church to its former position of power following the Revolution. Instead, democratic reforms were introduced. D is incorrect. French nationalism became stronger

following the Revolution, not weaker. Nationalistic movements also surged across Europe. E is incorrect. King Louis XVI was executed following the French Revolution in 1793.

Section II, Part A
SAMPLE ESSAY

1. A good response may begin with a discussion of industrialization as a driving force for change in England in the eighteenth and nineteenth centuries.

> While Document 1 offers a theoretical basis for this change in the eighteenth century, Document 2 presents a practical effect. Documents 3–6 present more dramatic effects associated with changes in the nineteenth century, but also present problems caused by the economic policies of the British government. These policies encouraged business owners to exploit workers for their own benefit.
>
> By 1750, trade was already strong in England, as was the demand for more goods. English merchants began to accumulate money and assets (capital) to invest in new technological innovations, such as the steam engine. Combined with new methods of production, such as the factory, goods could be created cheaply and efficiently. Smith's book focused on how the British government could support these innovations and help the country increase its wealth by adopting certain policies. He argued that laissez-faire ideas, which essentially resulted in the government letting businesses run without interference, would result in businesses being regulated by the forces of supply and demand, making regulatory laws unnecessary. However, Smith also recognized that the primary goal of business was to make money (Document 1). The lack of regulation meant that businesses could put their primary goal first without acknowledging the human or social consequences.

The first consequence in the eighteenth century was the loss of well-paying manufacturing jobs. Skilled workers in Leeds were replaced by machines that "could do the work of ten men" (Document 2). This meant that businesses could cut costs and improve output at the same time. Demand for raw materials increased, as did the need for new modes of transportation—canals and railroads—to get them to the factories. The shift in the economy meant that farmers and artisans moved to factory areas, which developed into cities, and became factory workers.

However, as Documents 3–6 reveal, the problems associated with this shift were significant. Laissez-faire policies meant that business owners could arrange working conditions however they wanted. Factory workers were forced to toil long hours and live in poor housing. Few had little if any freedom. Children, who were often apprenticed to factory owners, were hit especially hard because they could be paid less. They were often injured, abused, and imprisoned in a system similar to slavery (Documents 3 and 4). The problems of working hours and low pay extended into other English industries, such as coal mining, where dangerous working conditions and a lack of sanitation led to the further abuse of women and children (Document 5).

Along with the British government, social critics such as Charles Dickens began to call for change. Industrialization not only hurt people, it hurt the environment by polluting the air and water (Document 6). Ultimately, the rise of labor unions helped improve working conditions and allowed workers to gain political power. The industrial system remained firmly entrenched, however, and spread throughout Europe and eventually to the United States.

Section II, Part B

2. World War I caused the art and literature of Europe to change dramatically from the styles of previous generations. From the onset of World War I in 1914 to its aftermath in the 1920s, art and literature took on a completely new, modern, and often bleak character. Art inspired by the war tended to focus on the horrors of combat and the despair of the modern world, the destruction of past forms of art and belief, and utility and propaganda.

Many of the young artists of the twentieth century represented the horrors of war in their work. In previous wars, many artists celebrated bravery and gallantry, but World War I proved that modern war was a filthy, horrid, tragic event. Artists no longer wanted to portray war as glamorous or glorious. Instead, they focused on the grim realities of fear, pain, loss, hunger, and desperation. This is reflected by many of the authors of the generation, such as Wilfred Owen and Erich Maria Remarque, whose writings tell tragic stories of young men whose lives are derailed by violence and privation.

The dramatic changes in perception caused by the war led to equally dramatic changes in art theory. Prior to 1914, many artists created cheerful works that celebrated life and nature. After the war, art and society became disillusioned. Artists felt that prior art forms no longer applied to the modern world. Instead, artists began experimenting with new forms that expressed angst, confusion, and rejection of the past mind-sets that had led the world to war. This new way of thinking led to the flourishing of schools such as surrealism, Dadaism, and Cubism. Some of this art was ironic, startling, and even bizarre to people used to the sunny realism and harmony of the past.

In many cases, art also took on a more utilitarian use during the war years. Many artists stopped creating works that attempted to express their own emotions or universal truths and began creating propaganda. Posters and cartoons with nationalist themes became commonplace throughout Europe. Many created crude stereotypes of other nations, or attempted to instill fear or hatred to motivate enlistment in the armed forces or sales of war bonds. In addition, many artists were called upon to design methods of camouflage. Artists designed unique geometric patterns of shapes and colors for application to equipment and vehicles that would obscure their size, shape, and speed from enemy observers.

World War I had a dramatic effect on European history and culture, and almost completely transformed its art. During and after the war, artists tended to focus on the brutality of war, to reject past art forms, and to use art for nationalistic or utilitarian purposes. The changes made to art during this period have forever changed art and culture in ways still evident today.

3. Prior to the French Revolution, France operated under a system called the ancien régime, or the old order. This system was a very old tradition in the country, although it had developed three major shortcomings: economic inefficiency, social inequality, and unjust laws. These shortcomings created severe problems in France at the end of the eighteenth century, ultimately leading to the French Revolution.

Under the ancien régime, the French government was almost bankrupt. The cause of the shortage of money was primarily military expenses. The king had waged many wars and had pledged significant financial and material support to the American cause during the American Revolutionary War. The French treasury was almost bankrupt and the king had few options for getting more money. French aristocrats refused to accept tax raises or the reduction of any of their luxuries. Meanwhile, the poorer classes shouldered most of the tax burden but soon could not pay any more.

The economic problems highlighted perhaps an even greater shortcoming of the ancien régime, the problem of social inequality. Under France's old order, society was divided into three Estates. The First and Second Estates were made of nobles and clergy, while the Third Estate was the poorer classes of laborers and farmers. Although the Third Estate was the overwhelming majority, they received no extra representation in government and suffered the worst restrictions and taxation. In addition, the Estates General, the assembly meant to represent the Estates, almost never met. That meant that even those citizens who hoped to work for reform had practically no opportunity to do so.

Another problem relating to the social inequality was the unjust laws of the ancien régime. France had different courts that did not treat all Estate members equally. Additionally, the king and his representatives had the ability to imprison anyone at any time, often without charges or the opportunity for bail. Many citizens felt this was the ultimate insult and demonstrated the intolerable gap between the rights of the king and those of the people.

These major problems in French society quickly escalated in the late 1700s. When the king finally assembled the Estates General to ask for more money, members of the Third Estate decided to withdraw. Inspired by the ideals of the Enlightenment, they formed a new assembly and began drafting their own rules and demands. Meanwhile, peasants began to revolt against the ancien régime, leading to the French Revolutionary War. Revolutionaries made sure to capture jails such as the Bastille in order to release those who had been imprisoned without trial.

The ancien régime in France was rife with shortcomings that led to severe social problems. These shortcomings included inefficient economic policies, gross inequality in society, and unjust laws. Motivated by Enlightenment principles, French citizens began to protest the systems of the old order, which ultimately led to the French Revolution.

4. The Reformation and Counter-Reformation period is known for the dramatic religious changes that took place during that time. When growing religious differences mixed with political tensions, the result was often war. Military conflicts fueled by religious issues occurred in lands such as England, France, and Germany during the sixteenth and seventeenth centuries. These conflicts included the Spanish Armada attack, the French Civil Wars, the Thirty Years' War, and the English Civil War.

The Spanish Armada attack took place in 1588. The king of Spain, still a loyal Catholic, was angered by England's official acceptance of Anglicanism, a form of Protestantism. The Spanish thought that by conquering England, they could not only expand their own territory but also convert the English back to Catholicism. The Spanish Armada, a fleet of over one hundred powerful warships loaded with soldiers, sailed toward England. Its goal of invading England was doomed, however, by a brave counterattack by a much smaller English navy as well as inclement weather. The Spanish Armada was defeated and forced to return to Spain.

In France, Catholics clashed with Huguenots in a series of civil wars throughout the last half of the 1500s. Huguenots were French Calvinists, another Protestant branch. Powerful Catholic and Huguenot families fought for control of France and engaged in massacres and battles. At last, a Huguenot leader took the throne, becoming King Henry IV. Henry IV helped pacify future religious conflicts by accepting Catholicism while protecting Huguenots.

Shortly after the French civil wars ended, another religiously fueled conflict broke out in the kingdoms of Germany. This was the Thirty Years' War, lasting from 1618 to 1648. In this conflict, the Protestant and Catholic regions of Germany went to war, and they were joined in battle by armies from almost every major European country. Germany sustained terrible damage during this war and was ultimately left with continued sharp religious divisions.

Shortly after the close of that war, another war broke out in England. This was the English Civil War. This conflict had roots in political disagreements as well as the monarchy's mistreatment of Puritans. Kings James I and Charles I supported the Church of England and discriminated against Puritans, members of a branch of Calvinism. The kings made powerful enemies among Puritans, especially Puritan members of Parliament, which contributed to a long war known as the English Civil War, or the Puritan Revolt. In the end, a Puritan leader named Oliver Cromwell successfully overturned the monarchy and then became dictator of England.

The Reformation and Counter-Reformation period brought great religious changes and contributed to several major military conflicts in Europe. Conflicts including the Spanish Armada attack, the French Civil Wars, the Thirty Years' War, and the English Civil War, fueled by religious disagreements, causing generations of death and destruction in Europe during the sixteenth and seventeenth centuries.

Section II, Part C
(SAMPLE ESSAYS)

5. From 1965 to 1990, events occurred in Europe that helped bring about the fall of Communism. Some of the most important events of that period took place in Poland. There, decades of political and economic struggles led to growing discontent with the Soviet-backed leadership. Many people tried in vain to protest for reforms before a worker's union called Solidarity helped loosen the grip of Communism on the country. The work of Solidarity and other reformers led to the creation of a free Poland by the end of the 1980s.

After World War II, Soviet-backed Communists took control in Poland. Poland did not thrive under the Communist system and faced great economic and political difficulties. Polish pro-democracy reformers attempted to hold protests and strikes in the 1960s and 1970s. These reformers included intellectuals and students as well as workers, and they sometimes acted in conjunction with Czechoslovakian and Hungarian protesters. However, the protests in Poland were not successful and were promptly crushed by Communist authorities. Still, the Communists could not extinguish the spirit of rebellion.

In 1980, a group of Polish shipbuilders led by Lech Walesa formed a trade union called Solidarity. Solidarity demanded that the Communists loosen their regulations on Poland's economy and industries. Although Solidarity made some early progress, winning some concessions from the government, the Communists took exception. Its leaders outlawed Solidarity and arrested Lech Walesa. They also set up a system of military rule in Poland. However, many other countries denounced these actions and Communist leaders were forced to release Walesa and end their martial law in Poland.

In the 1980s, there were great changes in Poland. Communism began to weaken in the USSR and Eastern Europe. Soviet leaders began to cede some of their powers. In the USSR, the program of *perestroika* allowed citizens to start their own businesses, and the policy of *glasnost* allowed greater freedom of speech. In addition, Soviet leaders adjusted their foreign policies to increase disarmament and end conflicts. Polish protesters were able to voice their concerns more easily and make more progress.

In 1989, Poland finally won the right to hold free elections, and a party based on the Solidarity movement took control of the government. Shortly afterward, Lech Walesa was elected president of Poland. Although he and the Polish citizens still faced many difficulties, they had become the first government to defy the USSR. Many other governments followed their lead in the late 1980s and early 1990s, and soon Communist power in Europe was broken.

Between 1965 and 1990, many Polish reformers worked to defy Communist rule in their country. Although early protests were crushed and the Polish people faced many difficulties, eventually the pro-democracy movement flourished. Solidarity and Lech Walesa led the way for protests and reforms and eventually free elections. The reforms in Poland set the pattern for other countries to reject Soviet domination; ultimately, this brought about the fall of Communism in Europe.

6. The English Civil War, also known as the Puritan Revolt, was waged in the mid-1600s over political and religious disagreements. The conflict began during the reigns of Kings James I and Charles I, both of whom feuded with Parliament and Puritans. In 1642, a lengthy war began between supporters of the monarchy and supporters of Parliament. The war lasted almost ten years before Puritan leader Oliver Cromwell took over the country and declared it a republic. The English Civil War exemplified the Age of Revolutions because it involved resistance to traditional monarchies and the promotion of more democratic forms of government.

The major conflicts that led to the war began during the reigns of King James I and his son Charles I, who ruled England during the first half of the 1600s. Both of these rulers strongly believed in the Divine Right of

Kings, or the idea that monarchs are granted their powers directly from God and cannot be questioned. In addition, James and Charles both supported the Church of England and discriminated against Puritans, members of a branch of the Calvinist faith. Many members of Parliament were Puritans and they took exception to the monarchs' behavior.

The feuds between the monarchy and Parliament continued and escalated during the reign of Charles I, who demanded large sums of money to strengthen the military and wage wars. Parliament refused to grant him the funds unless he agreed to some democratic concessions such as getting the consent of Parliament before raising taxes. Charles pretended to agree but continued to act unilaterally, going so far as to dismiss Parliament when they refused to follow his plans and even having some of its Puritan members arrested.

Charles' behavior touched off the English Civil War, also called the Puritan Revolt, in 1642. In this war, supporters of the king, known as Royalists or Cavaliers, clashed with supporters of Parliament, known as Roundheads. The leading faction of the Roundheads was composed of Puritans, and they also gained the support of English commoners and various disaffected Protestants who were unhappy with the king's rule.

The leader of the Roundheads, Oliver Cromwell, was a staunch Puritan and an often-cruel authoritarian. He created and led a powerful army that eventually defeated the king and his supporters. Parliament convicted King Charles I of treason and had him beheaded. Cromwell declared that the monarchy had been destroyed and that England would instead be a republic called the Commonwealth.

Although Cromwell soon became a dictator and, after his death, England returned to a monarchical system, the English Civil War was an important event in the Age of Revolution. It involved a fight against the monarchy and the promotion of democratic ideals. It also established the idea that kings could only act with the support of Parliament, making the English government a limited monarchy. In that way, the English Civil War was an important event in the Age of Revolution and greatly changed European history.

7. During the Scientific Revolution, people began exploring new kinds of knowledge in new ways, resulting in major changes to life across Europe. Two of the most important scientists of the era were Galileo, an Italian astronomer, and Sir Isaac Newton, an English mathematician who made great contributions to the study of space and the planets. One of the main developments of the era, advanced by both of these scientists, was the scientific method, a logical process used to identify problems, create experiments, and draw conclusions.

Italian scientist and astronomer Galileo was active in the sixteenth and seventeenth centuries. He was familiar with the common belief that the Sun and planets revolve around Earth. That was the belief officially endorsed and protected by the Catholic Church. Feeling this idea was not sound, Galileo proceeded to test it scientifically. He built his own telescope and studied the heavenly bodies and their movements. Ultimately, after much observation and experimentation, he concluded that the widely held belief was incorrect—in actuality, Earth and the planets revolve around the Sun. Church authorities persecuted him and forced him to deny his conclusions. Since Galileo had used the scientific method, however, his observations could be easily replicated, and they were. Later scientists checked his work and realized that he was correct in his conclusions.

Isaac Newton advanced Galileo's work and discovered new knowledge of his own during the seventeenth and eighteenth centuries. Newton explained some of the mysteries of the stars and planets when he discovered gravity, or the invisible force that pulls objects toward large bodies such as planets. This helped to explain how and why Earth and the other planets revolved around the Sun. Newton also made great strides in mathematics, creating calculus, a system of advanced math. Like Galileo, Newton was a careful scientist who used the scientific method. Because of that, other scientists could check and expand on his conclusions.

Galileo and Newton were some of the first scientists to make the scientific method work. Prior to the development of this method, scientists drew their conclusions from ancient philosophies and religious teachings. Many of the ideas they held as facts were actually completely inaccurate because they had been reached without any real evidence or organized study. Later, however, revolutionary scientists such as Galileo and Newton undertook careful and methodical scientific studies. By using experiments and observations, testing facts, and documenting conclusions, these scientists helped create the scientific method that scientists still use today to reach highly accurate and verifiable conclusions.

About the Authors

Ira Shull is a history buff with a BA in creative writing from Oberlin College and an MA in English from the University of New Hampshire. Ira has spent the last 20 years in educational publishing, working as an editor and writer on a variety of K–12 projects. Additionally, Ira is a former college instructor who currently tutors high school students in AP European History and AP English, among other subjects.

Mark Dziak is a writer and editor whose extensive background in history, education, and English allows him to develop high-quality, engaging educational materials. Mark has spent the last 10 years working as an educational writer and editor for a variety of major publishers. He has a BA in English from King's College along with secondary teaching certification. In addition, Mark recently published a book on the American Revolutionary War called, *The Battle of Wyoming: For Liberty and Life*.

Also Available

My Max Score AP Biology
by Dr. Robert S. Stewart, Jr. • 978-1-4022-4315-8

My Max Score AP Calculus AB/BC
by Carolyn Wheater • 978-1-4022-4313-4

My Max Score AP English Language and Composition
by Jocelyn Sisson • 978-1-4022-4312-7

My Max Score AP English Literature and Composition
by Tony Armstrong • 978-1-4022-4311-0

My Max Score AP U.S. Government & Politics
by Del Franz • 978-1-4022-4314-1

My Max Score AP U.S. History
by Michael Romano • 978-1-4022-4310-3

My Max Score AP World History
by Kirby Whitehead • 978-1-4022-4317-2

$14.99 U.S./£9.99 UK

Also Available

My Max Score SAT Literature Subject Test
by Steven Fox • 978-1-4022-5613-4

My Max Score SAT Math 1 & 2 Subject Test
by Chris Monahan • 978-1-4022-5601-1

My Max Score SAT U.S. History Subject Test
by Cara Cantarella • 978-1-4022-5604-2

• • •

**My Max Score ASVAB:
Armed Services Vocational Aptitude Battery**
by Angie Johnston and Amanda Ross, PhD • 978-1-4022-4492-6

$14.99 U.S./£9.99 UK

To download additional AP, SAT, and ACT practice tests and learn more about My Max Score, visit mymaxscore.com.

Online Test Prep at Your Fingertips

Based on the Strategies and Refreshers of Dr. Gary Gruber

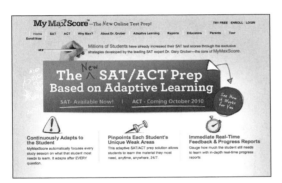

Discover the areas you need to improve and learn proven strategies to maximize your score

MyMaxScore is a truly innovative program that will revolutionize how students prepare for standardized tests. It's simply the best SAT/ACT prep solution out there! Each student receives an individualized experience focusing specifically on areas in which he/she is weak and spends less time on areas that have already been mastered.

Other test prep programs claim to offer truly personalized prep. The truth is that most programs diagnose your areas needing improvement one time—at the beginning of the course. MyMaxScore offers so much more than that—it actually adapts to your strengths and weaknesses after EVERY practice question! The program continually monitors your progress and serves up questions only in the areas you need to improve.

Online SAT/ACT prep adapts to you continuously

- ✔ How you answer determines what you study
- ✔ Focus remains on improving unique weaknesses
- ✔ Reports your progress at every step in real time
- ✔ No driving to classes. No more wasted Saturdays.
- ✔ 30 minutes a day
- ✔ Increase confidence. Raise scores.

Sign up for a FREE Trial

Go to MyMaxScore.com today to learn more about how you can max your score!

Essentials from
Dr. Gary Gruber
and the creators of My Max Score

"Gruber can ring the bell on any number
of standardized exams."
—*Chicago Tribune*

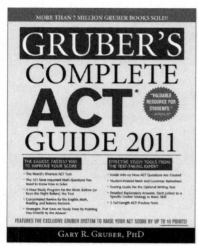

$19.99 U.S./£14.99 UK
978-1-4022-4307-3

$19.99 U.S./£14.99 UK
978-1-4022-5331-7

$16.99 U.S./£11.99 UK
978-1-4022-4308-0

$13.99 U.S./£9.99 UK
978-1-4022-5334-8

"Gruber's methods make the questions
seem amazingly simple to solve."
—*Library Journal*

"Gary Gruber is the leading expert on the SAT."
—*Houston Chronicle*

$14.99 U.S./£9.99 UK
978-1-4022-5337-9

$14.99 U.S./£9.99 UK
978-1-4022-5340-9

$14.99 U.S./£9.99 UK
978-1-4022-5343-0

$12.99 U.S./£8.99 UK
978-1-4022-6072-8

Notes